The
Secret
Life of
TYRONE
POWER

The

Secret

Life of

TYRONE
POWER

by

HECTOR ARCE

WILLIAM MORROW AND COMPANY, INC.
NEW YORK

Acknowledgments

IN THE WRITING OF THIS BIOGRAPHY, SPECIAL THANKS ARE DUE to three people:

To Bob Thomas, who, when he heard of my intention to write a book on Tyrone Power, laid aside his own plans to write about the same subject and gave me his years of accumulated research for use in this work. This gesture from one writer to another is unparalleled in its generosity, and I am flattered and grateful for the implicit trust he has placed in me.

To Patricia Fitzgerald, who collaborated on this project and searched out those whose lives were touched by Tyrone Power. Without her intercession on my behalf, I would not have been able to gain the confidence of many people who trusted that the subject would be handled with compassion and sensitivity.

To Joe Adamson, for lending his expertise as a film historian and critic in evaluating the body of Tyrone Power's work, the only criterion by which the actor himself would have wanted to be judged.

My gratitude also goes to those who shared reminiscences or offered their cooperation: James Bacon, James Bell, David Chierichetti, Olive Behrendt, David Bradley, Roy Bradley, George Cukor, Ty Culhane, Fitzroy Davis, Alice Faye, Edith Mayer Goetz, Henry Golas, Sara Hamilton, Smitty Hanson, Anne

Power Hardenbergh, Robbin Hauert, Allan Held, Gail Hensley, Rock Hudson, Eve Abbott Johnson, Kurt Kasznar, Alan Ladd, Jr., Elsa Lanchester, Jacque Mapes, Ruth March, Russell Orton, Taryn Power, Ginger Rogers, Walter Scott, Ray Sebastian, David Shepard, Maxwell J. Shapiro, Richard Simonton, Aubrey Solomon, Tom Stempel, Jan Sterling, Charles Walters, Barbara McLean Webb, Paul G. Wesolowski, Billy Wilder, and Wil Wright.

Because of the sensitive nature of some of the material, several people who spoke to me requested anonymity. They are people above reproach, whose names, if made known, would doubly confirm the incidents they supplied to me. To them, too, my deepest thanks.

H.A.

Introduction

I CAME TO THE ASSIGNMENT, PROPOUNDED BY MY LITERARY agent, Helen Barrett, with no preconceptions, other than the knowledge I was to write the biography of a romantic and noble actor who died before he could prove his capacity for growth. With it came the challenges. Could I reflect with both honesty and taste the tormenting contradiction of Tyrone Power's public persona and his quite opposite personal character? Would it be possible to accomplish this without causing his children any unnecessary pain? His two daughters had only dim memories of him and his son never knew him at all. Could they perceive that the revelations, needed if they were to present a true picture of their father, were being written in a manner both low key and unsensational? If they got to know their father after reading the foregoing pages, would they come to realize—as I was beginning to from my preliminary interviews with his friends and associates—that he was an extraordinarily decent man?

A few days before a memorial service commemorating the twentieth anniversary of Tyrone Power's death, in the West Hollywood apartment she shared with her man, Taryn Power talked about the time she'd moved to California and met some of her father's closest friends. "I was very surprised when I found out who they were," she told me. "One of them told me my father was a very tormented man . . . totally unlike the public image of him."

"Do you want to know the extent of that torment?" I asked.

"Of course," she replied. She was already aware of its nature. Her sister Romina was planning to write a book about it, too. "I was raised to think my father was a god," Taryn said. "I never knew him. I want to. I want him to become a human to me."

A few days later, over lunch, Bob Thomas discussed his plans, now canceled, in which he would write about the essentially tragic man he found Tyrone Power to be. When I asked him if he had planned to delve into the facts behind the whispers, he replied, "Yes. But, you know, it's going to be a tough job. You're going to get a lot of resistance."

Bob Thomas is a gentle man, but I'd never realized his capacity for understatement until then.

Friends and associates of Tyrone Power were eager to talk about him as a great and honorable man, but were cautious about discussing his personal anguish.

They opened up only after they were told several other books covering the same material were being written and were assured that I would treat Tyrone Power's life with empathy and understanding. I hope they will find that I have kept my promise to them.

HECTOR ARCE

North Hollywood, California
March, 1979

I am a man: nothing human is alien to me.

—TERENCE, *The Self-Tormentor*

The
Secret
Life of
TYRONE
POWER

CHAPTER

1

He never looked better; he never looked worse. He was in an exuberant mood; he was suicidal. He took only one scotch before dinner; he was drinking heavily. He at long last was emerging as a great actor; by playing in yet another potboiler he had come to grips with his limitations.

Contradictions abound in the reports of people who shared Tyrone Power's last days. For each one who found portents and ironies, there was another who gave them logical and mundane reasons. There were as many versions as there were witnesses to his impending tragedy.

All of his life, Tyrone Power had repressed his emotions, bottling in resentments and rages, rarely confiding in anyone as he labored to compartmentalize his professional, family, and secret lives. He masked true feelings with an easy Irish charm which couldn't bear close scrutiny, lest the sadness and the desperation show through. As a result, he was friend and stranger to all.

His mother had taught him to face life with an austere and stoical grace. Triumph and disaster were to be kept in their rightful places. He was to look on them both as impostors and bow to neither, facing up to them with no breast-beating displays of pride or despair. To be publicly self-indulgent was the cardinal sin.

Not for him the morbidly real posturings of a Montgomery

Clift, who cried out in anguish so often that he wore out the patience of those who loved him. Neither would he be party to the public buffoonery that Errol Flynn had come to represent as he ineffectually juggled booze and babes, some so young that they were almost in arms.

Tyrone Power had taken on, like a chameleon, the shodings of his backdrop, neither presuming nor daring to show his true colors to anyone. It was now too late to change. He couldn't have acted differently even if he'd known his days were dwindling, and this was a thought that surely was preying on his mind.

He had recently closed on Broadway in *Back to Methuselah,* his notices ranging from poor to lukewarm, when he had lunch in New York with his divorced second wife, Linda Christian, on that day in late April of 1958. After the tortures they'd put each other through, that they should remain friendly was proof of their forgiving natures. Linda asked him about the girl with whom he was being seen around town. Ty laughed off the question. He insisted he would never marry again. After two failures, he had come to realize he wasn't cut out for marriage, as well they both knew. He went on to casually describe a physical examination he just had. An irregularity in his heartbeat had been discovered by the electrocardiograph.

"You should be careful about that," Linda said. "I think you should have another."

Ty shrugged. "I'd rather not know."

A week later, he was married for a third time to Debbie Minardos, the girl he'd been seeing, and the divorced wife of a minor actor. Something had changed his mind in a hurry.

Despite the reams of publicity about his past marriages and affairs, each step of each courtship had been deliberately, if not sensibly, thought out. Ty was not a passionate and impulsive man. He was known for his methodical ways. He had once told a lover that much of his sex drive was expended in his work. He'd gotten no argument there.

For Ty to take such an important step, particularly when the paying of two alimonies and child support, as well as nursing care for his invalid mother, usually left him strapped, there had to be a reason.

He was regenerated, hopeful, apprehensive. He'd gotten a second chance. Would the fates finally reward him with a son to carry on the distinguished family name?

He and his new wife returned to California. He had to get himself ready for the $5,000,000 production he would be shooting in Spain that fall. They settled in Newport Beach, where Ty's forty-two-foot ketch, *The Black Swan,* was docked, and planned to laze the summer away.

A will was made out that July, in which Ty divided the bulk of his estate into trust funds for his new wife, mother, sister, two daughters, and his unborn child.

That dreary chore taken care of, Ty and Debbie could give their undivided social attention to such fellow sailors as Milton Bren and his wife, Claire Trevor; Robert Wagner and Natalie Wood; and Rock Hudson, who had spent some time with the Powers recently in New York.

During quiet moments, he prepared for *Solomon and Sheba.* He had recently decided that all future movies would be made on the basis of deferring his salary against a share of the profits. "It's the only way a star can make money," he told Bob Thomas of the Associated Press. "Let's face it. Nobody is going to get rich in these times, no matter how you work deals, I don't think that an actor always knows what is best for him. After all, we're not infallible. That's why I will always rely on the advice of producers and directors whom I respect." The deal on the upcoming picture was particularly sweet. He was assured $350,000 up front against a share of the profits. What's more, Ted Richmond, Ty's partner in Copa Productions, an independent company, had been engaged as producer of the film by Edward Small of United Artists. This gave Richmond an assignment while he and Ty got their own projects off the ground.

Already, Ty's favorite makeup man, Ray Sebastian, had created a slightly modified profile for him. "I designed the nose," he recalled. "Ty's had a little dip and a sort of little bump on the end of it. So I made a Jewish nose. Not a hump, but just a curve. A nice, almost a soft Roman nose, but it changed his whole countenance."

"Ty was looking forward to the film," Rock Hudson recalled. "He studied his script a lot. He was growing a beard for the part and getting in shape. He looked terrific."

What about the monumental drinking bouts that people later said Ty indulged in? "If he were a heavy drinker," Hudson said, "I'd remember it. I never saw him drunk. His deportment in public was unbelievable. He kept everything in. I never saw him blow up, explode, get angry, or lose his temper. This was to a point that I thought was unhuman. I think he died of kindness."

Professionally, Ty was suggestible if not downright weak. Leather-bound volumes neatly shelved in the library at Twentieth Century-Fox were filled with the Naugahyde words he'd been forced to pass off as real. If the new picture, in tandem with the birth of a son, was the start of another phase in his life, his pedestrian lines would be printed in yet another leather-bound book, to go on a new shelf at another studio library.

He was being asked to make love in pseudo-biblical and impossible language: "Thou art fair, my love. Thine eyes shine like doves. Thou art a lily of the valley. Thou art a rose of Sharon. Thy lips are like pomegranates. How much better is thy love than wine."

"If he resented the script," Hudson said, "he never said anything to me. Actually, such films take a better actor. You have to believe it yourself. Solomon was a man of great wisdom, so *he* had to be a man of great wisdom. To play a ruler takes a bit of doing. You have to be much more graceful in movement, plus move regally. When he worked in costume films, Ty was graceful as could be. When he had a business suit on, he had to work harder. With most other actors, it's the other way around."

In September, Ty and Debbie left for Europe. *The Black Swan* being transported by freighter for their only-on-Sunday enjoyment while filming abroad. When on location, you not only work longer hours, but also six days a week.

Prior to departure, Ty shot a promotional film for the American Heart Association. Sporting his new beard and wearing a dressing gown, he was the picture of suave urbanity as he sat in an easy chair. He picked up an hourglass and looked thoughtfully at it. Then he turned it upside down and, as the grains of sand started filtering through to the inverted bottom, he said, "For all of us, the most precious element we have is time. But time runs out all too soon for many millions of us, because of an enemy that takes more lives than all other diseases combined."

Because of a contractual dispute with Howard Hughes, Gina Lollobrigida couldn't work in the United States. The mechanization of the Israeli army created a shortage of horses there. *Ben Hur* was being filmed in Italy, and that country's facilities were operating at maximum capacity. The deserts of Spain and the armies of Generalissimo Franco stood in for ancient Israel by default.

The cast was international in scope. Ty's Midwestern accent established him as the good guy for American audiences; Lollobrigida's Sheba was patently Italian; George Sanders as Adonijah, Solomon's elder brother, was British and bored; the dying King David was played by Finlay Currie, a Scotsman. The effect, considering the quality of the dialogue, was a tower of babble.

Was it a sign of his usual expansiveness that he wanted his friends about him, or was there another reason for his unusual insistence that they gather around?

He'd already stopped off in London on his way to Spain, where Charles Laughton and Elsa Lanchester were appearing together in *The Party* at St. Martin's Lane Theatre. The Laughtons were staying in Ty's unoccupied flat off Brompton Road, their host even supplying them with the services of his British secretary.

Laughton had directed Ty in *John Brown's Body,* his only undisputed triumph as a stage actor, and the two men were quite close. The Laughtons and the Powers had dinner at a restaurant near the theater, one of Ty's favorites because of the way it prepared *osso bucco.* Miss Lanchester found nothing ominous about their last meeting. All she recalled was the strength in Ty's new wife. "She knew what she wanted and she got it in Ty. I suppose all of his women were strong."

Van and Evie Johnson had since arrived in England where he was to shoot a picture. Ty called Evie, the first girl he'd ever asked to marry him, and invited her to come down for a visit. "Annabella is also coming," he added.

Evie's husband, however, had the upcoming weekend off, and they'd been invited to spend it in the country with some British friends. She regretfully declined the invitation.

Actor Kurt Kasznar was finishing up a picture with Mario Lanza in Austria. He'd recently suffered a horrendous experience in a German stage production of *Arms and the Man*. "Don't worry about those Nazis," Ty wrote him. "We'll talk it out in Spain." Subsequently, Leora Dana, his wife of eight years, with whom Ty had starred in a play, asked Kasznar for a divorce. Again Ty advised his friend. "I love you both," he wrote, "but you shouldn't stay together. You're wrong for each other. We'll talk about it when you come down." This Kasznar promised to do as soon as the filming of his picture was completed.

Annabella drove down the first week in November from her farm in the French Pyrenees to the location in Saragossa. "He absolutely wanted to introduce me to his new little wife, whom he adored," she would later say about her former husband. When she returned home, she told close friends there was something terribly wrong with Ty, but she couldn't put her finger on it.

Ty hadn't told her, as he had Debbie, that he was feeling pains in his shoulder and upper left arm. He didn't think it was cause for alarm. He was playing a role too strenuous for his age, which might have activated a case of bursitis.

"When Annabella came to see us," Ray Sebastian explained, "we were filming the 'young' sequence. His beard was gone, and he was all bleached out from not being out in any sun. He had a light makeup on. He was supposed to be a very cultured, nurtured, young son of David. Maybe he looked pale to her.

"We were shooting in one of those old castles this one day and Ty walked onto the set. There was something of beauty in this man's face that I never saw before. It wasn't the face of a sick man. It wasn't a tired man. It was just something sort of at peace with the whole damned world. It left an indelible impression on me, and I never forgot it. I can see it any time I want to bring it back."

Whenever a star dies while making a film, studio spokesmen are quick to point out that he passed an insurance physical before he began the project. The death may cause the cancellation of the production and the insurance company must absorb the production costs.

Sebastian said, "They checked his blood pressure; had him running up the steps; they checked his urine . . . this, that, and everything. Ty said he'd never had such a going over in his life. They gave him a clean bill of health and Eddie Small was able to insure him for two million dollars. So don't give me that crap about a heart thing."

"It's automatic coverage," Rock Hudson, in contradiction, said. "You usually go to some quack doctor. He asks, 'Have you had any illnesses in the last year?' You answer no. He says, 'Okay.' He checks your pulse and takes your blood pressure. Then he gives you a form to sign and you're insured."

Ty wrote a letter to his daughters, Romina and Taryn:

I miss you both and I do so look forward to the time we can be together again . . . Be good girls and work well in school so that Mummy and Daddy can be proud of you . . . With kisses and hugs to you both, and all my love and a big hello from Debbie.

DADDY

Annabella had visited Ty and Debbie the week before. The production company was back at its headquarters in Madrid. It was the second month to the day that they'd been filming the biblical epic. Ty's work was about 60 percent completed.

The cold fall air hung heavily over mountain-locked Madrid that morning, as the company prepared to shoot the culminating action sequence of the picture.

Director King Vidor quickly got a couple close-ups of Ty. He already had a master full-figure shot of the duel with George Sanders. Next would be medium shots to capture facial expressions and dialogue, the camera pulling back to catch the choreographed swordplay.

How many times in the past had the two men faced off against each other in movie fights? The pictures, none of them distinguished, had run together in their minds, variations of the same theme in which heroic Ty vanquished the nefarious Sanders. The repeated combat had taken on the character of a grudge match. If Sanders was doomed to die, he understandably wanted the gory death to have the optimum histrionic effect. It wasn't beneath him to milk the scene dry.

In this version, it was brother pitted against brother, fighting for the right to rule Israel over the fallen body of the Queen of Sheba. Only Ty and Sanders were on call this morning, however. Gina Lollobrigida, in her nearby trailer dressing room, was preparing for her afternoon of work, in which she would miraculously rise from her previously presumed death to take the next scheduled chariot back to her homeland.

Over the next hour and a half, the two men, wearing heavy robes and working with real Roman swords weighing fifteen pounds, staged the duel on an elevated staircase landing. Sanders wasn't pleased with some of the angles being shot and asked several times that the scene be shot over. Ty voiced no objections, going through the exhausting paces time after time.

Finally, after the eighth take, he could stand no more. He threw down his sword. "If you can't find anything there you can use, just use the close-ups of me," he angrily said. "I've had it!"

Ray Sebastian had never heard Ty speak this way. He'd always been accommodating and generous with other actors. In the past, Ty had handled difficult actors by kidding them. "Come on, you son of a bitch," he would say, "let's get it right and let's get the hell out of here."

His makeup man saw that Ty was shaking uncontrollably, but didn't know whether it was from anger or exhaustion. Whatever the reason, something was wrong. He helped the actor down from the platform.

The cameraman reloaded his film as Sebastian took Ty to his

trailer dressing room. Inside, the small electric heater hadn't yet warmed up the drafty enclosure.

"I feel cold," the actor replied. He groaned. "I hurt all over. I think I'll lie down."

In the dozens of pictures and in the twenty-three years he'd worked with Ty, Sebastian never knew him to lie down between takes. He would either sit in his dressing room and read, conduct interviews, or trade small talk with the crews.

As Ty lay down on a small couch, Sebastian poured him a cup of hot tea, and added some rum, thinking the stimulant might be of help.

"Ty, can you hold your arms up?"

He tried. "Boy, they hurt!"

Sebastian asked a messenger to get the company doctor. A few moments later, the boy returned and said the doctor hadn't been on the set that morning. A Spanish girl who didn't speak English appeared with a beat-up first-aid kit.

In his limited Spanish, the makeup man discerned from the girl that the doctor had gone into town.

"This man is seriously ill," he said. "He belongs in a hospital."

Ted Richmond and two production executives had arrived by this time. Each of the stars and the director had been assigned a Mercedes Benz for the duration of the filming around Madrid. Gina Lollobrigida's was nearby. Having heard sounds of the emergency, the actress had come out of her dressing room. She watched in horror as an ashen-faced Ty was carried into the back seat of her car.

As the car sped off to the hospital at the United States Torrejon Air Base, the full force of the attack hit Ty. He cried out as his body lurched, then fell back. There were no signs of life when the car arrived at the hospital. Ty was immediately placed in an oxygen tent. None of the emergency measures provoked a reaction. In desperation, adrenalin was injected directly through his rib cage into his heart. This last measure, as usual, was a futile attempt to save a life. Tyrone Power, at the age of forty-four, was dead.

It was up to Bill Gallagher, Ty's secretary for over twenty years, to pass on the news to Ty's friends in Europe. Evie Johnson was devastated, her thoughts returning time and again to what might have been.

Post-production work on his film in Austria had delayed Kurt Kasznar's departure for Spain. He was in his hotel room when he received an urgent phone call from Mario Lanza, asking him to come to his hotel suite. The singer met Kasznar at the door, tears streaming down his face. He'd heard a radio report. "Tyrone is dead," Lanza cried. A sobbing Gallagher called Kasznar to confirm the bad news shortly thereafter.

Within minutes, word had spread around the world. Mutual friends offered condolences to each other. Laurence Olivier was vainly trying to cope with the emotional turmoil of his wife Vivien Leigh. Yet, his words to William Goetz, a studio executive, and his wife, Edith, the daughter of Louis B. Mayer, were typically sensitive and apt. Olivier said, "You tell your son two things: 'I am your father,' and, 'When there's a pain in your arm you go to your doctor and see about your heart.'"

Tyrone Power's father had never acknowledged to his son's satisfaction the first point—that a man should give of himself to establish a loving relationship with his children. Ty Power, Sr., had also suffered heart disease, and his strikingly similar death twenty-seven years previous hadn't sufficiently inscribed the second message in his son's mind. Now, Tyrone Power would neither pass on the message nor the great import he placed on the family tradition to a son he would never know.

CHAPTER

2

ONCE HE DECIDED TO FOLLOW IN THE FAMILY'S ACTING tradition, Tyrone Power constantly strove to shine through the tall shadows cast by his ancestors. To him, they were sacred, intimidating monsters. They were not the raw and fumbling talents that grew into people of achievement and distinction. Instead, they were full-blown and thoroughly accomplished, the sum total of their triumphs and not their stumblings along the way. They were a formidable challenge.

He was a boy of great beauty who grew into a man of quiet and cultivated charm. But was he an actor? He'd just as soon not be judged by those whose genes he inherited. His self-evaluation was merciless enough. Little matter that his fame was greater than theirs, when he continually sensed that several promises—an implicit one to the earlier Powers to continue a noble tradition and another to himself to develop his craft to the utmost—weren't being kept. His most overriding obsession was to be a great actor, equal to, if not better than, the Powers who had performed before him, to transcend their transcendence.

This—and not the inhuman pressures he was forced to endure

in attempting to fit into the gentle, noble, and manly mold that the public cast him in—was the tragedy of Tyrone Power's life.

No one ever accused publicists during the golden days of film studios of having any great respect for accuracy when it came to writing biographies of their players. They had a way of elevating and ennobling the backgrounds of those under contract to their studios. Because of his name, it was much easier to surmise the obvious, that his ancestors came from the Irish County of Tyrone. That county, however, is in Northern Ireland, whereas Waterford County, from where the Powers actually came, was on the southern coast, to the west of St. George's Channel, which separates Ireland from Wales.

Those at Twentieth Century-Fox who fashioned the company line on the actor missed an opportunity to trace Tyrone Power to fascinating noble roots and he, in turn, didn't know enough of the family background to fill them in. From 1630 to 1690, in the same Waterford County from which the future Powers came, there lived a Richard Power. He had been taken into Cromwell's "special protection," according to *Debretts National Biography,* "in consequence of his father, John, Lord de la Power (or de la Poer), having become insane and dying in 1661. His son succeeded as Governor of Waterford that same year and was created the first Earl of Tyrone in 1673. Six years later, in 1679, he was imprisoned, charged with treason, but released two years later because of insubstantial evidence. He converted to his king's Roman Catholicism upon the accession of James II to the English throne in 1685, and was named privy councillor the following year. James II issued the first declaration of liberty to all denominations in England and Scotland. The House of Commons vacated the throne in 1689, for it had been "found inconsistent with the safety and welfare of this Protestant kingdom to be governed by a popish prince." The Earl of Tyrone assisted in the defense of Cork against Marlborough in 1690. After the Catholic capitulation and the ensurance of Britain as a Protestant state, he was committed to the Tower of London, where he died the same year at age sixty.

Through primogeniture, the title was passed on and the name of

Tyrone was adopted as a middle name by those on the genealogical chart of the acting family. Yet, the title today still directly reflects the family's roots, for the Marquess of Waterford, John Hubert de la Poer Beresford, today sits as Baron Tyrone.

The first acting Power was reputed to be a minstrel of sorts in Ireland late in the eighteenth century. He was married to a Maria Maxwell, whose father was killed while serving with the British in the Revolutionary War. Their only child, William Grattan Tyrone Power, was born in Waterford on November 2, 1795. He was still an infant when his parents, feeling there was great opportunity where revolutions were forging republics, decided to move to America. The nest egg of the elder Power was small and his health was unstable. No sooner did the small family arrive at their destination than the father was bedded by a fever, from which he soon died.

Maria Maxwell Power, left with little money and a small child to support, decided to leave America. Once she reached Waterford, she decided to go with her son to Dublin, and then on to South Wales.

Mother and son settled in Cardiff. William Grattan Tyrone Power's education was haphazard at best. He picked up a smattering of French and German and filled his head with popular plays and romances of the day. However, the most indelible impression that Cardiff made on the young man was the first play he saw there. His mother felt he should aspire to a military career, but her son thought otherwise. He served notice of his plan by lopping two years off his already callow age, packing up, and running away.

Young Power was a scrawny sixteen-year-old when he made his stage debut in 1811, playing Orlando in a modest production of *As You Like It*. Claiming to be fourteen, he cut a rather precocious romantic figure.

Over the next five years, it was maturity and not so much well-fed prosperity that caused him to fill out. He had grown into a stockily built man, five feet eight inches in height, with fair coloring. As he reached adulthood, he fell in love with Annie Gilbert, whose lineage could be traced back to the Norman Conquest. She was expecting a small inheritance within two years, on which the couple planned to live. The young lady's guardian, a Doctor Thomas, was opposed to the marriage. Power's was a nonexistent career thus far, in a calling of extremely low, if not equally nonexistent, prestige.

The two eloped in January of 1817, and somehow, despite his weak but husky voice, he began to get a few more engagements in popular theatricals of the time.

For someone who was a rabid Irish patriot, it is curious that Power didn't attempt an Irish role earlier in his career. This he did in the summer of 1818, playing the comic Looney McTwolter in *The Review*. Critical response was lukewarm.

In June of 1819, the couple's first child, William, was born. The family couldn't live on Mrs. Power's small inheritance and her husband's occasional acting engagements. Power had no choice but to think of an alternative career.

Although an uncle had a high position in the Austrian army, Power couldn't get an officer's commission because he was burdened with a wife and child. In partnership with a British army officer, he decided to form a settlement in the African Cape territory instead. As the two set sail in June of 1820, Power started a diary, later lost, and began writing verses of farewell to his family and native land. He was beginning to hone a second craft by which he would also be known in the future.

The African expedition turned out to be a disastrous misadventure. Power, while on a foraging tour, was lost. He was missing for almost a year. When he was finally found, his matted beard and long hair would have ideally cast him to play Defoe's Robinson Crusoe, a tale already a century old.

He was reunited with his family in Ireland shortly thereafter. The happiness at seeing his loved ones was coupled with an exciting discovery. John Johnstone, the great Irish comedian, had just retired, and the field was open to younger actors. Power returned to his original calling. He rose slowly in public favor, and it was not until his return from his first visit to the United States in 1833 that he became an actor of consequence in London.

He brought to the United States, as William Winter wrote in *Tyrone Power,* the biography of the patriarch's grandson and namesake, "genial but refined humor, the merry twinkle of his

eye, rich tones of his voice, his skill in dancing, his happy variations of brogue to the different shades of character he represented."

In Power's first American appearance, at the Old Park Theatre
in New York, on August 28, 1833, he played Sir Patrick O'Plen-
ipo in James Kenney's comedy, *The Irish Ambassador.* He had to
overcome considerable trepidation to appear. Mrs. Trollope, in
her *Domestic Manners of Americans,* published a few years
previously, had given American theater audiences bad marks for
deportment. Yet, just as Americans were pleased to see that his
Irish characters weren't the predictable ruffians with black eyes
and straw in their shoes, Power was equally delighted to see "no
coats off, no heels up, no legs over boxes . . . a more English audience I would not desire to act before."

America had seen no equal as an Irish actor, and a review of
his American debut, which appeared in the *New York Mirror,*
presaged the scores of huzzahs coming his way over the rest of the
tour: "At all events, when compared to other attempts at Irish
character, it was a faithful and spirited sketch, filled up with great
ability and irresistible humor by Mr. Power. A style so peculiarly
comic, is seldom free from some intermixture of buffoonery. This
is not the case here—there is no straining, no unnatural effort; the
fun, though of the essence of the richest risibility, is perfectly
smooth, and the very opposite of forced conceits . . ."

Power's description of theater in America, as well as a lucid,
unprejudiced view of the state of the United States in the mid-
1830s, was charted in *Impressions of America,* published in a
two-volume set in 1836, which came to be regarded as the definitive social essay of the period.

Tyrone Power returned to the British Isles, fully qualified to
take his place as Ireland's national actor. He would pass on his
vocation to future generations, becoming known as the patriarch
of a theatrical dynasty now in its fifth generation.

Over the next few years, Power would make two additional
tours to America, "acting in many cities," as Winter put it, "prospering in all."

He had, in fact, prospered to such an extent that he was ready
for retirement as he approached his mid-forties. In the summer of

1840, he performed in London and Dublin before embarking on his third voyage to America. Power hadn't wanted to endure another arduous eight-month tour. The actor had accumulated considerable land holdings in Texas and had substantial bank accounts in other parts of the country, however, and these had to be tended to. As he sailed from Liverpool, it was announced that he would return in time to open at the Haymarket Theatre in London on April 12, 1841.

Power's tour ended at the same Park Theatre where he had made his American debut eight years previously. Two days after his closing on March 9, 1841, in the company of his friend, George Charles Lennox, Lord Fitzroy, he sailed on the *President*, a steamer, bound for Liverpool. An acting crony, the tragedian Edwin Forrest, didn't trust the vessel and had recommended that Power wait for another ship. The *President*, 273-feet long and with a 1600-ton burden, had crossed the Atlantic three times before without incident. Power scoffed at his friend's premonition.

One week later, probably not far beyond the Nantucket Shoals, the tempest-tossed *President* foundered, and 123 people died, Power and Lennox included. With his too-early death, the actor, who had cut a warm and comic figure in life, now became tragic and romantic, to be celebrated in song and story. As a headline in a London newspaper put it, "America has lost her President and England her Power."

The dead actor had fathered four sons—William Tyrone, Maurice, Harold, and Frederick—and an equal number of daughters, their given names long since forgotten.

The youngest son, Harold, had to overcome considerable family opposition to work in the theater. The Powers were now financially established and full equals of their titled cousins. Harold changed his name to Page so as not to embarrass them.

Motion-picture biographies of his grandson, the film star, described Harold Power as one of England's most famous concert pianists, the publicity machine suggesting that the family enjoyed one long unbroken line of successes. Such wasn't the case. The only son of Tyrone Power the Elder to make a career in the theater created minimal impact. Harold was most noted for the series of entertainments he mounted with his wife, Ethel Levenu, after he defiantly changed his name back to Power. The two performed throughout their native England before taking their act on the road or, in this case, the high seas, with their first trip to America. They were billed as "Mr. and Mrs. Power at Home," appearing at New York's Chickering Hall in November of 1877 and offering little playlets held together by their snappy badinage. The first part of the program was a series of funny lectures written by Harold Power and his friend, the lyricist William S. Gilbert. (Another close friend was Gerald Du Maurier.)

Harold's son, Frederick Tyrone Power, was the father of the subject of this biography. His career would be marked by a distinction which was beyond the grasp of his father Harold.

His father's reaction to the news that his son intended to be an actor, colored by the insecurity of his own life in the theater, was negative. Tyrone was taken out of Dulwich College, his education terminated, and he was shipped off to Florida to learn the orange-growing business.

Given his bibulous Irish heritage, it is highly unlikely, as his biographer William Winter wrote about Tyrone Power after his death forty-six years later, that his alcoholism stemmed from his days on the orange plantation. "Being an unsophisticated youth he knew nothing of the dire effects of intoxicating beverages," Winter wrote. "Scarcely had he arrived there than the plantation employees decided that he must become one of them. So they offered him rum and the young fellow, not accustomed to such things, refused. Then they bound him hand and foot and poured the vile stuff down his throat. That was the initiation which resulted in Tyrone Power being a slave to drink."

Tyrone's days as a citrus grower would be few. His new employer treated him no better than a servant, and Tyrone rebelled. He packed up his belongings and ran away to St. Augustine.

One of the little theaters in the city, the Genovar Opera House, was managed by a Ralph Bell, who engaged Tyrone for the company. He made his acting debut the following year, in November of 1886, as Gibson in *The Private Secretary*.

Within a few months, he decided to move to Philadelphia, where he heard there was an opening for a leading juvenile. Tyrone was seventeen now, but still considered too young by the manager. The adaptable young man bided his time in Pennsylvania until he was engaged by Mme. Fanny Janauschek for her company. He stayed there for three years, his salary eventually reaching thirty-five dollars a week.

Armed with a letter of introduction from Ellen Terry, he was engaged by Augustin Daly for his professional company at a salary of twenty dollars a week. He was getting less salary than in his previous position. Yet it was a decided step upward nonetheless, Tyrone soon after appearing as Sir Oliver Surface in *The School for Scandal*.

Daly was a martinet, retaining total control over every aspect of each production. He had a varied theatrical background as critic, playwright, and manager. It was as a director, however, that he became a major figure in the American theater, contributing to the final phase of American realism. He was also instrumental in creating such stars as Ada Rehan, John Drew II, and James Lewis. In Daly's 1867 production, *Under the Gaslight,* the hero was tied to railroad tracks for the first time. Next came such other innovations as a heroine locked in the stateroom of a burning steamboat. These were marvelous theatrical flourishes carried over to silent pictures fifty years later, as was his concept in the 1871 play, *Horizon,* of portraying the American Indian as a villain.

The year after he joined Daly, in 1891, Tyrone went with the company to London. It would take him two years before he was able to finance the staging of his own play, *The Texan.* Tyrone Power the Younger, as he was billed, played the leading role of William Plainleigh in the production, staged at the Princess Theatre in 1893. The production failed.

After a short tour of the provinces with the Herbert Beerbohm-Tree Company, Tyrone returned to the Daly Company, which was now headquartered in New York. For the next five years, he intermittently worked with Daly, periodically withdrawing because of "artistic differences."

Despite his disputes with the autocratic Daly, he could not deny that his greatest triumphs—primarily in Shakespearean roles—had been with him, and he had developed into a certifiable star.

His powerful six-foot-one-inch frame would have stood out on any stage. He was a robust player in the Edwin Forrest tradition, outsized in movement and gesture, and his voice was so resonant as to be sepulchral.

The theatrical world was consequently bemused when, in the fall of 1898, Tyrone Power joined the Harrison Grey Fiske Co. to tour with Minnie Maddern Fiske in the old chestnut, *Tess of the D'Urbervilles.* Although his part was newly written into the play, it was a virtual walk-on.

True, Power might have taken the part to underwrite his everyday expenses. He had recently married actress Edith Crane, a great beauty, who played with him as Marie in Daly's 1891 production of *The School for Scandal.* The newly married couple was planning to mount a production of *Macbeth,* in which they would star.

Actually, Mrs. Fiske wanted to be assured that Tyrone Power would be available for the next production of hers, *Becky Sharp,* which was still being written. It was an ambitious project, with thirty-two speaking parts. Maurice Barrymore—father of Lionel, Ethel, and John—was engaged as the leading man, and Power was to play the sinister Marquis de Steyne. In this portrayal, he appeared in only three scenes, but created an indelible impact.

A tête-à-tête supper scene with Becky and the Marquis, interrupted by Rawdon Crawley, the part played by Barrymore, resulted in twelve curtain calls for the three stars on opening night in September of 1899. The production could have run indefinitely had the Fiskes not been fighting the Theatrical Trust, which was closing theater doors on them with merciless impunity. Tyrone Power also could have played the part indefinitely, had he not decided to tour with the same production to his wife's native Australia, Edith Crane taking on Mrs. Fiske's role.

Nevertheless, despite the defection, Mrs. Fiske could think of no one else to play Judas in the production of *Mary of Magdala,* set to open in New York in October of 1902.

"The selection left another costly production at the mercy of a temperamental Irishman's whim," Archie Binns and Olive Kooken wrote in *Mrs. Fiske and the American Theatre,* "but Minnie felt that if *Mary of Magdala* could not continue without Power, neither could it begin without him."

The poet William Winter insisted that his name be kept secret when he translated *Mary of Magdala,* the German play by Paul Heyse. As he was seduced by the excitement of the theater, he stopped looking down his well-bred nose at its denizens. He had come sufficiently around in 1913 not only to begin the writing of a series of books to be called *Lives of the Players,* but to select Tyrone Power as the first such actor to warrant such treatment.

Winter felt that Tyrone Power's life had been one of exceptionally interesting adventure, and that in some respects it was as romantic as that of Edmund Kean, the great eighteenth-century English tragedian.

His near-veneration began with Power's portrayal of Judas. It was "the role of roles," Binns and Kooken wrote, "and Tyrone Power made the most of it. His sinister classic makeup was as sure a work of art as a Rembrandt painting, and his magnificent physique and voice completed his identification with the character." His performance was the most praised of the year.

For the second time, however, Tyrone Power left the Fiskes in the lurch. As they made plans for a European tour, he was signing with Charles Frohman to star in *Ulysses.* The Fiskes took him to court, but they lost the suit. Another actor was engaged.

When *Becky Sharp* was revived in September of 1904, George Arliss was playing the Marquis de Steyne. It had taken the Fiskes five years to find a replacement for Power.

Over the next few years, Tyrone Power's career was marked by mediocre work, with two exceptions. He enjoyed an enormous success as The Drain Man in *The Servant in the House,* which ran for two years, 1908 through 1910, in New York. Throughout 1911, he starred in a highly successful production of *Thaïs* opposite Constance Collier.

On January 3, 1912, Power's wife Edith died following surgery to remove a tumor near her heart. He forced himself a few days later to embark on a three-month tour in his hit of two seasons back, *The Servant in the House,* which opened in Detroit. Another actress took over his wife's part.

When he reached Cincinnati, he called upon Emma Reaume

and her mother. The two women had met the Powers when they appeared in Cincinnati before.

"Back then, a company would tour," Anne Power Hardenbergh, his daughter, said, "and pick up local talent to fill in the bits. Mother had met the Powers, and when the first wife died, she and her mother wrote him a letter of condolence. He wrote back and asked if he might take them both to dinner when he returned to Cincinnati. He did, and their romance went on from there."

According to a widely circulated story of the time, Tyrone Power had been deeply in love with his beautiful first wife. After her death, he developed an all-encompassing interest in the occult. He came to believe that his dead wife's spirit had selected Emma Reaume as the second Mrs. Tyrone Power.

Patty Emma Reaume—she dropped the first name while still a young girl—was thirty-one. Born in Indianapolis, she had taught theater arts at private schools in Covington, Kentucky, concentrating on speech. Then she toured in minor productions throughout the Midwest before she and the Reaume family settled in Cincinnati. Her aunt, Helen Schuster-Martin, founded a dramatic school there.

Tyrone Power, at forty-four, was thirteen years older. He was an imposing figure, a celebrated player, who despite his legendary drinking, must have been considered a good catch. Emma, a woman of the "arts," was no longer blooming with youth, and though handsome, she had never been considered a great beauty.

They were married within a year after Edith Crane's death. The new Mrs. Power combined her two given names into one, Patia, and went on tour in Shakespearean roles with her new husband. Patia Power soon became pregnant, but went on with the show, performing with her husband until two months before the lying in, when she returned to her mother's home in Cincinnati.

Their married life had begun at about the same time Tyrone Power was appearing in support of William Faversham's Antony in *Julius Caesar,* in which he played Brutus.

Faversham in the November 5, 1912, *The New York Times,* was praised for selecting players of mettle to contend for acting honors with him. He was lauded for "acting the role eloquently

. . . magnificent bearing, graceful in elocution, and consistently vigorous. It may be doubted whether his delivery of the speech over the dead Caesar's body has ever been equaled . . .

"In respect to his Brutus he (Faversham) has made a particularly happy choice, for Mr. Tyrone Power acts 'the noblest Roman of them all' in a manner to justify the phrase. His Brutus has nobility of bearing, is richly fluent in speech and movement and gesture, fluid in expression, and in practically every respect a reflection of the figure as the poet revealed him."

Despite the enthusiastic review—or perhaps because of it—Faversham and Power had an altercation, and the latter withdrew from the production.

Faversham stated to the *Dramatic Mirror* that "Power was a victim of jealousy and was annoyed because he had expected to make [a big hit] in the part."

Power took umbrage. In a letter to the editor, he wrote, "I am old-fashioned enough to believe what Mr. Faversham appears not to consider—that an actor should always remain a gentleman and that no salary is large enough to compensate for loss of self-respect."

Of that quality, he had a healthy amount. Paeans were still written about him, William Winter's at the forefront. "His figure is massive and imposing," the poet wrote. "His face is large, with strongly marked features, and is expressive of acute sensibility. His eyes, dark and brilliant, are communicative equally of tenderness and fire. His eyebrows (distinctively the actor's feature) are black and heavy, and they almost meet—like those of the wandering Jew, in representative ideal portraits of that mystical, lonely, wretched being."

Yet, a gradual evolution in the theater was in the making, which Power's old mentor, Augustin Daly, had been instrumental in starting. A new realistic drama was starting to dominate the stage, and Power's sonorous voice, larger-than-life presence, and too broad strokes with the makeup pencil would soon be making his acting style, and that of hundreds of others, passé.

The physical qualities that illuminated his art would, however, be a source of marvel for as long as he lived. These went along so well with the name he tendered his son, born May 5, 1914, at

five-thirty in the afternoon, at the Reaume family home at 2112
Fulton Avenue in Cincinnati.

His first conscious memory, as he later told an interviewer, was
of standing on a curb in New York while a delivery truck on the
street spun its wheels in a snowdrift. With him were his sister
Anne, fifteen months younger, and their nurse, Frieda Tracy, who
would take care of them until the boy started school. "I don't
know how old I was," he said, "but I was bundled to the eyebrows and so absorbed in the driver's efforts that I didn't know I
was cold."

The year was undoubtedly 1917, for Tyrone Power, Sr., had
brought his family with him to New York when he starred in *Chu
Chin Chow,* an Eastern musical spectacular with a plot suspi-
ciously similar to *Ali Baba and the Forty Thieves.*

It would be facile, yet accurate, symbolism to equate the snow-
bound truck—a visual image of his three-year-old awareness—
with this frail and often exhausted child, whose physical weakness
thwarted him from satisfying his lively curiosity.

"He's got too much energy and too little brawn," a doctor told
Patia Power shortly after his birth.

"Tyrone was not the most robust baby," his sister, Anne Power
Hardenbergh, said. "There was nothing medically wrong. Some
children are just born tiny and not terribly strong, whereas I was
born ten pounds overweight and screaming all the time."

"The pranks he played, even when he was still in diapers,
seemed inspired by the most destructive kind of malice," Howard
Sharpe wrote in *Photoplay* of July, 1937. "He was impatient
under punishment, self-willed in the face of opposition, and
loudly assertive when crossed." In those respects, he was very
much his father's son, as well as the Oedipal competitor for Patia
Power's attention.

Patia Power knew that her husband possessed the same negative qualities of other actors when she married him. He was irrita-
ble, restless, unreasonable, temperamental, totally self-involved.
He was also afflicted with the occupational disease of the actor—
alcoholism—and because of it she took on the role of his mother.
In drink the alcoholic often gives vent to his unconscious yearning

for a mother's protection. Only in her does the alcoholic actor find the unquestioning approval and admiration that become more difficult to elicit in audiences that have grown accustomed over the years to his bag of performing tricks. Only with his mother can he revert to a time when he is free from the inhibitions which, as an adult, hamper his development as a performer.

Tyrone Power would have to be as nurtured and protected as any infant. Since her son was sickly and her husband among the finest actors of his time, both required her constant and disproportionate attention. It's a wonder that she had any time left over to foster an acting career of her own.

In being cast as the mother to her husband, as well as to her actual son, Patia Power inadvertently contributed to the reawakening of the wandering eye of Tyrone Power, Sr. Now that he had his substitute mother's total support, he could again search for esteem and excitement from other females, more compliant and less complicated.

Young Tyrone was only a few months old when the Powers signed a contract with Famous Players to make some silent pictures in New York. Frieda Tracy was engaged as his nurse at that time.

The senior Tyrone Power was separated from his family for the first time when he went to Chicago early in 1915 to play The Drain Man—"a powerful yet humble being synonymous with the work of the world, its suffering and its glorious service"—in the Selig adaptation of his theatrical triumph, *The Servant in the House*. He stayed on there to start a second silent film, *Whom the Gods Destroy*. His pregnant wife and son were not asked to join him.

In April of 1915, during an interview with John Sheridan of *Photoplay*, he described his attempts to adapt to the hurly-burly of the new medium, particularly when it involved filming on city streets:

> I am, invariably, more rattled than a stage-struck girl in a first appearance in her hometown. I can't get used to having my fervor [*sic*] dodge a street car or sidestep a baby carriage. I feel like an actor doing *Hamlet* with the scenery indecently falling

down around him, or a leading lady losing her skirt in the midst of a grand rage . . . I am embarrassed because my audience is continually walking in and out on me, or just *past* me, which is worse.

"I believe I speak from the personal standpoint of the actor in general when I say that the most appealing thing to the legitimate player who turns to pictures is the resident feature of the business. The actor becomes a citizen instead of a nomad. He spends his money for a garden hose instead of tipping bellboys. He actually sees his children going to school—you bet he does, for he leaves for the studio at the same time they leave for morning classes. He gets acquainted with his wife, and if she is a player, there is usually work for her too . . .

In Chicago I am living at a hotel for the reason that my time here is very uncertain, but if I go to California Mrs. Power and I have the bungalow thing absolutely planned to its smallest feature. We have maps of Los Angeles and the printed seductions of at least twenty real estate men. We are going to have a home! This, of course, will not interfere with my Eastern home, which is my permanent place of residence, but it is comforting to think of crossing the continent and playing in anything long enough to simulate a home and homelike atmosphere.

The Eastern residence, actually a summer house, was a two-story frame building called Two Elms, located at Ile-Aux-Noix near Quebec. The building would be destroyed by fire in a few years, but Tyrone Power, Sr., continued to return to the area, staying at a nearby inn on the Richelieu River.

Most of his theatrical contemporaries didn't feel movies would be the art miracle of the twentieth century, as Tyrone Power, Sr., did. "Mrs. Power and I have a little son," he told an interviewer, "and naturally all our hopes are centered on him. And when he grows in years, the art of motion pictures will do much for his education."

Yet, one man who came to agree with Power's assessment was the greatest actor of his generation. "The actor of today has an opportunity to get variety of work through acting in the films," John Barrymore wrote in his 1925 book, *Confessions of an Actor.*

"In the beginning a great many persons of the theater and out of it looked upon the movies as an inferior art. It isn't . . . Not only may the actor gain variety of expression and work through appearing in the pictures, but he can earn enough money so that he may retire before he is too old. A man never knows when he is too old to play Romeo."

Barrymore was considerably more plain-spoken about movies in real life. Despite the "silly, scented jackasses" he was forced to play in costume epics at Warner Brothers, he told friends, "It's so much better having a nice house here than farting around the country playing King Lear."

The Powers were reunited in California, where Ty, Sr., had contracted to make additional pictures for Selig. Their daughter Anne was born there on August 26, 1915.

In June of 1916, Tyrone Power, Sr., repeated his role of Brutus in an outdoor production of *Julius Caesar,* mounted before audiences of twenty-five thousand at the Temple of Jupiter in Beachwood Canyon, the forerunner to the Hollywood Bowl. William Farnum starred as Antony in the production, and others in the cast were De Wolf Hopper, Frank Keenan, Mae Murray, and Douglas Fairbanks, Sr. He stayed on to make several silent pictures in nearby Universal City, before accepting the offer to star on Broadway opposite Florence Reed in *Chu Chin Chow.* It was a popular entertainment, unlike the classical roles that had predominated throughout his career, and Tyrone Power chewed up the scenery at the same time he was smacking his lips over Bertha Knight, a leading interpretative dancer in the show.

When the seriousness of her husband's infatuation with another woman became known, Patia Power didn't rail at the past sacrifices she had made for her errant husband. The family doctor had been advising Patia to find a balmier climate for her delicate son, and she could withdraw from the distasteful situation with her dignity intact. The marriage was virtually ended.

If the principals often don't know the full reasons for the breaking up of a marriage, their children know even less.

"When you're a child, you don't really know," Anne said, "and in my day children were just not kept informed. You just assumed someone came and someone left. I don't know when it happened or what happened. All I knew was that they were apart. I had no trauma at all. Nor, as far as I know, did Tyrone."

Nevertheless Patia told him he had to be moved to a more temperate locale. That this migration with his mother and sister coincided with the separation of his parents may well have created unavoidable guilts, so that he felt it was he and not a situation of which he was unaware that caused the estrangement. He was partly right.

Only later did Ty discover how necessary to his well-being the move actually was. As he told his close friend, Edith Mayer Goetz, it was the recurrence of rheumatic fever, which he hadn't known he'd had, that confined him to bed for long periods of time, and which necessitated the move to a climate where fresh air and sunshine were plentiful. There were no immediate symptoms that his heart was permanently damaged, but these could be quiescent for years until the long-range effects of the disease took their probable toll.

Patia and her children settled in San Diego about the time the first American Expeditionary Forces were landing in France. World War One troops were mobilizing in and about San Diego, and she resourcefully organized the Power Players, a branch of the Stage Women's War Relief unit of the Red Cross. Plays, vaudeville shows, and concerts were mounted by her and her associates on military bases in the area.

Frieda Tracy was delegated to care for the children while Patia performed her war relief work. Young Tyrone and his sister grew stronger and browner on the sands of Coronado Beach. Because he was frail, they were nearly physical equals and preferred each other's company to that of other children. Brother and sister remained inordinately close for the rest of his life.

When she had time to spend with her children, Patia concentrated her energies on her son. Despite her claim that she was born screaming, Anne screamed on the inside, for she was never the disciplinary problem her brother was. She was stolid and calm, almost a stoic in her lack of reactions, even when Tyrone at the age of four cut off her long brown curls.

"I don't know that I was that unemotional," his sister says today, "but perhaps I didn't show it as a child. Why does a child do anything? I think he said, 'Let me cut your hair.' I said, 'Go on ahead.'"

Patia, through her own training as a teacher, was a strict disciplinarian. Perhaps unconsciously, she tried to remove any traces of her estranged husband's weaknesses in their son. The test of two strong wills—the mother's and the son's—made the household a miniature hell. Tyrone lacked any immediate male role models to intercede on his behalf. As he grew older and Patia was able to reason with him, he became more malleable. Tyrone Power's mother finally succeeded in shaping him to her satisfaction and in so doing she broke his defiant spirit.

Her Little Lord Fauntleroy had become a boy of blind obedience and impeccable breeding. But most striking of all was his beauty.

"Isn't it sad the boy got all the good looks?" Patia would ask of those who commented on his dark and perfect features. She didn't seem to consider the effect this thoughtless remark would have on her daughter, Anne, a sweet and agreeable girl whom her brother adored. The feeling was ardently returned, and Anne didn't outwardly resent the way Tyrone was singled out for notice.

"I believe Tyrone was personable even when very young," his sister said, "of slender build, dark of hair and eyes, independent and resourceful of nature. When one looks at one's brother one does not really notice what others may notice; but I believe there was no time when he was not attracted to and attractive to the girls. He was as mischievous as little boys always are, animated and not averse to a good scrap if the situation arose . . . as it usually does when one is young." The situation hadn't arisen often, however, for Tyrone was too sheltered thus far to be exposed to much roughhousing.

This would change somewhat after Patia moved with her children to Alhambra, after the end of the war. She was engaged to play the leading-lady role of Señora Josefa Yorba in John Steven McGroarty's *Mission Play*, which was staged annually at the San Gabriel Mission. Since she was also in charge of casting, it was to be a year-round job. Coincidentally, the children's first exposure to the theater came four years previously when their father played the role of Father Junipero Serra, founder of the California missions, in the same pageant.

The people in the predominantly Methodist town of Alhambra were unusually public-spirited, and the Mission Playhouse in nearby San Gabriel was an integral part of their lives. The pageant was equal in every respect to the better-known Ramona pageant in San Diego, and Alhambrans basked in the achievements of their neighboring town. Orange groves abounded in Alhambra, as did packing houses where Mexican immigrants worked. The children of the town would prankishly rub their noses on each other's clothes, for soot would accumulate on their faces from the smudge pots used by the growers to ward off the winter cold.

Standing in the center of the town was the high school, along with a library with a stereopticon department more extensive than that of any other suburb of Los Angeles.

A spirited rivalry existed among the town's six grammar schools and their total enrollments of over one thousand students, particularly in the track meets held every fall. If Tyrone didn't participate as an athlete, it was because there were chores at home after school every day.

Collectively, the boys of the town gathered scrap iron for recycling during the first world war. Not feeling this was enough for the war effort, they volunteered to do more. Chief of Police Ben Parker decided that relays of these boys could guard the bridge over Arroyo San Pasqual every evening from six to nine, because there would be no regular officer on duty at that time and "that's just the time saboteurs might choose to do their work." That the bridge was of no strategic military importance was beside the point.

The war over, several community organizations joined forces to clear up rubbish before planting trees and building pergolas to create Alhambra City Park. On Friday nights, families congregated there for picnic suppers prior to a program presented by playground children.

In contrast to the children's unconventional and insecure touring existence of the past, they were deposited in the midst of wholesome Americana. Because of Alhambra's many open spaces, a child could hear his mother calling him from several blocks away. Patia Power, with or without her husband, was finally making a permanent home for her children.

Tyrone Power, Sr., in the meantime, carried out his six-year-old threat to William Faversham to mount a New York production of *Julius Caesar,* in which he again enacted Brutus. It ran for a week in March, 1918, with Walter Hampden as Antony, Cyril Keightley as Cassius, Howard Kyle as Caesar, and Alma Kruger as Portia. Then, he began discussing the possibility of marriage to Bertha Knight. Their engagement would last for three years.

Patia Power suffered nobly and silently. She had become the chief, if not the sole, breadwinner of her family. Her estranged husband's child-support payments came in erratically, if at all. The children were approaching school age and were told they no longer needed a nurse. In truth, Patia could no longer afford to pay Frieda Tracy. "We were not told of such matters," Anne said. "I know that our mother had an earned income, but as to the extent of my father's contribution to us I have no idea."

Patia quite simply was forced to throw herself into her work in order to support her children. Her dressing room would serve as a playroom for Tyrone and Anne during the run of the play every season, and as a classroom during the rest of the year. The children hadn't started grade school as yet, but their theatrical training had already begun.

Patia Power taught Tyrone and Anne breathing exercises and had them study enunciation, pronunciation, and articulation. Testament to the effectiveness of her method was her son's being awarded the 1946 International Sound Research Institute award for diction, one of the few film actors to win that award.

Unlike the stage-mother stereotype, Patia was not even remotely manipulative. She didn't resort to stratagems and cajoleries to get them to do her bidding. Her approach was totally direct and disobedience was unthinkable. Having been exposed to backstage life, the children knew practice as well as theory in stage conduct. "We were always theater people," Anne said. "When you live in that environment as a small child and then through subsequent years . . . and when both parents are professionals . . . you accept it as a way of life and not a remote realm of glamor . . . you know the value of the work, that you're always on time in the theater, that you owe an obligation to your profession."

In 1920, Tyrone, Sr., and Patia Power were finally divorced. That same year their son entered Granada Grammar School. He and his sister, who'd spent virtually all their lives together, were separated for the first time as Tyrone stepped out into the big world. He made immediate friends with two classmates, Olive Ponitz and Roger Wellman. The boy would die quite young leaving a shocking void in the lives of both Tyrone and Olive. "I don't remember that he had any other particular little boy friend," Olive, now Mrs. George Behrendt, one of Los Angeles' most distinguished civic and social leaders, said. "Nor do I remember him participating in sports as others did."

Because she was Jewish and he was a Catholic, they were among the few of their classmates who didn't congregate every Sunday at the Methodist church.

"It was another thing we had in common," Olive Behrendt said. "I don't remember ever meeting Ty. I always knew him. He was my best friend . . . no argument. There's always a child in school who everyone thought was fine and good and lovely. That child was Tyrone.

"As a child," Olive Behrendt continued, "I wasn't aware of the beauty of others . . . except for Ty. It came from within, the expression from the eyes. Those wonderful brows and those black eyes! The eyes don't change. That was always evident in Ty. He had presence, even as a little boy. People would say, 'Look at that lovely boy! Look at that face!' I always felt the face never changed. He was as beautiful as a grown man as he was as a child. There was no vulgarity in his face . . . a fineness. Yet, I never felt he was self-centered, nor aware of his beauty. If he were it would have made him an entirely different child. I never had the impression that he was an unhappy child, nor did I find him to be a happy one.

"He was a very fine boy . . . gentle . . . genteel. He listened. Very few people do. I think that speaks very well of his mother. She must have done something wonderful. Her children had strong cultural interests. Her standards had to be high. Ty must have had good relations with her. He was very much loved."

Mrs. Behrendt recalls Patia Power as "a handsome and nice lady. She was darling to me. Most of all I remember her being very strong. I never spent much time with her. She must have been working. All I remember is asking if Ty could do this or that. As I look back I'm sure it wasn't easy for her.

"I was aware his mother and father were divorced. Mother said, 'My, the strength of Mrs. Power!' I know Ty had pride in his father, and I'm not sure his sister Anne would know its extent. Yet, he spoke very infrequently about him, and only when I would prod. There were things you simply didn't discuss."

Relations between Patia and her ex-husband had turned extremely bitter since the divorce. They didn't improve when, in February of 1921, Tyrone Power, Sr., married Bertha Knight in a New Jersey civil ceremony. He was fifty-one and his third wife was thirty-four. Yet, Tyrone's mother didn't belittle his father in any way. Her children were early made aware of their father's singular talent. If they later came to know of Tyrone Power, Sr.'s, weakness in spirit and the flesh, they were not to talk about it. Life's vicissitudes were to be borne without self-pity and complaint. They were an unfair burden to place on anyone else. The boy learned his lesson well. He would spend a lifetime being outwardly placid and holding in grievances.

The Powers lived in a Spanish bungalow south of Main, one block from the grammar school, while the Ponitz family lived a few blocks away, north of the street where those better off Alhambrans lived. "I know they were not people of means," Olive Behrendt said, "but I never thought of this as a division. I was never aware of who had or didn't have anything. The Power family was very close, and I don't think their mother let them feel they were in need or want. They wouldn't have talked about it if they were. They were very private people. I can't remember anything about their house, nor did I get to know Anne well, which suggests that many of the things we did together happened at our house.

"Some children are not loud and not noisy. Ty was like that. He had an open quality, but he was modest and shy. My mother adored having him near."

Olive and Tyrone shared a love of music and opera. "They say that by the age of seven your passions are set," Olive Behrendt said. "Well, these were our passions, and culture had nothing to do with it."

Culture nevertheless had been ingrained in the young girl since infancy. Her family was the most cultivated in Alhambra. "Ours was the house where everybody came," Olive Behrendt said. "Privilege in our family was how much you learned. We were always putting on performances at our house: dancing, imitating operas, musicales. My cousin Lydia Marcus was a pianist, and my brother played the violin. He was four-and-a-half years older than Ty and I. We wanted to become part of his life, but he wanted no part of us. Yet, it was a wonderful life. My dear husband George once said that the most abnormal thing about me was that I had a wonderful childhood."

Tyrone was often invited along when Olive and her family went to Los Angeles to concerts and the ballet, as well as to the movies in downtown Alhambra.

"All this is what we shared. So many children keep secrets. We told each other everything. He shared my dreams about music and dance. As children we talked make believe, not acting. I never heard him overtly say he wanted to be an actor, yet I expected him to. I didn't tell him, but he wasn't surprised either when I studied opera."

He would make his stage debut some ten years before Olive made hers at the San Francisco Opera. In his second year of school, at age seven, Tyrone was cast as Pablo, a neophyte of the Franciscan fathers.

He was emotionally prepared for a life of celibacy, having recently learned about sex and being totally unimpressed. That attitude drastically changed within a few years.

Olive Behrendt was also recruited for the *Mission Play*. "I remember Ty's excitement. 'Can you come?' he asked. He went to my mother and asked if I could be in it on a Saturday. I played an Indian. My love of wanting to be in theater makeup started then."

Tyrone Power, Sr., continued to flirt with silent films during his son's primary school years. *Footfalls* was one of the few pictures of this period in which Power had the leading part, that of an old blind cobbler whose sharp ears can recognize an acquaintance by the sound of his walk. The photoplay, as were so many others of the period, was highly melodramatic. The old man hears a fight upstairs between his son and a lodger. One kills the other and attempts to flee with a satchel containing a large amount of money. A lamp is overturned during the fight, setting fire to the house. The dead man is burned beyond recognition. The old man seizes the escaping man on the stairs and grabs the satchel from him. Police, because of identification found on his body, identify the dead man as the lodger. The old man nevertheless waits for the killer to return for the money. When he does, the blind man chokes him to death. Then it is revealed that the killer is the lodger and not the son, and that the old man awaited the killer's return to exact revenge.

"Only in a few scenes does the picture become at all impressive," The New York Times said in its review of September 9, 1921, "despite the fact that Tyrone Power, as the old cobbler, has the face and figure suited to the part and, while not a subtle pantomimist, is yet sufficiently definite and vigorous to make the role acceptable."

Apparently film makers didn't find him definite and vigorous enough. If he was slumming in the brawling infant medium, his new associates hardly noticed his condescension. A player of no small distinction on the stage, Tyrone Power was further reduced as a mature character actor to performing in support of younger, less steady talents.

He was delighted, and grateful, to be able to return to the stage soon after. The kudos his son received in his first appearance were also enjoyed by the father when he opened as The Wandering Jew. The production had had an enormous success in London the previous season, and was presented in New York by A. L. Erlanger in association with David Belasco. In it, Power was required to go through strenuous paces, completely changing clothes and makeup between acts, the drama spanning more than one thousand years. He played four distinct characters, each centuries apart in customs and habits, while conveying the impression that they were possessed with the same individuality.

Power's performance was a tour de force. In a statement to an interviewer which could apply word for word to his son some thirty years later, Tyrone Power, Sr., said, "I have been wearing the trappings of costume parts for so long a time now that I feel more at home in them than in ordinary street dress. That may seem strange to you, but it's a fact. It's like anything else that you are closely identified with for a long time. It is bound to become second nature to you."

In a separate interview, he made one last plea for his possibly outmoded approach to acting. "There isn't any such thing as a new school of acting," he said. "If there is I want to see it. So far as plays containing everyday life are concerned, I want a shot at one of them myself . . . Oh, they refer sometimes to me in newspaper stories as the old-time actor. I don't know why. Faversham and Skinner and I play young parts when we care to. The only difference is that when we begin studying a play, we treat it seriously, and when we speak our lines you can hear us past the front row . . . What some of our younger actors today call their new school will be the old school next year . . . What we need instead of new or old schools is quality, accomplishment, real ability on our stage . . . When a great moment comes in a great play, a man has to go. He can't whisper when the climax is reached. You would think to hear some people talk about my voice that I'm something covered with hair—a wild animal. My God, I'm not that, am I?"

Despite his awesomeness, his son didn't consider him as such when he visited Tyrone Power, Sr., and his new wife during the show's run. The father didn't like the slight effeminacy he noted in his son and gave him a football to take back to California.

When he returned to Alhambra, Tyrone's schoolmates were fascinated. None of them had heard of the game. He appointed himself captain of the team and they played on a vacant lot every afternoon after school. He had been grounded for throwing a baseball through a living-room window in the past. He was forced to scrimp in order to pay for the damage. Since he liked the sound of breaking glass, he limited his destructive acts in the future to breaking bottles with his baseball bat.

Back in New York, on the strength of his success in *The Wandering Jew,* Tyrone Power, Sr., was in the enviable and unusual position of sifting through several offers.

In the summer of 1922, Mrs. Fiske asked him if he would appear with her in a revival of *Becky Sharp.* "Half a lifetime later, Power was remembered best for his performance in Mrs. Fiske's company," Archie Binns and Olive Kooken wrote in *Mrs. Fiske and the American Theatre,* "and belatedly he realized the magic of the school-marm-looking little woman who could call up in an actor greatness which no other director was able to call up afterward."

Power opted instead to appear in the Players' Club all-star revival of *The Rivals,* with Robert Warwick, Francis Wilson, John Craig, and others. He wasn't willing to commit himself to a long run with Mrs. Fiske when a more enticing project was at hand. With his refusal of the engagement with the formidable actress, all their previous plans to appear together in *Macbeth* evaporated.

In addition to appearing with Maurice Barrymore in *Becky Sharp,* Tyrone Power, Sr., had once portrayed Frederick in a production of *As You Like It,* starring John Barrymore's father. Now he was being asked to play Claudius, at $875 a week, to the son's Hamlet. John Barrymore would be receiving $1,000.

During rehearsals, Barrymore electrified his associates with his Oedipal interpretation. "By God!" Ty Power, Sr., said. "He's going to make the hit of his life in this part . . ."

The production opened on November 16, 1922, at the Sam H. Harris Theatre under the aegis of producer Arthur Hopkins. Never had the Broadway stage witnessed such an enthusiastic reception for a classical role. Barrymore's interpretation was hailed as a landmark in the theater, and his fellow player's contributions, Ty Power, Sr.'s, included, were virtually overlooked.

When a deputation of elderly actors called on Barrymore during the run, asking him to stop his performances so as not to break the record of one hundred performances set by the master, Edwin Booth, Barrymore laughed them out of his dressing room.

"Gentlemen," he reportedly said, "I think it about time that you stop living in the past. That's what is wrong with the world. It is run by a lot of persons who keep bitching up the present by applying only the rules of a dead past. I am compelled to inform you that I shall play Hamlet for exactly one hundred and one times."

This he went on to do. Barrymore had been losing interest in the role as the run progressed, but after defying the elderly actors, his vitality returned and he ended the engagement in triumph. The same couldn't be said about Ty Power, Sr. There's a theatrical saying that the great actor triumphs in a tour de force, as Tyrone, Sr., had so recently proved, while the lesser actor is forced to tour. Ty Power, Sr.'s, change in fortune was so abrupt that he wasn't deemed good enough to do even that. Hints that he was unreliable and that he performed while drunk were not very subtly veiled.

To Anne's knowledge, her father was not an alcoholic. "I never saw any evidence of it. Where you don't have a family life, such unawareness is to be expected. But I don't feel he was a drinking drinker. You can't stay in any art profession and continue to produce indefinitely, as my father did at his age, if you are undermined alcoholically. It takes a terrible toll, and would impair one's work."

His daughter didn't realize it, but this was exactly what had happened. Film director George Cukor, getting his start in the theater in the early 1920s, recalled meeting Tyrone Power, Sr. "He was an old gentleman, on his uppers, and he seemed rather faded. I remember seeing him in some of his great roles. He had a beautiful voice and a noble carriage . . . all in all a very distinguished man."

It became public knowledge that he wasn't doing well financially when Patia, in June of 1923, bowed to her own everyday pressures. She had him arrested for nonsupport of the children. At issue was $1,600 in arrears. The action was filed in her legal name, Emma R. Arper (or Emma R. Arpel-Power [*sic*] as later reports put it), strongly suggesting that she had another husband before Power. Two weeks later, the sum was paid and the action against the actor was dismissed.

His path seemed to cross with his ex-wife and their two children as Ty Power, Sr., resorted to the inevitable, and headed West for additional work in silent pictures. Over a four-year period, from 1922 to 1926, he appeared in about a dozen such movies. He was a mature character actor in support of Florence Reid in *The Black Panther's Cub;* Eleanor Boardman in *The Day of Faith;* Dorothy Dalton and Jack Holt in *The Lone Wolf;* Marion Davies in *Janice Meredith* (in which W. C. Fields was also lesser billed); Dolores Costello and John Harron in *Bride of the Storm;* Agnes Ayres and Antonio Moreno in *The Story Without a Name;* Reginald Denny and Marion Nixon in *Where Was I?;* Ernest Torrence and William Collier, Jr., in *The Wanderer;* Raymond Griffith and Mary Brian in *A Regular Fellow;* Priscilla Banner and Nellie Bly Baker in *The Red Kimono.*

As for Patia and her brood, she was able to use the $1,600 settlement to return East in 1923 to Cincinnati, where her family lived and where she could expect to receive the emotional support that had been lacking in her life for the last several years. She took the job of assistant dean at the Schuster-Martin Dramatic School run by her Aunt Helen. The accredited school was noted for its large dance department, and Patia was now being entrusted to improve the other theater arts at the school.

Aunt Helen was considerably younger than Patia's mother, whom her grandchildren called Mudgie. Her husband, Grandfather Reaume, dead long before Tyrone and Anne were born, had worked as a railroad conductor and had been badly injured in a railway accident. He was an invalid for years before his death. Patia's brother, Charles, was an absentee member of the family, through his several marriages having created several additional families of his own. He'd been successful selling background music for Station WLW in Cincinnati during the earliest days of radio.

It was Mudgie who was matriarch and head of the surviving, totally female family that surrounded Tyrone.

At the age of nine, Tyrone shared his father's belief in predestination and the occult, as well as other influences, beyond his control or comprehension, that govern the behavior of a person.

For those who don't believe in such matters, it might be considered hindsight—based on dozens of fan magazine articles—for Margaret Malock to analyze the hand of the film actor, which she reported in the December, 1946, issue of *Photoplay:*

"Tyrone's early life is mirrored in his fate line, which starts deep on the outer part of the hand and brings to mind the picture of a boy given to dreaming . . . The broken marriage of his parents is clearly etched in the early formation of the fate line and the shock of this to his happy nature is recorded. Until the age of ten, a strong but painful influence appears and with it a great disappointment. It is my conclusion that it was at this point that he began to understand the erratic nature of his father, accepting his many weaknesses, putting behind himself his childhood illusions and even loving him in a curious, shy way.

"His sister gave him comfort and companionship during the years when the adult world of his father and mother seemed harsh and terrifying. Tyrone was a physically weak child and since there was only a slight age difference, he turned to his . . . sister to assuage his loneliness."

The flat Patia took with her children, in the Walnut Hills section of Cincinnati, was in a building that tumbled in a ramshackle fashion along the side of a hill. There was no mistaking its extreme modesty. With justifiable bitterness, Patia was no longer circumspect about discussing her ex-husband's failings. They had been hugely responsible for his as well as her straitened circumstances. But, then, he wasn't being discreet either, and the theater world had pretty well written him off. It wasn't that his alcoholism prevented him from performing. He simply wasn't able to summon up the suitable passions of the past, and his fellow actors had to, figuratively if not also literally, carry him.

Patia enrolled both Tyrone and Anne at the Sisters of Mercy Academy, the boy entering the fourth grade and his sister the second.

California had done wonders for the boy's health, and Granada Grammar School had given him a good educational foundation. Olive Behrendt found him to be her equal, and she was a highly intelligent and accomplished girl.

Although his love of play-acting remained, he somehow had lost his interest in schooling. He was no longer a listless child, but when it came to the classroom, he was a disinterested one. The Sisters of Mercy, much as they admired his manners and tried not to notice his beauty, nevertheless were forced to fail him.

At considerable financial sacrifice, Patia sent him off to St.

Xavier Academy, an all-male school, where he finished his elementary education. A male environment, after a lifetime thus far of being in totally female control, seemed to be what he needed.

Ty was particularly impressed with one of the brothers who seemed to have eyes in the back of his head. As he was writing on the blackboard, his back to the class, he would suddenly sense who was misbehaving. He would spin around, calling out the offender's name, flipping the piece of chalk between his thumb and forefinger at the miscreant. "He never misses a shot," the boy told his mother. "Catches me on the nose every time. He's swell!"

During this time, Ty seemed to wage a highly conscious effort to become all-boy. He played football in the afternoon with four neighborhood boys, as well as five Italians and three blacks from across the tracks. Patia forbade him to play with them.

"I'm not a snob," she explained to him, "but you have to draw the line somewhere."

Disobeying her orders, Ty continued to play with the same boys. During a tackle, he broke a finger. When he returned home, he said nothing. Over the next few weeks, the bone set in such a way that the finger became misshapen. When Patia discovered the injury, she carted him off to a doctor, who rebroke the finger and reset it properly. She didn't have to say much to her son about his disobedience. Retribution itself had spoken.

He was next sent to the preparatory school of the University of Dayton, a parochial school under the supervision of the Brothers of Mary. He was now approaching puberty, which some of his older classmates had already experienced, and sexual thoughts lay heavy in the air. He was a pretty boy, and subject to the advances of older fellows, but he avoided any entanglements by claiming ignorance—and rightfully so.

It was during this period that a flap involving Ty's father became so well publicized that it reached Ohio and other points west.

Writing in *Damned in Paradise,* John Kobler told of a letter Tyrone Power, Sr., had written that year, which was released to the press. In it, he reproached John Barrymore: "I think you know that I have always admired your art, on occasions I have called in your dressing-room and expressed my admiration of your performance. Though I disliked the part of the King in Hamlet, believing—as I still believe—that it is a difficult and thankless role, still when I undertook Claudius in your production I did all I could with it; it may not have been very much yet it was the best I could do. I played through your entire run, never missed a single performance, never slighted my work or played with indifference. It was all uphill work for me, but I was loyal in my effort to assist you, and to please your audience. Surely you will subscribe to this? I arrived here in London after an absence of twelve years, eager to again see my oldest and dearest friend Edmund Footman —in whose house you have been. Naturally we spoke of you . . . I was deeply wounded, hurt beyond measure when he said, 'Fred, in this room, sitting in this very chair, I was asking Barrymore about you, and he said, "I didn't bring Fred over because he is absolutely unreliable through drink and not to be trusted."' I cannot believe that you whom I have known since you were a boy, who was a friend and fellow-player with your father could have made such a statement. Uttered by an actor of your standing, it bears the stamp of authority, and calculated to ruin me in my profession . . . Until I hear from you I absolutely refuse to believe you would injure a man with a story without foundation of truth . . ."

Barrymore immediately wired Power, claiming the impression was erroneous and a letter was following. "In the first place," it read, "it is impossible for me to talk about any other actor in such a fashion, and in the second place I have far too much affection for you personally, as an old friend of my father's and myself to indulge in such an absurdity. The only thing that could possibly have been peculiarly misconstrued that I can imagine having happened, and I say this in order to palliate what was evidently a misconception on the part of Mr. Footman, whose hospitality was kindly tendered me, was some allusion intended to be humorous, in what I considered practically the bosom of your family (at least warm and loving friends of yours) to an occasional mutual potation we enjoyed together in the sanctity of my dressing room as the performance was in progress. Inasmuch as Shakespeare did the same with Burbage [the Elizabethan actor] that seems to establish a pretty good precedent for both of us, in whichsoever capacity either of us wish to cast himself.

"I think we are both old enough to realize that these contretemps happen in the best regulated domestic circles for varieties of reason, and should make no difference to friends of such long standing as ourselves . . . ."

Nevertheless, Barrymore had not retained Power and others in the American cast when he prepared for his London engagement of *Hamlet* in 1925. An all-British cast of supporting players was hired instead.

Ty returned from Dayton to Cincinnati to enter Purcell High School, also a Brothers of Mary Institution. He became fast friends with Wil Wright, who would later own the chain of southern California ice cream parlors bearing his name. He was one year behind Ty in school and had yet to enter Purcell. They met at the Schuster-Martin school, in a dramatic class coached by Patia.

"She was very domineering," Wil Wright said of Patia, "a power and a presence. As a kid I was scared of her. As long as you did what she wanted, you got along fine with her. She believed in strict discipline."

Students at the dramatic school, as Wright recalled, learned how to speak and to read various plays. Then they toured the nearby towns of Ohio in their amateur theatricals.

"In her way, she tolerated me," Wright said. "I know my family was fond of her."

Patia couldn't help but approve of her son's friendship with young Wright, as she had of his closeness to Olive Ponitz. Both were products of distinguished, more privileged households. Wright's father was a prosperous lumber dealer.

"We lived in a very nice house," Wright said, "in a much better area. It was apparent we didn't have financial problems. Mrs. Power had to support the kids, and yet her pride was enormous. Ty's childhood was pretty spartan. He was never a complainer, though. Ty was a good son. I didn't see any big family problems. His mother pretty much gave him his own head."

Yet there was the unspoken void of a father's absence. "We did not see a great deal of our father as we were growing up," Anne said. "He would periodically come through town to see us. My brother and I would go to Chicago to see *him*. We saw him in *Othello*. I was deeply impressed and, of course, quite proud." (The Moor and Macbeth were his favorite Shakespearean roles.)

"I believe I also saw him in *Diplomacy*, but I have no clear recollection of this," she stated. In that 1927 play, one of a record 268 Broadway productions that year, Tyrone Power, Sr., starred with Charles Coburn, Helen Gahagan, Cecilia Loftus, and his one-time nemesis, William Faversham.

During that period, Power was enjoying a last flurry of theatrical successes. Another 1927 production in which he appeared was the Players' Club revival of *Julius Caesar*. If his acting style was passé, you wouldn't have known it by the cheers of the audiences. "Tyrone Power made of honest Marcus Brutus a man among men," an overview of his career in the *New York Sun* read, "who wore his honor like a shula even as he drove his dagger home."

A personal tragedy blotted out the successes for him that year. His wife Bertha, only forty, died suddenly at the theatrical hotel on West Forty-sixth Street where they were living. Her death took more out of Ty Power, Sr., than he would admit, but he persevered.

The following year, he starred in *The Unknown Warrior*, and Bide Dudley of the *New York Evening World* was moved to write, "His diction is marvelous and his great sense of theatrical values admirable. Even his whisper is impressive."

Despite the recent successes, the influence of his voice and acting style had similarly faded to a whisper, though hardly impressive, for additional New York offers weren't forthcoming. "He saw all around him actors without a tithe of his talent and personal attributes making fortunes by means of the art which he was a master," Roy Day, Librarian of the Players, wrote in *The New York Tribune*. "Tyrone Power was patrician in appearance. His countenance and demeanor were noble. Withal he was simple. At times he was boyish and this was noticeably evident when he felt he had been wronged. His quarrels with managers were many

. . . He resented the spirit of tyranny and was ever with the underdog. His treatment of the subordinate actor was considerate and kind."

Wright found his friend Ty "happy and wild. Later he was not so happy, but our life was very uncomplicated when we were kids. There was nothing at all unusual about his high school years. Ty wasn't a follower, nor did I ever think of him as a leader. He had no causes. I don't recall his ever pressuring anyone to get his own way in anything.

"That was the way we were brought up. We would never think of going downtown without a coat and tie. This was an era when there weren't many fads. I remember, though, that in high school we would get into some horseplay. You'd walk up to a fellow and grab him by the shirt, and rip it off. We all went along with it."

Ty had to earn his spending money. He took a job as a delivery boy for a drugstore near Peeble's Corner, an intersection close to downtown.

These years, 1928 to 1930, were when skirts were their shortest and trousers their fullest. The young people of Cincinnati congregated at Ault Park, on the hills overlooking the river. A pastry-cake pavilion with a marble floor and surrounded by terraces was situated in the midst of a grove of trees. An orchestra played for dancing. Admission was twenty-five cents, and each dance cost a dime.

"I remember Ty coming over on a Saturday afternoon," Wright said. "We'd wash the family car and go out on Saturday nights." There was no particular girl in Ty's life, nor in Wright's, but young men of the period weren't as forward then as they are now.

Occasionally, until he was able to buy his own oil-burner, Ty borrowed Patia's car. He had begun working as an usher in a theater by this time, and he went to his mother one night, asking to use her car to take a girl home. He'd met her at the movie theater. Patia suggested the girl be brought up to their apartment. She was about to show in not so subtle fashion how complete was her influence over her son.

His mother could see why Ty found the girl attractive. But those tinny bracelets, and that giggle, and all that perfume . . .

When they were ready to go, Patia took a long breath. "It's so very warm tonight—would you mind if I came along too for the ride? I'll sit in the back seat."

Tyrone looked at her calmly, his eyes expressionless.

"Very well, mother . . ."

Patia sat in the tonneau and stared straight ahead, knowing how miserable she was making the young people.

Her courtesy to the girl was faultless. She didn't imply by word or tone or attitude what she thought of her.

The girl, intimidated by the formidable Patia, lost her poise completely when they stopped in front of her modest house on the wrong side of the tracks. Patia felt pity for her, but she had to demonstrate to her son how unsuitable the girl was for him.

On their way home, Ty stopped the car, motioned for his mother to come up into the front seat with him. "Okay, you win," he said sheepishly. Patia suddenly felt exhausted, as if she'd been running uphill for hours.

Tyrone Power, Sr., as well as the movies, now had a voice, albeit in his case it was over sixty years old. It would be competing with the panoramic vistas and cinematic effects envisioned by director Raoul Walsh for a Fox picture, *The Big Trail,* as well as with the talents of a studio stunt man being given his first chance to star in a picture. His name was John Wayne.

The younger actor portrayed a scout for the wagon train heading from Missouri to the West. He too would be juxtaposed against a buffalo stampede, Indian attacks, the fording of a river, the lowering of cattle over steep cliffs by rope, thunderstorms, blizzards, and burning desert sands.

The tyro handled his assignment well. "Mr. Wayne acquits himself with no little distinction," Mordaunt Hall wrote in *The New York Times* of October 29, 1930. "His performance is pleasingly natural and even if he is somewhat fortunate in settling matters in a closing scene with the ignominious Red Flack and his cohort, Lopez, one feels that he is entitled to this stroke of luck."

Power portrayed Flack who "has a voice that reminds one of Captain Hook in Peter Pan. He talks in English to Lopez, who replies in Spanish." If his notices weren't as positive as Wayne's, they were nevertheless respectable and offered Power the hope that he could spend his declining winters ensconced in mild and temperate southern California, with summers to be spent in Quebec.

His son Tyrone had starred in *Officer 666,* the senior class play at Purcell High School. Like so many before him, he had been seduced by the applause. He wasn't bold and presumptuous, and he'd rarely sought out his father's attention. Ty Power, Sr.'s, only son had always been afraid of this stranger, whose voice was resonant and whose manner, if not angry, was certainly stern. Ty nevertheless wrote his father in California as he was finishing the picture with John Wayne, telling him of his desire to follow in the family's footsteps. He was surprised that the older man answered so quickly. Ty Power, Sr.'s, thoughtful, rambling letter suggested Ty might want to spend the upcoming summer with him in Quebec, for some fishing and high-flown actor talk. Along with the letter, he sent an abridged version of Hamlet's advice to the Players, which he thought was as good a guide to acting as any:

> Speak the speech I pray you, as I pronounced it to you, trippingly on the tongue; but if you mouth it, as many of your players do, I had as lief the town-crier spoke my lines. Nor do you not saw the air too much with your hands, thus, but use all gently; for in the very torrent, tempest, and as I may say, the whirlwind of passion you must acquire and beget a temperance that may give it smoothness . . .

Ty was eager to make himself ready after he graduated from high school that spring. Academically, he wasn't an overachiever, a fact he well realized. The women of his family nevertheless gathered to discuss what college he wanted to attend. There was his mother, Patia Power; his great aunt, Helen Schuster-Martin; and his Grandmother Reaume.

"I want to become an actor," Ty told them.

Patia was pleased. She had, after all, coached Ty and his younger sister since they were small children in California.

"How do you plan to accomplish it?" she asked.

"Father wants me to come to Quebec with him for the summer. He says he'll coach me."

Both Mudgie and Aunt Helen groaned.

"Absolutely not!" Patia said.

"But, Mother," Ty protested. "How am I going to get any experience?"

It was the quality of that experience that Patia dreaded. Granted, the father could prepare his son admirably for the stage, but there were more earthly pursuits she'd rather Ty not learn as yet.

Then there was Ty Power, Sr.'s, melancholy existence. He had always been a hard-drinking womanizer, and Patia Power had spent the last eighteen years wondering why she ever married him. Since his third wife's death, he was disoriented and lost.

His reputation for unreliability, due to his alcoholism, made it difficult enough to get acting assignments. But his florid acting style—the sepulchral voice and exaggerated gestures—also held him back.

That Patia finally agreed to Ty's joining his father was as much an act of kindness on her part, giving her ex-husband a sense of purpose in the form of their son, as it was due to Ty's uncharacteristic insistence.

Now that the matter was settled, he could tell his closest school friends, Wil Wright and Ben Hamilton, of his plans.

With Wil, Ty had long shared a love of dramatics and a general disinterest in sports.

With Ben, it was another matter. Sexual experimentation had led to what his friend considered a deeper relationship. There'd been no talk of a long-lasting commitment between them. The idea was ludicrous to them both. Yet, Ben expected they would be going on to college together, where they would be roommates and their friendship would continue.

Wil wished him luck, and the two promised to keep in touch. Ben, however, was very hurt.

"You never said anything about this," he told Ty.

"But you knew I wanted to become an actor," Ty replied.

"You never said so."

"We'll still see each other," Ty said, trying to mollify him.

The two boys parted on a rather formal note. Ty had always been a private person, although others tended to reveal their innermost thoughts to him. Because he hadn't confided in Ben about his plans, his friend was in a black mood. Ty charmed him out of it. Charm was a commodity he plentifully possessed.

The journey from Cincinnati to Quebec, with its layovers and transfers to different trains, took more than a day, a hot and humid one. Ty occasionally reread his father's letter on the trip. The metallic taste in his mouth and the curiously full feeling of his stomach, despite his not having eaten on the trip, were symptoms of the apprehension, excitement, and doubt Ty Power, Sr., generated in his son.

His father welcomed him at the train with a happy bit of news. He was engaged for a short season in repertoire at the Chicago Shakespeare Festival, under the direction of Fritz Lieber, which would be conducted in the fall. His son was also being offered a job.

During the summer in Quebec, Ty Power, Sr., put into practice what he had verbalized in his letter, and Ty received a cram course in acting. He would never feel emotionally close to his father, the years of estrangement having taken their toll, but he appreciated the way Ty Power, Sr., extended himself for him.

When the Chicago season opened, Ty Power, Sr., was playing a supporting role in *The Merchant of Venice,* the lesser billing denoting his humbled circumstances. His son—whom the company called Young Ty—was playing an even smaller part as a friend of the Doge. Ty didn't know what his father's salary was, but he was delighted that he was getting forty dollars a week.

The play had proceeded into the fourth act, where Shylock, the Jewish money-lender, was about to exact his pound of flesh.

"And you must cut this flesh from off his breast," the actress portraying Portia proclaimed. "The law allows it, and the court awards it."

Fritz Lieber as Shylock responded, "Most learned judge! A sentence! Come, prepare!" Lieber apparently had forgotten Hamlet's instructions to the Players and sawed the air too much with his hands. The knife he was holding flew out of his grasp across the stage, barely missing Young Ty before it stuck in a scenery flat.

Ty Power, Sr., was standing next to his son. "You're not hurt, boy. Keep on playing." He nodded to Portia, cuing her to continue.

"Tarry a little," she resumed. "There is something else . . ."

It was Young Ty's baptism in the centuries-old ritual that the show must go on.

No mention was made of the near-disaster when the *New York American* made passing notice of a new actor in the ranks. Under a headline, TYRONE POWER III MAKES STAGE BOW, a one-paragraph item read: "Tyrone Power made his debut on the stage as a Shakespearean actor with the Chicago Civic Shakespeare Society Monday evening in *The Merchant of Venice* under the tutelage of his father Tyrone Power. Tyrone Power III will be seen in small speaking parts." Ty also played a page in *Hamlet* and a Roman soldier in *Julius Caesar* during the few weeks of the season.

From there, father and son went on to Hollywood, where Ty Power, Sr., was signed to play the title role in the Paramount talkie, *The Miracle Man*. Ty was engaged for a small part. Shooting under the direction of Norman McLeod started in mid-December of 1931.

During the week after Christmas, Tyrone Power, Sr., sent a note to William Faversham, in which he extended New Year's greetings to the other actor. By sending the message, Power showed that their past rancor, if not forgotten, would from that point on be ignored.

On Tuesday, December 29, Paramount-Publix was forced to cut salaries of all featured players by 10 percent. The Depression had finally hit Hollywood, two years later than the rest of the country. The action couldn't have pleased an actor plagued with continual money problems.

The day's shooting of *The Miracle Man* ended at nine that night, Ty Power, Sr., and his son had already eaten dinner at Paramount, and they retired to the quarters they shared at the Hollywood Athletic Club. His attorney, Francis D. Adams, joined them briefly, leaving at about eleven that night. Both retired shortly thereafter.

In the middle of the night, Ty Power, Sr., called out to his son, complaining of pains near his heart. Tyrone called Dr. John Scrobby. It was apparent to the physician that the actor had suffered a massive heart attack. Emergency treatment was to no avail. Frederick Tyrone Power died at six the following morning, at the age of sixty-two. All his earthly possessions were in the pocket of his pants. They totaled three dollars and fifty-one cents.

The body was removed to Los Angeles Crematory. After conferring with his father's attorney, Ty scheduled the funeral for the following day, Thursday, December 31, at the Maynes-Fitch Funeral Parlor in downtown Los Angeles. Tyrone's sixteen-year-old sister Anne did not come from Cincinnati for the services. The rites were severely simple, according to the deceased's wishes. Tennyson's "Crossing the Bar" was read, followed by a eulogy delivered by actor Ian Keith. Fellow actors H. B. Warner, Arnold Lucy, and Lawrence Grant acted as pallbearers, along with directors Rupert Julian and Sidney Olcott.

His ashes were sent to his former home—Isle Aux Noix—in Canada.

On January 1, 1932, in the *Los Angeles Examiner,* Louella O. Parsons prattled, "As the old year went out Tyrone Power, splendid actor, passed on. Fine that he should have died with the knowledge that he was the one to have played 'The Miracle Man.' Death is easier for actors when they feel they are still in harness. When Theodore Wharton, director, was passing, Paul Bern sent a scenario to the house, and he died believing he was to direct a great masterpiece. Now a new 'Miracle Man' will be chosen. In memory of Tyrone Power, I hope that someone in the picture business who has been here a long time will be chosen."

CHAPTER

3

THE POWERS AT PARAMOUNT-PUBLIX HEEDED LOUELLA Parsons' recommendation when they hired Hobart Bosworth to fill in for the late Tyrone Power, Sr., as *The Miracle Man.* The replacement, whose performance was described by *The New York Times* as "a careful and thorough portrayal," had made his first silent picture in 1916, and his most prestigious film thus far had been *The Big Parade,* generally conceded to be the greatest war film up to that time, in which Bosworth costarred with John Gilbert and Renée Adorée. The current picture, however, was designed as a vehicle for Sylvia Sidney, a big Paramount star, and the great and good friend—as columnists used to write—of studio production head B. P. Schulberg. Others in the cast were Chester Morris and Boris Karloff. Nepotism, however, ended with his father's death, and the part originally assigned to Tyrone Power, Jr., was abolished.

Francis D. Adams, his late father's financial adviser, told Ty there was no estate whatsoever for him and his sister Anne to claim. In fact, Ty's only legacy from his father was the letter he'd received six months previously. He would carry it with him until the paper disintegrated. Adams generously offered the young man money if he wanted to stay on in California. Ty gratefully accepted the loan, and set out to find other movie roles.

He had little luck while making the rounds of studio casting offices. Should he be given an appointment, it would invariably be with an old-timer who wanted to reminisce about the brilliant achievements of Tyrone Power, Sr. Ty was proud of the heritage, but it was turning out to be an obstacle. He was slim and delicate in appearance, while his father had been massive and strong-featured. Casting agents had difficulty reconciling the father's legend with the son's too-human, though admittedly handsome, presence.

In order to survive, Ty took a job as a chauffeur for humorist Arthur Caesar, who had been a friend of his father's. It was a cushy job, requiring no responsibilities. Ty was actually a free boarder, having use of the Caesar Lincoln to tool around town and down to Laguna Beach, where his benefactor had a second home. He would lie on the sand, discussing his future plans with a contemporary named Curtis Kenyon. His friend's Uncle Charles had written *Kindling,* a then-famous play, and he also aspired to become a writer. He promised Ty he would one day write a great part for him. Soon after, Curtis took a job as a steward on an ocean liner going around the world. Ty never saw him again.

Another promise was soon made to Ty by an executive at Universal Pictures. If he did well in an upcoming picture, he would get a studio contract and consequently more work.

Thus, Tyrone Power kicked off a major film career in May of 1932 with a minor part in the most minor film of a major director. He was eighteen when he was cast as one of the older cadets bullying the young *Tom Brown of Culver* in the picture directed by William Wyler, whose name would later be associated with such classics as *Dodsworth, Dead End, Wuthering Heights, The Little Foxes, The Best Years of Our Lives, Ben-Hur,* and *The Collector.* With his eleventh billing in the virtually all-male film went a salary of $150 a week for eight weeks of location work in Indiana.

The New York Times, when the picture was released in July, approvingly observed that "the boys act like boys instead of like road-company Hamlets."

"With the exception of a few momentary appearances in unimportant and incidental bits, such as nurses in a hospital, there are no women in the entire picture." Thus started a review in the

Hollywood Herald. "It is a man's world indeed, more particularly a boy's world. And in addition to the entire personnel of the Culver school (Indiana Military Academy) some of the best and most popular juvenile screen actors enact the principal roles with magnificent spirit, gripping sincerity. They include Tom Brown in the title role; Richard Cromwell, the Long Beach boy who was catapulted to fame when Columbia selected him for the sound version of 'Tol'able David'; Ben Alexander, who has a screen record of importance dating 'way back to tadpole days'; Norman Phillips, Jr.; Tyrone Power, Jr.; Dick Winslow, Kit Wain, Matty Roubert."

Despite his respectable showing in the picture, no additional work was forthcoming at Universal. Ty went for months without further employment. Francis Adams, his father's financial advisor, handled receiverships in his capacity as an attorney. He arranged for Ty to live in one vacant building after another, he being allowed to stay at each place until litigation concerning the property was settled and the new owners took possession.

Circulating in Hollywood, often without enough money for food, he was approached by several wealthy homosexuals. It wasn't prostituting himself in the strictest sense to grant sexual favors in exchange for a warm meal.

One such benefactor recalled, "He was one of the nicest boys you'd like to meet. I don't think homosexuality was his preference. It was just something he had to do in order to eat. He certainly didn't seek it out, and he kept quiet about it."

Soon, however, he was included in the circle of lyricist Lorenz Hart, who was working in Hollywood with composer Richard Rodgers on *Hallelujah, I'm a Bum.* Hart was a small man with a big head, an imp and a practical joker whose good cheer didn't totally mask a deep and brooding sadness. "He was a funny, ugly, dear man," said a mutual friend of Ty's and Hart's.

In the Beverly Hills mansion on Bedford Drive, which he shared with his widowed mother, Hart's entertainments were much talked about. On one hand, he was a host to all of Hollywood, being so lavish as to once bring home Paul Whiteman's band for the amusement of his guests. On the other, he catered to amenable young men. Young Tyrone Power was among the more evident of this group. He spent much time at the Harts's house, raiding the refrigerator and charming Frieda Hart, Lorenz' mother.

In a feature story about the Harts's black maid, Mary, which appeared in the *New York World Telegram* in 1937, three years after Hart returned to live in New York, the situation was described in this way: "The Harts' guests never fail to plague Mary. There was Tyrone Power out in Hollywood. Mary had to keep the broom out for him. 'I have to chase Mr. Power out of the kitchen all the time; he's always after sandwiches. They don't eat in California—just sandwiches and bread.'"

Larry Hart was almost twenty years older than Ty, a jaded man consumed by emotional problems, which in turn caused him to consume inordinate amounts of alcohol. He died tragically some ten years later, his career terminated when Rodgers turned to Oscar Hammerstein II as his collaborator. The composer had been forced to do so, because the situation with Hart had become untenable.

Ty didn't approve of the notorious homosexual hangouts Larry Hart was known to frequent. He was too conventional and circumspect to "come out" in this way. Nor did he approve of the unspoken contest between Hart and another homosexual song writer, Cole Porter, to determine who could publicly flaunt, in the toniest gathering places, the company of the town's most handsome men.

Still, Ty continued to associate with Hart, who was nothing but kind to him. He'd tried to help Ty get acting jobs through his friends at Metro-Goldwyn-Mayer, where he was working, but to little avail. If the novice actor was an opportunist, the opportunities apparently weren't coming through Larry Hart. Basically a New Yorker temporarily working in an alien medium, Hart didn't possess the clout of resident Californians whose entire lives were devoted to the business of motion pictures.

Ty wasn't remotely near to being a Machiavelli. He hadn't presented himself to the men of influence who could have helped him. He hadn't proven an adage, that an actress is more than a woman and an actor is less than a man, by surrendering a portion of his masculinity on the casting couch.

In the summer of 1978, syndicated columnist James Bacon wrote about a Gay Mafia taking over Hollywood. His piece was much talked about and Middle America was shocked at the revelation, while most of Hollywood wondered why little mention of homosexual influence in the movie industry had been made by columnists in the past.

Homosexuals have always been a highly influential substrata of Hollywood life, their voice in the industry disproportionate to their numbers. Many prominent male actors today would rather not talk about the subject. Now that they are established, they are uncomfortable remembering what they had to do to get their starts in the business.

A few years ago, I was invited by a producer and his wife to a party. They were among the more prominent members of the Bel-Air Circuit. This consisted of studios loaning films to movers in the industry for showing in their home screening rooms. The practice was abolished because of an ensuing epidemic of film piracy. The twenty-year-old picture shown after dinner starred two of Hollywood's greatest stars. Its director was one of the most distinguished in the history of films. But filmmakers of accomplishment can be as predatory as the Sammy Glicks, and this one was widely known to be a homosexual. The guests laughed as the film was run, because the then prominent star of a television series and one of the world's top box office stars were playing bit parts. Everyone surmised what they had to do to get the jobs.

In Pasadena during the spring of 1933, at about the time that southern California was recovering from the devastating Long Beach earthquake, a troupe of twenty performers was working under Leonard Sillman, rehearsing a satirical revue to be known as *Low and Behold*. Each was getting paid one dollar a week for his services and happy to be included. The Pasadena Community Playhouse was considered good exposure for entertainers, since studio talent scouts took in every production.

Among those involved in the earliest rehearsals was a showgirl named Eunice Quedens, who would later change her name to Eve Arden, and dancer Charles Walters, later to direct such major MGM musicals as *Good News, Easter Parade,* and *Lili.* He was one of a group of aspiring performers who had "dumpy little apartments in Hollywood. A lot of us knew each other.

"Tyrone was always the best mannered. That drew me to him early. He was a young gentleman, and I like to think I was, too. It attracted us to each other. He had more class and breeding than the others."

Yet, Chuck Walters didn't find Ty as much fun to be with as others in the group. "He was on the quiet side. All of us kicked up our heels more than Tyrone. Even as a kid he was quite serious. We were all ambitious, but I think Ty showed it more."

There was much borrowing of clothes among them. "We loaned each other sweaters mostly," Walters said. "If we'd worn one four times to see an agent, we'd borrow somebody's blue alpaca or maybe a suit. Ty was good looking, but he didn't have much style at the time. He blossomed with success and self-confidence."

Some of Ty's acquaintances were preparing for the show. "We did sketches, individual things, and also were in the chorus," Walters recalled. "It was that kind of revue. Tyrone wasn't working. He was really starving. I wasn't doing too good either, but he was really on his ass. As we would learn the routines I would teach them to him. He wasn't a dancer, but he was young and energetic and attractive. As we were rehearsing I found out they needed another kid in the chorus. I said I had a friend who knows the routines. Tyrone got the job."

He joined his friends, most of them eighteen and nineteen, who met every day at a designated street corner in Hollywood, to hitch a ride with one of the few in the group to own a car.

The opening number of the show had the entire company singing about what not to do in Pasadena, while it proceeded to do everything that was forbidden.

Kay Thompson, a well-known radio singer, shared star billing in the revue with Marguerite Namara, an opera singer. Sillman cooked up a comic routine to showcase Ty's good looks during Miss Thompson's solo. He had Ty and Miss Thompson behind a music stand, the handsome young man turning the pages of the sheet music as she sang. She attempted to flirt with him throughout the song, but he looked straight ahead with a deadpan expression.

Before the show moved over to a Hollywood theater, both Chuck Walters and Ty Power were offered full scholarships at the Pasadena Playhouse. "We talked about accepting them," Walters said, "but neither Ty nor I could wait that long. We were both too ambitious. We had to make a career, and we had to get going."

Low and Behold played in Hollywood for a couple of months. Cast salaries were raised to thirty dollars a week. On the strength of the success there, Sillman decided to take the show to New York, and offered jobs to any member of the company who happened to be in the East later in the year. Naturally, he couldn't afford to pay their transportation there.

Eunice Quedens and Chuck Walters moved with the show, which was renamed *New Faces of 1934,* and which also introduced Henry Fonda and Imogene Coca to the New York stage.

Ty couldn't afford to go East. Walters went on to become a featured dancer, singer, and actor on the Broadway stage before becoming a film director. The paths of the two rarely crossed again.

"I knew Ty and now as I talk about him I realize how much I didn't know him," Walters said. "There was an element of secrecy to him."

When I asked him about Ty's homosexual activities, Walters replied, "I know he went with a few gay guys. What happened I don't know. I think that's what kept him under wraps. It's an extra burden. You want the fame and fortune, and you have this awful load to carry."

A homosexual who was a member of the *Low and Behold* troupe amplified on Walters's thoughts: "Most of the dancers must have known that the people they worked with were also gay. But there was a paranoia at the time. Today it doesn't matter. You played it straight then with everyone except your sex partner. Some kids would come off the opening number. One of them would say, 'Holy Christ! Wait until you get a load of the crotch-watchers in the front row.' I thought I'd die if I knew one of them, and he came backstage later."

Ty, during the time he was being openly seen with homosexual men, was also having an affair with a tall, handsome girl in the show. Some of the troupe surmised Ty was using her as a front, particularly when the girl began openly complaining that nobody loved her. It was evident to everyone that the girl loved Ty more than she was loved. He wasn't purposely cruel to her, yet he wasn't able to make the total commitment her insecurity demanded of him.

Walters recalled a weekend at his parents' home in Anaheim, where Ty and the girl shared the guest room. "We were just kids," he said. "How broadminded my parents must have been to let them share the room."

Now that Anne had finished high school, Patia Power decided to move with her daughter to California to be closer to Ty. The two settled in Santa Barbara, where a distinguished and artistic enclave flourished. Soon, Patia became associated with the active community theater there, and her son commuted the eighty miles from Hollywood to appear in some of the productions.

He had recently rented a garage in Hollywood, near the hall where the Sillman troupe regularly rehearsed, which he planned to convert into living quarters. While he whitewashed its walls and tried to make it habitable, he bunked with Roy Bradley, a ballroom dancer who had worked with Irene Castle, and who would later be the noted host at Don the Beachcomber in Palm Springs. Bradley was then appearing at the Club New Yorker on the roof of the Embassy Restaurant in Hollywood.

"Tyrone was very simple," Bradley recalled. "He was conservative about everything he did. He was more serious about working than anything. He didn't have much, and because we were the same size, I let him wear my clothes."

Within a short time, Patia and Anne moved to Hollywood, taking an apartment around the corner from Ty's garage, not far from the intersection of Hollywood Boulevard and Highland Avenue. His mother, surprisingly, proved more effective getting work than her son, being cast as a character actress on several dramatic anthology series on network radio.

Ty continued doing the rounds, but made little impression on those in authority. One talent scout who believed in Ty's talent was Lela Emogen Rogers, head of the New Talent Acting School at RKO, where her daughter Ginger was already beginning to emerge as a major studio star. Mrs. Rogers's other protégés included Lucille Ball and Jack Carson.

About Ty, Miss Rogers commented, "I was never witness to any of this, because I was too busy at the time. But my mother said Tyrone Power was at the acting school at the time, and that he appeared in several little plays they put on. I never met him."

The only job worth mentioning came early in 1934, shortly before Ty celebrated his twentieth birthday. He was signed to play his second cadet in as many films, this time in *Flirtation Walk,* starring Dick Powell and Ruby Keeler. The Warner Brothers picture was directed by Frank Borzage, who already had *Humoresque, Seventh Heaven,* and *A Farewell to Arms* as impressive notches on his belt. It was nominated by the Academy of Motion Picture Arts and Sciences as Best Picture of the Year. Ty didn't make much of an impression. His bit part, after all, had required only one day to shoot.

Ty discussed his continuing frustration with his mother, who agreed that he should go to New York to try to get work in the theater. Movie people seemed to have more respect for actors recruited from Broadway. Until studio executives came to their senses about him, she felt, he could get seasoning and training in the theater. Patia advanced him some money, which Ty supplemented with loans from friends, and he left southern California in the summer of 1934.

Ty stopped over in Chicago to see old friends from the Civic Shakespeare Society troupe, and decided to stay on for a while. Roy Bradley was dancing at the Drake Hotel, and Ty stayed with him for a while. "I introduced him to Irene Castle," Bradley said. "That was the beginning of his better connections." When his dancer friend went on tour, Ty moved into a South Shore apartment with four other actors and began looking for work.

The Century of Progress Exposition was underway, and he landed a job with "The Circuit Theater Productions," as his studio biography read. Actually he was nothing more than a carnival shill, luring tourists into the "Glimpse of Hollywood" concession, which promised to show them how movies were made. The concession consisted of a nonfunctioning movie camera and four canvas directors' chairs.

He also tried radio work, meeting an already-established personality, Don Ameche, with whom he worked on a program called *Grand Hotel*. In addition to acting in dramatic plays, he was also engaged to appear on a religious hour sponsored by Sears-Roebuck and was even required to read the Sunday funnies over the air.

Toward the end of the year, he was engaged to appear in Luther Greene's production of *Romance,* playing Freddie in support of Eugenie Leontovich. The production ran eight weeks, closing in January of 1935.

Wil Wright, his school friend, came to Chicago to visit Ty while he was appearing in *Romance.* Wright did not see the play. "Ty was living in some Bohemian loft," he said. "I thought how glamorous it all was." Nevertheless it wasn't exciting enough for Wright to sidetrack his more prosaic plans to become a businessman.

During that period Ty met another actor, Robin Thomas, appearing in the Dahlberg production of *The Green Bay Tree*. They had much in common. Both were the same age. Robin had been the stepson of John Barrymore, with whom Ty's father had appeared in *Hamlet*. The two became lovers. When Robin returned to New York, Ty agreed to follow soon after, and they would live together.

Two years before her death, Diana Barrymore appeared at the Sombrero Playhouse in Phoenix, Arizona, then operated by Russell Orton. As the producer recalled, "She did *Laura* there." The two became friends and continued seeing each other until "one month before she killed herself."

Although he liked John Barrymore's actress daughter, Orton didn't always believe her. "Yet, I always knew when she was lying," he remarked. She could lie about herself, but was scrupulously truthful about others.

She adored her half-brother Robin, who, according to her autobiography, *Too Much, Too Soon,* "was to have a tragic life. He was born three centuries too late. He should have lived in the days of Louis XIV, a courtier in lace cuffs and powdered wig. Robin was Dorian Gray come to life. He was elegant and exquisite, and he loved the elegant and exquisite. His face was angelically beautiful. His eyes were startlingly blue, his features small and perfect, his pale skin so translucent that I felt if I were to push my finger against his cheek, I would touch not soft flesh but the finest Dresden china."

Because Michael Strange so obviously favored Robin over her older half-brother Leonard Thomas and herself, Diana resented her mother.

Robin had tried his hand at writing, painting, studying music in Vienna, publishing an avant garde magazine in London. Now, in April of 1935, he had just returned from Chicago. He showed Diana a photograph.

"I looked at it," she wrote. "It seemed all eyes at first. Then I saw a beautiful young man with enormous black eyes and incredibly long lashes that actually cast shadows on his cheeks gazing dreamily out at me. I knew of whom he reminded me. Mother had a bust of Apollo in the sitting room. This was it come to life."

When Ty arrived in New York, he was invited to stay with Robin's family. Michael Strange, after her divorce from John Barrymore, married Harrison Tweed. The fourteen-year-old Diana, away at school, came home weekends.

She told Orton her publishers would not permit her to describe the actual details of the relationship between Robin and Ty, as well as her uncensored experiences with other living celebrities. The book as published was half the length of the original manuscript.

Ty and Robin were indeed lovers, and they lived together in the Tweed house. Michael Strange adored the idea. She understood and fostered it. They were the two most beautiful people together Diana had ever seen. They showed their affection openly. When she walked into a room she'd find them embracing, with no secret or apology.

Patia Power would neither have understood nor tolerated such a display, as her son well knew. Coming from a private family, each of its members kept his thoughts and worries from the others. "My personal problems are my own," Ty later told columnist Radie Harris. "I can't even discuss them with my mother or sister, Anne, much as I adore them both. I just keep things bottled up within myself . . . . I wish I weren't such an introvert."

Ty, for the first time, felt liberated enough to reveal his homo-sexual leanings to a woman, and she was Michael Strange, whom some described as George Sand reincarnated, and his lover's mother. How she would have reacted had he simultaneously been having an affair with a girl as well as her son was another matter altogether.

Staying with Robin at the Tweed residence, Ty had no major expenses. He budgeted five dollars a week for transportation and incidental expenses, while he looked for work in the theater. At first, he had the same bad luck he'd experienced in Hollywood.

Ted Peckham, a friend of Robin's, was then running an escort service, which hired Yale, Harvard, and Princeton men as escorts for ladies desiring them. Robin thought Peckham might hire Ty. Such wasn't the case. Ty didn't have the proper school tie.

It was a wet and miserable day when the rain-soaked Ty, card-board in the soles of his worn shoes, again made the rounds of the casting offices, "where they know how to say no in forty different ways . . ."

He walked into the office which handled Katharine Cornell's productions because he recalled it was usually warm. Since the staff took so long to get around to anyone looking for a job, Ty thought he'd have a good chance to dry out there. The woman behind the desk took down his name while he settled in to dry out in a straightbacked chair. He had barely sat down when he was called to see Stanley Gilkey, one of the managers of the company.

He was immediately offered the job of understudying Burgess Meredith in *Flowers of the Forest*. His salary would be fifty dol-lars a week.

When he returned to the Tweed residence, he found a note to call Gilkey. Ty feared that the offer was being withdrawn. He poured a drink and sank into a chair. When he couldn't postpone hearing the bad news any longer he dialed Gilkey.

"What do you want?" he asked.

"I got your note to call."

"That was this morning—didn't you come in answer to my note?"

"No—" Ty was going to add that he'd gone there only to get

dry. Instead, he repeated, "No—I just had a hunch you wanted to see me."

"Good thing you did," said Gilkey. "Right after you came in, another fellow whom I could have used dropped by. Lucky you had a hunch, otherwise he'd have got your job."

The conversation was accurate as far as it went. Ty hadn't known of a note actress Helen Menken had sent Katharine Cornell in the fall of 1931, when he was appearing with his father at the Chicago Civic Shakespeare Society: "Tyrone Power's here with his tall handsome kid. The boy's green but watch out for him; he's got the stuff."

Neither did he delve into the Guthrie McClintic-Katharine Cornell marriage of convenience, for each had lovers of the same sex.

"Where Guthrie was indiscreet, he was also secretive, and one could not always be sure which of his young male friends were or had been lovers." So wrote Tad Mosel in *Leading Lady,* a collaboration with Miss Cornell's most intimate friend, Gertrude Macy. "His affairs seem to have been of fairly short duration, ending without rancor or unpleasantness, the young men often staying on to perform peripheral production jobs."

This is not to say that Gilkey was one of those young men, but McClintic's associate was well aware that his employer had an eye for handsome, virile young men, and engaged them, whether or not there was a chance of having a sexual affair with them. Neither McClintic nor Cornell was foolish enough to risk his or her esteemed reputation on those who couldn't deliver before an audience. Consequently, many of today's most prominent actors were hired by the company early in their careers. Among them was Tyrone Power, Jr.

Flowers of the Forest, an antiwar play by John van Druten, had its out-of-town tryout in Baltimore before coming into New York. It was the first Cornell production in ten years not to be directed by her husband, van Druten insisting on using his old friend Auriol Lee instead. The part Ty was understudying was that of a dying young poet with second sight, the leading male role. Burgess Meredith played every performance. Ty observed and absorbed for as long as the play ran. That he didn't learn as much as he wanted to was due to the production's early demise, for *Flowers of the Forest* stopped blooming May of 1935 after an eight-week run.

When the shortened season with Cornell ended, Tyrone took a job in summer stock at West Falmouth, Massachusetts, within commuting distance of New York and Robin Thomas. He was assured of an engagement in the fall, having signed a contract to play Benvolio in Miss Cornell's revival of *Romeo and Juliet,* which would open at the Martin Beck Theatre before embarking on a tour of almost three months.

It was while at West Falmouth, where he made a hit in the role of Jerry in *On Stage,* that a studio representative approached him. Ty declined to discuss the possibility of returning to Hollywood at that time, feeling he wasn't ready. He still had much to learn from McClintic and Cornell, and this he would begin to do in *Romeo and Juliet.*

"In one scene," Tad Mosel wrote in *Leading Lady,* "Tyrone Power had to separate a fighting Montague from a fighting Capulet with a single upsweep of his sword between theirs. At rehearsal, in his desire to show Guthrie how hard he had been working and how deft he had become, the young and future Zorro raised his foil as directed and then for a fillip brought it down in the X that formed when the other two swords came together again, forcing one of them across the eye of the young actor playing Romeo's man Balthasar, Shelton Earp (who was, in this distinguished company, nothing less than a descendant of Wyatt's). The point just brushed his forehead and cheek, and when he was carted off to the hospital and dabbed and stitched, his eye was found to have escaped all injury, but he was never able to face the hazard of the duel again and happily retired to civilian life in Baltimore, where he came from, sending Miss Cornell a good-luck telegram on opening night in New York."

The production played in Baltimore and Philadelphia before opening in New York. Because of the size of Ty's part, he received few critical notices, but it was of sufficient human interest to a Baltimore reporter that a son was following in his father's footsteps. Patia Power had come East to see Ty perform.

"I was pleased with the way Tyrone held up his part," she

stated. "He really gave excellent support to the more experienced players—gave them line for line—and never let them down once. I was really proud of his work, both as a mother and as an instructor. When we talked it over afterward I impressed upon him how much work he must do in order to keep up to the high standard he had set in the tryout."

Ruth March, who was later taken under Miss Cornell's wing, joined the company in New York. It was her first job in the theater. She was one of the dancer-citizens of Verona, and would later act as the leading lady's stand-in during lighting rehearsals. "Tyrone was a very sweet, dear, young man. He had lots of talent. He was good-looking and handled himself well."

Another newcomer to the company, cast as a lady of the court, was Evelyn Abbott, a vivacious and statuesque brunette, who came from Miss Cornell's hometown of Buffalo, where the venerable actress had known the girl's father. Eve Abbott later married actors Keenan Wynn and Van Johnson.

"We played in New York a short run," Evie Johnson recalled, "so that we could say it was the original New York company when we went out on one-night stands on the train. Katharine Cornell adored Ty. He was such a charmer. While taking the train from one play-date to another, he would tell these stories, mostly about his father. Miss Cornell would come in from her private car where the rest of us were, just to hear Ty tell these stories. He was a great mimic; he could pinpoint the essence of the person."

"I used to watch the shows from up front. Tyrone had marvelous stage presence. This was his first real part. He had to fence. And he had this marvelous resonant voice. Ty told me his father's voice was like that, too. He wasn't just a pretty face. He had genuine acting ability."

And then there was his singular charm, unique in one so young, that deep and sincere interest in the problems and aspirations of others, no matter what their station in life. His body language was that of a totally accepting friend. His warm chuckle, the way he touched and fondled people as he talked to them, his acceptance of them in a nonjudgmental way . . . no wonder he could so effortlessly make others melt.

When Evie Abbott commented on his extraordinary way with people, Ty laughed, "A little tactfulness goes a long way."

"He truly was charismatic," she said. "When he talked to you, you thought you were the only one he was interested in. Then he would turn to someone else in the group and flash a smile, and they knew they were included, too. He had this incisive ability about people. He would defy you not to like him." Mrs. Johnson fell in love with Tyrone Power while they were touring, and they became lovers.

She adamantly denied that Ty was a bisexual, although she did recall that Robin Thomas was in Chicago when the troupe was playing there. "Ty innately loved women, sexually and spiritually. No one was closer to him than I was. He had this wonderful knack, this wonderful rapport with people, and the need for people to love him."

The plot of *Quicksilver,* a *roman à clef* work by Fitzroy Davis which was published in 1942, is considered by many the finest novel on backstage life. It revolved around this particular *Romeo and Juliet* tour, in which Davis was the single extra hired for the Chicago engagement. In the book the author described a homosexual affair between the actors playing Romeo and Benvolio.

When *The New York Times* reported that I was writing this biography, Mr. Davis considerately sent suggestions on whom I might interview. He also added an answer to my unasked question: "The homosexual relationship . . . between the actor who is playing Romeo and the one who is playing Benvolio, had no reference whatever to the real life situation in the Cornell company. Ty was never the lover of Maurice Evans." He went on to identify the real-life principals in the fictionalized affair.

When the tour ended, Ty went into rehearsals for the next McClintic-Cornell production, *St. Joan,* which opened at New York's Martin Beck Theatre in March of 1936, in which he was cast as Bertrand de Poulengey. He was now earning sixty dollars a week.

"I was cuing him when he got his sides," Evie Johnson recalled. "His first line was, 'What? No eggs? No eggs?' He read it eighty-five different ways. He was always the perfectionist."

Again, his performance wasn't singled out by the critics, but one admirer of his performance was his friend from Alhambra, Olive Ponitz, with whom he'd kept in touch. Now they were young adults. "I'd gone on to UCLA," Olive Behrendt said, "and I got a call from Ty. Could I come to the opening of *St. Joan* in New York? I must say my family was not surprised that he was gaining success. My mother let me go. I was going to study music in New York anyway. I was so much in awe of Tyrone and his performance, but not surprised. I've never been prouder of anybody."

His dashing presence caught the attention of Joe Pincus, a scout for Twentieth Century-Fox, who arranged for a screen test. The studio was casting the romantic interest opposite Alice Faye in *Sing, Baby, Sing,* a 1936 studio production whose main distinction would be the introduction of a comedy team, the Ritz Brothers, as Twentieth's answer to Metro's Marx Brothers.

Ty's test was shipped to the coast. Production head Darryl Zanuck and William Goetz, the second in command, screened it.

"Take it off," Zanuck ordered the projectionist. "He looks like a monkey!" Ty's eyebrows were so bushy that they almost grew together over his nose. In addition, the scene was so harshly lit that the young man had a sinister look, in direct odds to the matinee idol the studio was looking for.

"Wait a minute," Goetz said. "A little thing like that can be fixed. Let's have a whole new test made, with softer lighting. And shave and pluck those eyebrows."

When the second test arrived, Zanuck said, "That's something else again." Goetz had seen a spark in Ty and his potential.

"He did have very heavy eyebrows that almost covered the bridge of his nose," Evie Johnson said, "but all they had to do was pluck them. Ty wanted to go to Hollywood. The money appealed to him. He needed it."

Ty consulted with others in the troupe. "Brian Aherne advised him to stay in the legitimate theater and build a solid reputation as a stage actor," Tad Mosel wrote, "while from the next dressing room Maurice Evans advised him to grab whatever chances came his way while he could."

It was an understandable conceit when Ty told an interviewer years later, "The greatest thing anyone ever did for me was Cornell letting me out of my contract when I got the Hollywood offer." He was, after all, a most minor player, and there were hundreds of fledgling actors who could have filled in.

He and Evie came to an understanding. Their affair was put on hold until he established his film career. "He enjoyed making movies," she stated, "but he said he would never give up the stage, which he never did."

One bit of unfinished business was left for Ty to handle before he left for California. Robin Thomas. Ty knew his career would always come first. What's more, he had come to realize that, while he desired sex with males, he didn't feel comfortable with the concept of an exclusive emotional and sexual commitment to another man. His sensitivities were primarily directed to women.

Not only had Robin lost a lover, but another actor had been found more talented and desirable than he. Their separation would mark the beginning of his end. When a subsequent lover killed himself, Diana Barrymore's half-brother set out to do the same thing.

"How did Robin die?" she wrote. "He literally destroyed himself. In his Connecticut home he drank and he ate, and there was no stopping him. He took sleeping pills to sleep, and Benzedrine to wake, and he lay in bed for days, his guests coming and going, and he drank straight whiskey, the cases piling up outside his bedroom, and one morning he was found dead. He had died in his sleep. He was twenty-nine years old."

When she herself was at the alcoholic depths, she called Ty, during a time she was in California, and asked for a cash loan. Ty quickly sent over the money with his driver. Diana was disappointed that it was only one hundred dollars, when she had been expecting one thousand. Her drinking had long since become public knowledge, and it would have been foolhardy to send a large amount that would accelerate her killing herself, as she later came to realize.

"I never had the feeling Diana was bitter against anyone," Orton said. "I don't remember her being bitter at all about Tyrone Power." He had forfeited part of his personal life to take advantage of an exciting professional offer. Any dedicated actor, after all, would have done the same.

Tyrone Power at the age of two, sitting on the lap of his famous actor father, Tyrone Power, Sr. Patia Power holds the infant Anne.

At the outset of his film career

His first featured role, opposite Loretta Young in *Ladies in Love*

Tyrone Power in his first starring role, *Lloyds of London,* in 1936

The young Twentieth Century-Fox star looking at a photograph of his mother taken during her stage career

With Alice Faye and Ethel Merman in a scene from *Alexander's Ragtime Band*

On the set with his mother and an unidentified visitor

At the premiere of *Alexander's Ragtime Band* with his mentor and sponsor respectively, Darryl and Virginia Zanuck

On loan-out to Metro-Goldwyn-Mayer, opposite Norma Shearer in *Marie Antoinette*. Ty Power was outshadowed by the sumptuous production, and Darryl Zanuck vowed never to loan him out again.

Filming with his future wife Annabella in *Suez*

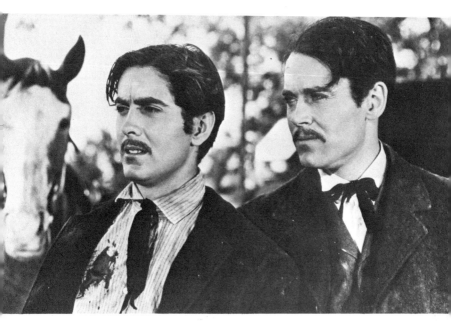

With Henry Fonda in *Jesse James,* the picture that made a star of Fonda

With Rudy Vallee and Sonja Henie in *Second Fiddle,* 1939

A scene from
The Rains Came

An evening out with
Annabella, 1941

Dueling with Basil Rathbone in *The Mark of Zorro*

With Rita Hayworth in *Blood and Sand,* in which the actress made her first impact as a sex symbol

A scene from *Blood and Sand* with Rita Hayworth and Anthony Quinn

With Betty Grable in a scene from *A Yank in the RAF*, the first successful World War Two film

CHAPTER

4

In 1933, Joseph Schenck, the president of United Artists, and Darryl Zanuck, head of production at Warner Brothers, formed a new company, Twentieth Century.

The production company came into being with considerable assistance from its future competitors in the film business. To begin with, it was agreed that United Artists would distribute its pictures. Schenck's brother, Nicholas, had become president of Loew's, Inc., the parent company of Metro-Goldwyn-Mayer, in 1927. Another tie-in was the $100,000 investment in the new company made by Louis B. Mayer, who ran MGM's Culver City studio. When he delivered the check, he in effect was buying a job as Zanuck's executive assistant for his son-in-law, William Goetz, then an assistant director at RKO.

Twentieth started with a small core of stars: Constance Bennett, Loretta Young, and Raymond Griffith. Mayer agreed immediately to supply MGM contract players. Three of them—Wallace Beery, George Raft, and Jackie Cooper—appeared in Twentieth's first production, *The Bowery*. At some future date, it was agreed that Clark Gable would also make a picture for Zanuck.

The chief of the new studio produced twelve pictures during Twentieth's first year of existence. He brought George Arliss over from Warner Brothers, where the British actor had starred in *Vol-*

taire and *Alexander Hamilton,* and proceeded to make him into Twentieth's house impersonator of historical figures in such pictures as *House of Rothschild* and *Cardinal Richelieu.* In the future, Tyrone Power would supplant Arliss, who had succeeded Tyrone Power, Sr., in Mrs. Fiske's revival of *Becky Sharp,* as Zanuck fashioned historical figures into younger, handsomer, less credible and more profitable reincarnations.

In 1935, the small and prospering Twentieth Century merged with Fox Pictures, which, despite having the two top box office stars in films—Shirley Temple and Will Rogers—was a decaying dinosaur. Other studio stars were Janet Gaynor, Warner Oland, and Warner Baxter. Sidney Kent, whom Ty would come to think of as a father, came over from Fox as president of the new company, Twentieth Century-Fox. Schenck became chairman of the board and Zanuck took charge of production.

Will Rogers died in a plane crash that year, leaving Shirley Temple as the chief moneymaker for the merged studio. Over the next five years, she grossed $30,000,000 for Twentieth.

Schenck negotiated the purchase of 208 acres from the Los Angeles Country Club, located on the edge of Beverly Hills, which was added to the studio's adjacent 108-acre facility. Eleven soundstages were already in existence. In 1936, an additional $4,000,000 was spent by the studio on construction of eight additional soundstages and a three-story office building. A $10,000,000 storage addition would be added the following year.

This extraordinary amount of activity presaged Zanuck's ambitious plans to make Twentieth Century-Fox a major factor in the film industry. That he so quickly succeeded in his goal is amazing.

Tyrone Power was just another contract player when he arrived in Hollywood in the spring of 1936. The hundred-dollar-a-week salary he was earning, respectable enough for a beginner, was light years away from that of Shirley Temple's, who had earnings of over $300,000 that year.

He was given the part he tested for in *Sing, Baby, Sing*—that of a newspaperman named Ted Blake—and posed for studio stills.

Filming began. Sidney Lanfield, the director, found the new player too pretty, too soft, too mannered, his gestures just short of being effeminate. Lanfield bluntly told Zanuck the boy didn't have the balls to play the part of a tough newspaperman.

Ty was dropped and Michael Whalen, another contract player, was named to fill the role. Ty was nearly suicidal. Alice Faye felt badly for him, and took him to the Tropics Restaurant in Beverly Hills. As he drank himself into insensibility, she tried to soothe him.

"Don't let this setback get you down," Alice said. "I have great faith in you. You're going to be a big star. All this means is a delay until you find it out for yourself."

To this day, she doesn't know why Ty was dropped. "He had enormous appeal from the start," Miss Faye recalled. "He was very talented. Of course, we all needed direction. He was just a baby. We were all kids. I adored Ty. We went out a lot together, but there was no romance. My mother was crazy about him, too. She used to cook special dinners for him."

He also became a close friend of Bill Goetz and his wife Edith, the daughter of Louis B. Mayer. "I grew up with film stars all my life," Mrs. Goetz said. "Ty didn't have the virility, or the sex appeal, of a Clark Gable. I always felt Tyrone was not strong or well. He was never a powerfully built man. He was more delicate. I never thought he was earthy. But to me, Tyrone was a member of the family, and it's hard to tell what he had in addition to his exceptional handsomeness. I just wanted him to make good."

Despite Alice Faye's comforting words and Edie Goetz's belief in him, Ty's standing at the studio couldn't have been lower. He was next given a minor role in a distinctly minor film by a decidedly minor director. He did his walk-on during the week he celebrated his twenty-second birthday, and it was a hell of a way to celebrate. This was the kind of assignment any contract player would get before his six-month option was dropped and he was out entirely.

Girls' Dormitory, directed by Irving Cummings, although personally produced by Zanuck, was designed as a modest, coming-out film for the recent French import, Simone Simon. Ty's one scene was the last one in the picture. He walked on and asked, "Could I have this dance?" The European actress received enthusiastic notices, but it was Ty to whom film audiences gravitated.

"His name wasn't even on the screen," Hedda Hopper later wrote of Ty's initial impact. "I know because I sat through the picture twice to find out who he was. Then I left the theater without knowing. It seems thousands of Americans did the same thing. So much mail accumulated at the studio for the unknown young man, they didn't know what to do with it. So it was all taken to Mr. Zanuck's office, who saw the light quickly and put him into a small part in *Ladies in Love,* where he first met Janet Gaynor."

Actually, Tyrone Power, Jr., was tenth billed in the picture. Zanuck upped his billing to seventh in *Ladies in Love,* which was shot in the early summer of 1936. Perhaps this Tyrone Power had a future as a featured actor, the slick-haired effete type who loses the girl to the unquestionably masculine hero in the last reel.

The picture was to be the first in a series of Zanuck formula films. They were divided into two categories, Remakes and Sequels, Zanuck believing the film audiences couldn't get too much of a good thing, or even of a fair to middling thing.

Edward H. Griffith's *Ladies in Love,* based on a play by Ladislaus Bus-Fekete, was the first in a series of studio films about young ladies banding together to seek out rich husbands. They pool their resources to rent a fancy apartment, and from there they intend to make advantageous marriages. The motif was repeated with Don Ameche and Betty Grable in *Moon over Miami* and with Marilyn Monroe, Lauren Bacall, and Betty Grable again in *How to Marry a Millionaire.*

With the 1935 merger, Zanuck inherited Fox star Janet Gaynor, whose talents he publicly belittled. He found greater potential in two younger actresses, Loretta Young and Simone Simon, who were also assigned to the picture. Constance Bennett was hired to supply glamor, as well as to broaden the appeal of the picture so that it couldn't be considered a star vehicle for Gaynor. Zanuck was noticeably contemptuous of the few stars on the studio roster, with the exception of Shirley Temple. His only male lead, Warner Baxter, had a contract paying him many times his box-office value every week, and Zanuck got rid of him as soon as possible. It wasn't that these people weren't stars; they just weren't big enough ones to help accomplish Zanuck's grand design.

In *Ladies in Love,* three Budapest women shared a flat. Constance Bennett played the wisest of the three, a modiste's clerk whose affair with the urbane Paul Lukas ends when a sixteen-year-old, Simone Simon, steals him from her. Tyrone Power played a count whom Loretta Young attempts suicide over, after their affair ends. Janet Gaynor was romantically teamed with Don Ameche, who played a doctor. In Ameche, a former radio announcer, Zanuck felt he was creating his first male studio star.

Despite the presence of the actors in the cast, it was virtually an all-girl show. "Paul Lukas, Tyrone Power, Jr., and Don Ameche play the passive lovers with complete resignation," Frank S. Nugent wrote in *The New York Times,* "gratefully accepting the few dramatic crumbs the ladies brushed off their makeup tables."

Ty's presence was noted in passing by other critics. Archer Winsten of *The New York Post* said he was "as handsome as everyone seems to think Robert Taylor is." Another dismissed the actor as having "the screen manners one associates with the young men from Ted Peck's Escort Bureau [*sic*]." Ironically, Ty hadn't qualified for that job in real life.

Where it counted most, however, a momentum was developing. It wasn't Zanuck who solely decided to give Tyrone Power better roles. It was the clamoring public. A goodly amount of fan mail continued to come into the studio. Zanuck's estimation of him, however, hadn't changed. Neither had his low estimation of Janet Gaynor. This would be her last picture at Twentieth. She'd been, in the early 1930s, the old Fox studio's most consistent box-office star, but her contract had ended and Zanuck didn't renew. One evening, she packed her makeup case and left the studio for the last time. There were few well-wishers to bid her farewell, certainly none from the front office, her departure a total contrast to the fanfare that accompanied her arrival on the lot only a few years before. She would, of course, go on to even greater stardom under David O. Selznick's aegis in the classic 1937 production, *A Star is Born,* but her future at the moment was much in doubt. The example of her shabby treatment wasn't lost on Ty, but yet he longed to reach the heights from which his one-time date had so precipitously plummeted.

Unhappy and confused, fearing he would continue to be consigned to minor roles as he'd been in the Cornell company, Ty asserted himself.

Based out of a corner office in the new administration building was a vigorous Virginian and stern moralist named Henry King. The young actor called on him.

Ty got to the point. "I'd like to work with you."

King, whose fifty-year acting and directing career came to include the famous *Stella Dallas, The Winning of Barbara Worth, Twelve O'Clock High, The Gunfighter, The Snows of Kilimanjaro,* and *Love is a Many Splendored Thing,* had cast Tyrone Power, Sr., as Richard Barthelmess's father in *Fury,* his 1922 production. If other directors found Tyrone Power, Jr., a fop who didn't register strongly as a male, King saw something else. He liked the exceptional good looks of the boy, as well as the way he deferred to the older man. Most of all, he was impressed by the dedication. "Ty was a very sweet, wonderful person," King recalled. "He was just as simple at the end as he was when he started. He wanted to be a good actor more than anybody I ever saw in my life."

Ty was handed the script for *Lloyds of London,* and told to read it at home that night. He was surprised when he opened its blue cover to discover that it was based on a story written by Curtis Kenyon, his acquaintance at Laguna Beach during the year after his father's death. It was a good omen.

Knowing that Freddie Bartholomew would be starring in the picture, Ty thought that his grown-up interpretation of the same character, Jonathan Blake, would be a small part. As he read the script he discovered the adult role, despite Bartholomew's star billing, was actually the leading one.

Because Don Ameche, while filming *Ladies in Love,* had also been featured to good effect in *Ramona,* which King also directed, Zanuck thought he was ready for his first big part. He asked King to test him for the costume epic, which was to be made for $850,000, then a large budget for a picture.

The stock collars flattered Ameche, as King could see when he shot the footage. It was screened before a group of Zanuck and his sycophants.

"This is wonderful!" Zanuck enthused. "The boy is marvelous."

King agreed that the actor handled himself well, but as he later said about him, "Ameche is a character actor and will always be a character actor."

"Isn't it great?" Zanuck continued. "We made the first test and we got the right fellow."

"I'd like to make another test," King said.

"Why, Henry," Zanuck responded, "make as many tests as you want, but isn't it wonderful we got the guy right the first time?"

"What the heck!" King exploded. This was the extent of the straitlaced director's profanity. "Listen, I'm not making these tests for fun. They cost money. It's a lot of work. I'd like to make another test to compare with this."

"Of course," Zanuck said, "make all the tests you want. But isn't it wonderful—"

"Not if you're going to take the man right off the bat," the director interrupted. "There's no use in making the test. I'm thinking of someone else."

"All right," Zanuck said. "If the test isn't good, then we've got this to fall back on. Maybe the other man will be better. Who are you thinking of?"

"A young fellow that you have in the stock company called Tyrone Power."

If none of Zanuck's employees actually groaned, their silence was even more deafening. They knew what their boss thought of Power.

Zanuck mulled the suggestion over. "Sure," he said. "Go ahead. I think it's fine. Make a test of the boy."

King used the identical scenes he'd shot with Ameche, and he tried to use as many of the same actors as well. It took him three days to get the test to his satisfaction. Then he called Zanuck.

"Let's run it at two in the afternoon," Zanuck said, "in the big projection room."

King called Barbara McLean, one of the few women editors in the business at the time, and they arranged for the showing.

The scenes, covering five different stages of the story, with the actor starting as a youth and ending as a seventy-year-old man, ran more than twenty minutes. When the lights came on, Zanuck sat in the projection room without saying a word. Then he turned to his yes-men. "Which one do you like?"

All said they preferred Ameche. Zanuck then turned to King. "Which one do you like, Henry?"

"This boy."

"Why?"

"Because," King said of Tyrone Power, "this boy is younger. He's better looking. He handles himself better. I can do more with him. The most important thing is that this studio is short of talent. In two years this boy could be the biggest young leading man in the motion picture industry, and God knows we need stars here instead of borrowing them from somebody else."

Zanuck then asked Bobbie McLean, "Which one?"

Although she liked both actors, whom she hadn't met, she thought Ty wore the clothes well and moved better in them.

"This one," she said, referring to Ty.

"All right," Zanuck said, "put him in the picture before I change my mind." With his new prominence, Ty's salary was raised to $250 a week.

Loretta Young balked at taking the lesser assignment of Lady Elizabeth, and British-born Madeleine Carroll was already signed in her stead. George Sanders would be playing her dastardly husband, one of his first roles in urbane villainy.

Lloyds of London was Twentieth's most ambitious production up to that time. The front office wanted to showcase the new star as effectively as possible. Makeup man Ray Sebastian received a note, instructing him to handle the problem with the eyebrows so that Ty could be acceptably photographed.

Sebastian acquired an eyebrow plucker which had an airhose attachment. He shaped the eyebrows with it, then shaved off the area over Ty's nose. He didn't pluck the hairs there, because this might cause swelling.

"Every time I got Ty down in the chair," Sebastian said, "he'd get up swearing. 'I'll kill you!' he said. Those damn brows nearly drove us both nuts."

Shooting had been underway for two weeks when Zanuck called King into his office one morning. He walked around the room, swinging his polo mallet as he talked. "Henry, I've been watching the rushes very carefully. This boy up to now is good. He's just perfect. I know you have a tight schedule. I just want to give you this authority. I want you to know that I don't want you to hurry with this boy at any time. If we went out and got Fredric March or somebody of that kind we would have to pay him $150,000. We're paying this boy peanuts. Take your time on every scene. If you go over budget or go beyond, don't spare anything on this boy. He's going to be a star. That's all I wanted to tell you. Keep the good work going. Do the best you can. But don't hurry him."

He gave similar instructions to his female film editor. "Now, Bobbie, play him, because we're going to make a star out of him. If you ever want anything shot over, or anything like that, tell Henry and he'll do it."

Now that Ray Sebastian had worked on him, she had no difficulty bringing out Ty's good looks. "He had no bad angles," Bobbie McLean, who later married director Robert Webb, said. "He was just plain good-looking. You didn't have to worry about photographing his bad side. He didn't have any."

Although she didn't recall that the scenes required many takes, Bobbie Webb recalled that they proceeded to work at a slower pace. Had there been more of a rush, there might have been some energy in the picture, particularly in Ty's portrayal. Seen today, it's not clear how *Lloyds of London,* a dreary historical epic ranging from 1770 to 1805, could make a star out of anybody. Ty was adorned in everything but petticoats, his scalp hugged by a wig so tight it pinched his whole face, with enough makeup on the lips to make one understand why he and his future costar would be dismissed as "Pretty Miss Young, Pretty Mr. Power." The ponderous plot structure and his starched costumes had as much bearing to reality as the gliding marionettes on eighteenth-century clocks. It was perhaps the most mannered role of Ty's career. Yet, he carried himself as well as had been expected and didn't seem to be "acting." He belonged to the clothes he was wearing. What was lacking, what the world discerned anyway, was his enormous charm. King shrewdly held back in exploiting Ty to the optimum, lest his exaggerated stage-trained mannerisms earn him the label of *The Lavender Pimpernel.* The director settled for the love affair the camera was having with Ty's fabulous face. In future pictures, as the movie audience got to know him better, Ty's full arsenal of looks and dash and charm would be deployed. For now, the audience was getting to know him, while it appreciated the historical authenticity King was attempting to deliver in the period piece. It was what film people today deride as photographing the doorknobs.

"Suppose I'm doing a story on London," King once explained. "You'd bring in a set designer, of course, but you can't expect him to have everything at his fingertips. Consequently, I've got books that tell everything about London, from the kinds of doorway architecture to the different street lamps of different stages of history. I've got detailed descriptions of the crown jewels. They tell which ones are to be used for what occasion and even describe each jewel in each piece."

Hardly a jewel is out of place in the picture, and the last thing you would want to criticize is the street lamps. An exciting prologue featured Freddie Bartholomew and J. M. Kerrigan as the young boys Jonathan Blake (fictitious) and Horatio Nelson (historical) in an England scene perpetually shrouded by fog. It proceeds to Lloyds Coffee House and the birth of modern-day insurance, all of it patiently explained by Guy Standing, the action becoming less and less involved with ships and more and more involved with pieces of paper and announcements on bulletin boards.

Freddie Bartholomew loses little of his charm as he grows into Tyrone Power and his life maintains a mystical, unspoken connection to the life of the less charming Admiral Nelson, but that form of charm sits more fittingly on the English Bartholomew than it does on the American Power (whom King didn't require to try for an accent). The movie, like real life, gets slower, heavier, and more weary as it draws near its end, which seems to take longer than its allotted two hours. It's hard to be strung along for that length of time on nothing more soul-stirring than the relation of English shipping and English commerce to the development of the English empire.

Power is the ambitious youth who can see so far ahead of the old fogies who head Lloyds that he can very nearly predict the crash of 1929. He's also a ladykiller. He has Madeleine Carroll as the cultured Lady Elizabeth, who longs for the union with Power that class barriers make impossible, not to mention a previous engagement as George Sanders' wife. Also there's Virginia Field as Polly, the barmaid, so identified by her cleavage. It's a hopeless triangle that remains unresolved at the end, so unresolved in fact, that in the final close-up, as Power stares dreamily out the window at his future, it's not clear which of the two blond ladies is crowding into the shot with him.

Wil Wright, now graduated from college, came out to California while Ty was filming *Lloyds of London.* "He was living at La Ronda, which was an apartment house just below Sunset," Wright said. "I stayed with him two or three months. I was still there when the picture was released, and I went to the premiere."

Before Ty had a chance to contemplate the effect his first starring role would have on the public, he was plunged into a Zanuck formula picture, this time the Total Remake, in which the locale was changed and characters were transposed. "Only relationships and plot remained the same," Mel Gussow wrote. "The theory was that there was only a limited number of plots in the first place. *Love Is News,* which Zanuck made with Tyrone Power and Loretta Young, was about an heiress who falls in love with a reporter who has been criticizing her. Zanuck remade it as a musical, *Sweet Rosie O'Grady,* in 1943, with Robert Young and Betty Grable, and again, in 1949, as a straight comedy again starring Tyrone Power. He briefly considered naming it *Love Is Still News,* but changed his mind and called it *That Wonderful Urge.* Gene Tierney played the girl." The plot hadn't even originated with Zanuck. Its most successful interpretation came in 1934 with Columbia's *It Happened One Night,* starring Clark Gable and Claudette Colbert.

That a successful career was in the making was evident by the press's interest in the young actor. During one of his earliest interviews as a film player, Ty was asked why there was no girl in his life. "Why should I marry when all I dream about is work?" he responded. "It's adventure, experience, excitement, all the romance I need. Work is my passion, my beloved mistress who takes all I have to give and who's welcome to it. Of course, if somebody changes my mind, that'll be that." One wonders if he actually talked that way.

He dutifully went on to say that he was delighted to be working at Twentieth. While touring with *Romeo and Juliet,* he'd seen Bruce Cabot in *Show Them No Mercy,* and the picture made a great impression on him. It had on few others. "I thought that if I ever got to Hollywood, I wanted to work at the studio that made that picture."

One of his first studio-arranged dates was with Rochelle Hudson. Ty told Bill Gallagher, who had been hired as his secretary, to buy a corsage of gardenias for the lady. When he picked her up to go to the studio function at the Biltmore Hotel, Ty noticed the actress was wearing a corsage of orchids instead. "Mr. Power," she said, "how sweet of you to send me these beautiful orchids." Ty later joked that Bill had been pretty generous with his money.

Shooting on *Love Is News* hadn't been completed when *Lloyds of London* was premiered. Tyrone Power was fourth-billed, for the first time without the Junior.

He stood at the window of his West Hollywood apartment, as the floodlights beamed across the sky from the Carhay Circle Theatre a mile or so away, where the film was opening. He got into his rented tuxedo and drove to the theater in a car the studio had loaned him.

When the picture was over and the house lights came on, a spotlight played on him, and the audience rose to cheer the birth of a new star. The next morning, his overnight success finally registered on him, Ty had but one thought: Now that I've arrived, can I stay?

Largely because of him, the picture—overblown and overlong —was a smashing success. It would go on to be Twentieth's top moneymaker in 1937. Audiences related to his sincerity and decency. Here was an apparently nice young man, handsome to an extreme, who didn't carry with him the eyes of most great actors. Not for him their bluster and swagger. What he had unknowingly created, which audiences would eagerly accept, was his own brand of reality. No other actor in films of the time could carry himself as well in such impossibly artificial situations. Critics flailed out at *Lloyds of London,* but were kind to him.

"Where sheer action and character delineations are concerned, he is excellent," *The New York Times* review read. "That he is required by the frequently lofty script to utter occasional passages which seem addressed to a hearkening posterity is, of course, beyond his control."

Variety spoke in plainer fashion: "He's okay. He's going places. He has looks and he has acting ability. The women ought to go for him in a big way."

Lloyds of London set the precedent for future productions, the Partial Remakes in Zanuck's formula, in that a major ingredient of a successful picture was used again as a plot device. Zanuck told his biographer Gussow that this was first done in 1936 in *Lloyds of London:* "the story of two young boys who loved each other . . . and then . . . parted; one became a famous man and the other became more or less insignificant; but the insignificant one made possible the greatest victory of the famous one."

Because Darryl Zanuck had a prejudice against making any movie he hadn't already made at least once before, the basic recipe was to dominate Power's career for the next fourteen years. These ingredients, used with varying consistency, would include a boyhood prologue. It was apparently felt that delaying Power's entrance into his own film by at least three or four reels enhanced its effectiveness.

Then there would be a loud proclamation of the requisite Republican virtues: What's good for business is just the thing for the destiny of every chimney sweep.

Add to that a love triangle, involving a girl of breeding and a girl of sensuality, generally left unresolved except for coy looks and smart cracks.

Stir into the cauldron a main character of phenomenal drive and dedication, characterized more by the evidence of our ears than the evidence of our eyes.

Place him in a locale where everyone speaks present-day American regardless of the time or place specified by the subtitles (the actual language spoken colloquially only by newsboys and man-servants with throwaway lines).

Titles are superimposed over engravings of the period, with one reserved to acknowledge the appropriate historical society for its assistance and encouragement. As a fillip you may use actual historical personages as chronological landmarks and in-jokes. In *Lloyds of London,* Napoleon and Benjamin Franklin served as convenient reference points; in the later *Suez,* Franz Liszt and Victor Hugo do celebrity walk-ons that look like *Tonight Show* promotions for new masterpieces.

But was Tyrone Power one to cavil, in late 1936 or ever? That wasn't his nature. In nine short months, he had progressed from one line in his first studio film to full stardom in his third. Overnight, he had emerged as Twentieth Century-Fox's dark-haired, fair-haired boy. He was suddenly a major factor to be considered in all studio casting, judging from the clawing, squealing, adoring females who thronged about him whenever he appeared in public. Their highpitched voices, their gurgles and sighs, made him feel as if he'd been deposited in the midst of a screeching aviary. What had he done to deserve such violent devotion? The constant noise numbed his brain, though his eyes remained clear and smiling. What more could he deliver to satisfy their fanatic passions? A warm look, a shy smile, a gentle pat, a gracious thank you, his every small gesture was magnified and glorified. He was suddenly a god. He was only twenty-two.

CHAPTER

5

He is six feet tall; weighs 155 pounds. He is a handsome youth with dark brown hair and luminous brown eyes. He is a thoroughbred in all that the name implies. He is a distinctive addition to the screen's roster of eminently worthwhile players.

He is not married. Prefers blondes. Has no favorite type of girl, but says he will know her when he sees her.

His favorite flower is the white carnation. His favorite superstition is whistling in the dressing room [sic]. His greatest fear is that of being shut in, as in a cave or a mine—claustrophobia.

Among the classic authors he prefers Hugo, and Shakespeare is his favorite classical playwright. Of the moderns, he prefers Maxwell Anderson. His favorite historical character is Cyrano de Bergerac [sic].

His favorite classical orchestration is "Tales in the Vienna Woods" [sic]; favorite classical painter, Van Gogh; favorite illustrator, Petty; favorite modern painter, Grant Wood; favorite modern author, Thorne Smith; favorite play, Ethan Frome.

Reads incessantly—anything that is interesting and constructive and to keep in touch with contemporary magazines likes to read the Reader's Digest.

His favorite color is blue, any shade of blue. His favorite fruit is the avocado—very fond of them.

He is especially fond of outdoor sports and is a football fan. Always wanted to play football when in school and would go out every season for a tryout but did not make the team "because he was too skinny, just a beanpole of a boy."

His hobby is amateur photography with a sixteen millimeter camera. He swims, plays tennis, and rides horseback when not engaged at the studio.

He says if he should leave Hollywood he would return to New York and the stage, and, perhaps do some writing, a talent in which he excels in a measure almost parallel with his acting ability.

AND SO THE PUBLICITY MACHINE, WITH THE CREATION OF A new star, had added reason to double its efforts. The verbiage was inflated throughout, even in referring to Ty's height. Matinee idols, it was believed, had to be at least six feet tall, regardless of their actual height. Ty was of average size. Walter Scott, the set designer of many of his pictures, who often had to scale settings according to the height of the stars, said Ty was no taller than five feet ten inches, and probably closer to five feet eight.

Studio flacks, taking their cue from the movie audience, started to build the image of Ty as a guy who was regular, noble, romantic, *and* tall. He didn't object to enumerating the minutiae of his life. "This is what I'll let you know," he seemed to say, "as long as you don't probe any deeper."

No one, least of all he, had anticipated that he would become the idol of millions of females. His romantic image was thrust upon him before he experienced actual romance in his personal life. The bulk of his sexual experiences thus far had been with other men. He didn't have to be told by anyone at the studio. That aspect of his character was to be deeply submerged. Immediately. No gaudy plumage. No flamboyant gestures. Modulate the voice into a virtual monotone. Develop an interest in such manly pursuits as horseback riding, sailing, football. Be a man and become a star. Do exactly what the studio tells you.

Accommodating, reliable, untemperamental—these were adjectives that would never have been used to describe Tyrone Power, Sr. Patia Power had taught her son better, to be a gentle, as well as extremely private person. Ty was work-directed and goal-oriented. Now that he was well on his way to becoming a major star, he might even be able to develop as an actor. His public accepted his limited talent, asking nothing more of him than the outer package. It would cause Ty great frustration later when he realized that his fans didn't require him to expand his acting range. He never turned his back on them, however.

"Ty was a man of great patience," Ray Sebastian said. "He loved people. No matter where we were, if someone spotted him and asked him for his autograph, he'd always stop for them."

Not only would he give autographs willingly, he'd thank the fan for asking for it.

Once, Sebastian asked him, "Ty, don't you ever get tired of it?"

"No, I don't."

"I'm glad to hear you say that," Sebastian said, "because when they quit asking you, mister, it won't mean anything."

"That's why I do it," Ty replied. "Besides, what the hell, they can't say something nasty about you. They can't say I was a shit."

In one respect he was as sexually repressed as the millions of shopgirls mooning over his glossy photographs. Caution and discretion in his homosexual activities were the bywords. Of all the actors of his time, given the courtly and romantic image the public had foisted upon him, Ty had the most to lose by revelations about his bisexuality. If the gossip mill talked about Errol Flynn's occasional sex acts with other men, the talk couldn't harm his image as much. Given his reputation for extreme randiness, it was expected that the scope of Flynn's activities would run the gamut from high school girls to knotholes in a fence. Another actor coming along in a few years, Montgomery Clift, was afflicted with so many brooding aberrations that homosexuality would be considered the least of them.

But not for Ty. As his studio banked more and more from his films, it came to bank more and more *on* him. Twentieth had no other male stars, and Zanuck consequently was to star Ty in everything: historical romances, contemporary comedies, musicals, Westerns. The actor knew the extent of his responsibilities. Ty cooperated in fostering the persona so carefully being built up for him. His clothes were now tailor-made, of conservative cut, to underscore and not overpower his delicate good looks. He drove around town in his new black Cord phaeton. Well-publicized dates with Twentieth contract players—Simone Simon, Loretta Young, Janet Gaynor, Sonja Henie—were arranged. Fan-magazine conjecture about these "romances" followed.

He was like the light-skinned Negro in the South, trying to "pass." Sex with other men wasn't something Ty could either take or leave alone. He risked losing everything should it become public knowledge, and yet he continued having such affairs. He not only had to hide this facet of his sex life from the masses, but also from the sedate Hollywood crowd he'd taken up with. Despite its freewheeling image, Hollywood after the thirties was ruled by a strict code of behavior extending far beyond the morality clauses of studio contracts. The world was paying court to film people, royalty and other notables stopping by to visit, and personal conduct was expected to be exemplary. Homosexuals had never been condoned, even during the early twenties when Hollywood was considered a second Sodom. Many of its most distinguished citizens had since been forced to mute themselves. It was an extraordinary strain to live under, a thousand times greater than that suffered by any small-town homosexual of the period, particularly because of the conservative Beverly Hills establishment Ty associated with. A great percentage of these people were Jews, who'd been taught that sex with another man was the ultimate taboo.

These were everyday and immediate pressures, multiplied a millionfold because Ty was becoming a world-famous man who would come under great public scrutiny. He loved the feeling of great triumph, yet, because of it, his life was turning miserable and totally repressed. He was bound by unseen shackles, being tortuously twisted one way, only to have the bonds loosened so that he could be twisted in another direction. Ty's sex life was not one of excess, but it certainly was one of equally disreputable extremes. A man close to Ty in those days noted that whenever it came time for bedding any of the females he met at a party, "He went for the bum every time . . . the biggest tramp in the room." Some might analyze this propensity as a symptom of his own unworthiness. The jaded would say only women a cut above streetwalkers could cater to his offbeat appetites, whatever they were. A more obvious analysis was that these sex partners made no demands and created the fewest complications of all. Ty didn't want to be distracted in his work by emotional commitments.

The responsibilities of stardom were eagerly undertaken by Ty. A one-time male lover, who feels the actor was basically homosexual, said, "The building of the name, the career, the fulfilling of the wishes and demands of the studio heads . . . Zanuck didn't foist it on him. Ty wanted it . . . badly.

"He also knew he had to have a pretty girl on his arm, and he lived in the constant fear of destroying everything if his affairs with men were found out. I'm sure he loved his wives. But deep? Total? Or as a friend? He knew he had to do this, that he had to find someone who would fit the image."

As for his affairs with women before and during his subsequent marriages, his friend thought Ty had to prove his masculinity to the outside world. "If someone said he was a homosexual, there were plenty of women who could deny it. He could perform with women and he often did.

"That he gravitated to the broads is quite understandable. In his torment, he related to them. Perhaps that's what he really would have liked to have been. Here they were, tramps and whores, available to everyone. It wasn't the idea of great sex. I think maybe he felt the association. The thought of other men there before him might have excited him. Maybe he reversed the role. He became the tramp, having sex with many men by proxy."

Actor Kurt Kasznar, one of Ty's closest friends, agreed that the more sexually active a woman, the more desirable Ty found her. "A real whore in bed excited Tyrone," he said.

Ray Sebastian once jokingly told him, "Don't ever marry a virgin, Ty. She'll go home to her mother before midnight."

His accommodating nature also applied to any woman who wanted him badly enough. Sebastian recalled that once, while filming, a girl was camped out on Ty's doorstep every night.

"Go on home," he'd tell her kindly. "I just don't have the time. I have work to do."

One night, the girl was particularly insistent. "I've got to see you. I've been saving myself for you."

Sebastian recalled, "Well, Ty had been working pretty hard. He hadn't been laid in some time. He didn't want to get involved. But it went on for four or five nights."

The girl wound up being one of Ty's more enduring affairs. Whatever his motivations, Ty seemed impelled to transform his easy partners into highly respectable ones. Odds that he could achieve such a transformation in the women he bedded were overwhelmingly against him. And should he succeed, it could only lead to a different kind of frustration. The eroticism he felt toward the beautifully soiled and shop-worn could abruptly end if they regenerated into born-again virgins. It would take a woman of extreme artfulness to be both the madonna and the whore with him.

Ty was attempting to come to grips with his omnisexuality at the time when three older actors were noticeably failing at keeping their own problems under control. He might have seen some disturbing signs in these now-fallen idols. He was later to play variations on the themes of some of their old movies. They had indulged their carnal senses—as Ty's father had done—while ignoring their common sense. Their flesh was weakened, and the piper was now exacting payment. These once-great stars were mired in self-pity and alcohol, from which there was no escape. In the offing was a more immediate example. Ty, during his teenage days ushering in a Cincinnati movie house, recalled seeing a picture twenty-eight times, which starred Dorothy Mackaill and Jack Mulhall. That same Mulhall, years later, was an unbilled stretcher-bearer in a movie where an injured Ty was carried to an ambulance. Such are the vagaries of the acting life.

John Barrymore, Robin Thomas's one-time stepfather, was spending most of his lonely nights on his insular mountaintop. Two others—John Gilbert, the great lover, and Douglas Fairbanks, the swashbuckler—were also in various stages of lingering deaths. The excesses, once considered part of their charm, were too much in the public consciousness. Different responses were triggered, and the three reacted in varying ways to their new roles of self-parodists.

Barrymore would never outwear his public welcome, capitalizing on his new radio roles of tragedian turned buffoon, even though the doors to the film colony's distinguished homes were no longer open to him. Hollywood knew too well how his story would end. The syndrome of the alcoholic actor is depressingly predictable, and what was making Barrymore's case depart from the norm was the far greater height of his inevitable fall.

John Gilbert had become the greatest of stars with the smallest of talents. The parallels with Ty's ability thus far were obvious. Gilbert did absolutely nothing to develop his craft and doomed himself to become the most famous victim of the new technology. In January of 1936, Gilbert of the high-pitched voice went to a party. Midst the revelry, his toupee was snatched off his head. It would have been an unthinkable prank to play on him in his prime. He was found dead in his home, which shared the same hilltop as Barrymore's, the next morning.

Douglas Fairbanks wouldn't die for three more years. But at fifty-three, his swashbuckling days were long over, and he hadn't learned to make the transition to older roles. Trying to revive past glories, he became embroiled in a seamy affair in England, where he'd made his last picture. Mary Pickford and the court at Pickfair were not amused. The acrobat of the drawing room soon found himself to be a man without a country. America turned its back on him. His career ended.

There was a younger generation of actors—Fredric March, Edward G. Robinson, Clark Gable among them—who were in their prime and didn't appear to be following the example of the immediate past generation of stars. They seemed to be in total control of their careers.

Coming up at the same time as Ty were two other uncommonly handsome men—Robert Taylor and Errol Flynn—caught up in the public's adulation, unheeding and unthreatened by the examples of the older members of the acting fraternity. The corollary expounded by Orson Welles applied to these young film stars as well. "Versatility was always expected of any stage actor, unless you were a matinee-idol type, and nothing to be done about that."

The first indication of Ty's new standing was the top billing he was given in *Love Is News,* which was released in March of 1937. His costar, Loretta Young, was understandably displeased. She'd left Warner Brothers four years previously, at the age of twenty, believing Zanuck was grooming her to replace Janet Gaynor, the ingenue of the decade. Although Miss Young was generally regarded in Hollywood as one of the most synthetic and packaged of stars, she had extensive knowledge of the technology of the business. It was said she could tell if her face was properly lit for a scene by the degree of heat she felt. She also had a huge following. The public didn't care whether she could act or not; most critics didn't feel she could. She was bland and beautiful, they said, but Tyrone Power was felt by many of them to be the same.

Shirley Temple continued to be Twentieth's biggest star, Number One at the box office. Now, an import from Scandinavia, Sonja Henie, had emerged as the studio's second biggest star, ranking eighth in 1937 among the top ten.

Despite her resentment, Loretta Young's first costarring picture with Ty—they had been only featured players in their previous film—was such a popular success that the studio began publicizing them as the only love team on the screen. Ty, however, got the better notices. His effortless charm was very effectively showcased. "This handsome young man," *Life* magazine said, "was lifted to stardom only a few months ago by *Lloyds of London*. *Love Is News* will probably establish him as the leading contender for the romantic juvenile laurels now worn by Robert Taylor."

One review praising both stars appeared in the usually carping *Time* magazine: "Acting with a kittenish zest precisely suited to her appearance, Loretta Young does a job as good as any in her long career. Tyrone Power, Jr., in his second important role and his screen debut in farce, gives surprisingly mature restraint to a role which might easily have slipped into frantic mugging."

Ty made three more pictures in 1937, securing his position at the studio. All were flimsy. He played a commoner who pretends to be a prince in *Café Metropole;* a prince who pretends to be a newspaper reporter in *Thin Ice;* a millionaire who remarries his remarried ex-wife in *Second Honeymoon*. The best that can be said about these roles is that they gave him a chance to get into modern clothes and fresh dialogue, to better show off his natural charm. His ability to take a line like "You get a little attached to these noses after you've had them a few years" and deliver it with grace and believability, making the contrived masquerade look as natural and pleasant as everyday chatter, served the films better than the films served him.

The best Darryl Zanuck could say about them, as he did years later, was that they evolved into a predictable money-making formula: "In the old days you could schedule three Tyrone Power pictures a year. No matter what they were, you were assured a big gross and you could anticipate just about what it would be."

"You may sup lightly at . . . *Café Metropole,* taking more pleasure in the service than the fare," Frank Nugent of *The New York Times* wrote. He felt that the talents of the farceurs were more engaging than the farce itself.

The most profitable of Ty's comedies that year was *Thin Ice,* in which he costarred with Sonja Henie. On the strength of one previous low-budget picture, *One in a Million,* which had already grossed $2,000,000, the three-time Olympic champion was being paid $100,000 for her second picture. This assignment was the test to determine whether she was just a flash in the pan, and she was being teamed with an actor receiving an average of five thousand fan letters a week.

The picture, with its three elaborate ice ballets, was a huge success, and Miss Henie's future in films was assured. Perhaps because it was directed by Ty's old nemesis, Sidney Lanfield, his role called on him principally to grin a lot and to intrude his handsome face in the proceedings as facelessly as possible.

The happiest development from the picture was his very real love affair with Sonja Henie after several studio-manufactured ones. She was high-spirited and pert, as well as shrewd and aggressive. What's more she spoke in a delightful foreign accent. Friends noticed that Ty tended to gravitate to foreign-born girls.

For a reason that neither of them would talk about, the romance abruptly ended. Did she become suddenly aware of his bisexuality? She was too well-mannered to remark on it. "She has always been a happy type," Louella Parsons later wrote about her, "with the exception of that time . . . at the start of her Hollywood career when she was so in love with Tyrone Power. Sonja never did tell what went wrong between her and Ty."

The actor threw himself into more work. His next co-starring role opposite Loretta Young, *Second Honeymoon,* described by the studio as a society romp, didn't have the wit to be called a screwball comedy. It also had the misfortune to be released the week after *The Awful Truth*, starring Cary Grant and Irene Dunne, an instant classic, and it could only suffer by comparison. The love team that Zanuck had attempted to build was doomed for divorce.

On the strength of his recently gained stardom, Ty was hired to perform in a Sunday night dramatic series over a national radio network. His boss, Darryl Zanuck, introduced him on the program. The first production, in October of 1937, was *Her Cardboard Lover* opposite Margaret Sullavan. Most of the later shows were formula plot situations, much like his recent movies, and the public lost interest. Ty had a fine voice, but its appeal was minimized when it was so disembodied. At a later date he would get Eve Abbott cast as his costar in a Lux Radio Theater production of *Men in White*, which was broadcast from Radio City Music Hall in New York. He was extremely helpful in getting work for his friends, especially when they had talent.

It was at about this time that Patia Power went to her son and told him of a conversation she'd had with Hedda Hopper, who'd recently started writing a syndicated Hollywood column. The two women hadn't seen each other in twenty years, when both of their husbands were in California making movies. Hedda Hopper had been one of actor De Wolf Hopper's many wives.

"Was your husband's tour in *The Servant in the House* successful?" she asked Patia.

Ty's mother was amazed at Hedda's long memory. "How did you ever know about that?" she asked.

The columnist laughed. She said that her husband had always been a spendthrift. After much pleading, he promised not to lend any more money to down-and-out actors without first consulting her.

Hedda was waiting for her husband in the lobby of the Alexandria Hotel in downtown Los Angeles one June day, in the company of the first Mrs. Douglas Fairbanks. Hopper was very late.

He was apologetic and, in the presence of Mrs. Fairbanks, so that his wife wouldn't make a scene, told her of lending five hundred dollars to Ty Power, Sr., to help finance the tour.

"Wolfie," she said, "do you know what day this is?"

"Why-er, yes . . . it's Tuesday."

That was the final straw. Her husband had not only broken his promise about lending money, he had also forgotten her birthday.

A few days after the conversation, Patia invited Hedda Hopper to lunch. She handed the columnist Ty's personal check, canceling out his father's debt to Hedda's former husband.

"For the first time in my life I was speechless," the columnist recalled. "I thought it some kind of a gag . . . but it wasn't."

Zanuck was planning to mount Twentieth's answer to Metro's *San Francisco,* the enormous hit which had starred Clark Gable and Jeanette MacDonald. At last it looked as if Louis B. Mayer would keep his promise to lend Gable to Twentieth for *In Old Chicago,* which would do to the Chicago fire of 1870 what the Metro picture had done to the San Francisco earthquake of 1906. As a lagniappe, Jean Harlow would also be coming over from MGM. The screenplay by Lamar Trotti and Sonya Levien had been written with Gable in mind. He would play Mrs. O'Leary's errant son. Mayer, in return, wanted the services of Twentieth's Shirley Temple to star in *The Wizard of Oz.*

Once it looked as if the mutual loan-outs were agreed to, director Henry King took a trip to Honolulu, taking the script with him. It was his regular practice to go away for two or three weeks to work on a script before he held his preproduction meetings.

While in Hawaii, Zanuck cabled King to return immediately to California. Because of a ship strike, the director wasn't able to get back for some days.

As soon as he consulted with Zanuck, King was told that *In Old Chicago* was being postponed. Could he direct *Heidi* with Shirley Temple in the meantime?

King wasn't enthralled.

"Why can't we do the Chicago picture?" he asked.

"We can't get Gable yet," Zanuck replied. "We certainly wouldn't do it without Gable, would we?"

"Suppose Gable had died?" King asked. "What would you do?"

"We have determined that we're using Gable," Zanuck adamantly said.

"Let me tell you something," King said. "Gable will do more to ruin the picture than he will to help it."

"That's the silliest idea I ever heard in my life," his boss said.

"I'll tell you why," King persisted. "You have his mother taking in washing for a living and he comes in and goes through the linen of the other people's laundry and picks out a shirt that will fit him and puts it on. And he is at the age at the end of the story when he crawls up into his mother's lap and asks for forgiveness. If she doesn't kick him right under the chin or right in the teeth, the audience is going to get mad at her. He's too old. I'd put a kid like Tyrone Power in."

Zanuck dismissed the idea.

Ten days later, he called a meeting in his office.

"Boys," he said, "all of you are wondering why you're here. Ten days ago Henry King came back from Honolulu with the most cockeyed idea I've ever seen or heard in my life. But the more I think of it, the more I think he's right. I think we should do what he suggests and start the picture immediately."

Thus, Tyrone Power was cast for the role. Jean Harlow, in the meantime, became ill—she would die soon after—and had to be replaced. Alice Faye was hired. As for the loan-out of Shirley Temple, that was canceled and Metro decided to cast a child contract player, Judy Garland, in *The Wizard of Oz*.

Ty played the owner of a saloon, and Alice Faye was his star entertainer. Don Ameche played the good O'Leary brother, and Alice Brady was their mother.

In Old Chicago was to become the typical Twentieth product of the late 1930s, a massive melodrama based on flimsy facts, lively and colorful, with at least one spectacular episode.

Chicago was indelibly sketched as a place where things happen quickly. Less than two minutes after the titles are off the screen, a family in a wagon is racing a locomotive. The father, holding the reins, is dragged over rough turf as the horses bolt from their fastenings to the wagon, leaving Mrs. O'Leary a widow with three boys to raise. Two of them grow up to be Tyrone Power and Don Ameche, who enter separate walks of life with separate visions of their personal futures and the future of Chicago. Yet they maintain a bond of family loyalty despite their differences. "We O'Learys are a strange tribe," is the often repeated statement.

The pace begins to flag just short of breathless only minutes before the great Chicago fire breaks out, forcing the actors to tie up three or four plot threads while racing through the streets to save their mother from the flames. The growth of the meat industry, the corruption of Chicago's government, changing values, filial devotion, and the fire itself are all tied together in a way that alternates reckless growth with calamitous ruin.

When the fire has been exploited to its fullest, a stampede of stockyard cattle is introduced, the animals too being milked in not their accustomed way. The final speeches—"Nothing will lick Chicago" and "What it stood for will never die"—represent a cynical attempt to tack an optimistic ending to an orgy of destruction. What did Chicago stand for exactly—corruption and cows?

Ty was too fresh-faced to make a convincing scoundrel. He didn't seep corruption from every pore, and the audience had to take in everyone else's dialogue to know what a bounder he was. There was a hollow ring to many of his lines, due less to his deficiencies as an actor than to the ridiculous dialogue. In one scene, he's bleeding profusely at the temple. He utters, "It's just a scratch." His wasn't a problem of not being able to deliver the line. It was the script's problem, for the line was undeliverable.

In the picture, Ty began to assume the role of Zanuck's alter ego, the brash young man who hurdles all obstacles to achieve his vision of success, doing his bit for the growth of commerce and the creation of large industries out of small ones which are in the way. If corners are cut and ethics are bent, it's more palatable that a handsome and charming stand-in for Zanuck and his business philosophy be used. In this picture, the interpretation was split with the idealistic Ameche portrayal, the two representing the restless and the conventional sides of Zanuck's personality. Their joint characterization of Zanuck, however, wasn't the one that received the widest notice. It was Alice Brady as Mrs. O'Leary who won the Academy Award that year for Best Supporting Actress.

There was no question, nevertheless, that Ty had arrived at the

studio. He and his associates developed an unusual sense of cama-
raderie.

Because there were fewer stars than at Metro, Twentieth was
the Avis of this particular solar system. "I loved Ty Power, Don
Ameche, and John Payne," as Alice Faye put it, "and they loved
me, and this teamwork, this desire to make the movie as good as
possible, made those pictures.

"Twentieth was much more of a family affair. Darryl Zanuck
was the boss, a very brilliant man, but he wasn't part of the family. He was Mr. Zanuck. I thought we did very well. Our pictures
made a lot of money.

"Of course, today, I look at those Warner pictures directed by
Busby Berkeley and starring Ruby Keeler and Dick Powell, and
the pictures with Fred Astaire and Ginger Rogers. I didn't think
much about it then, but those musicals far surpassed anything Fox
did."

Yet the Fox musicals were greater financial successes. Technicolor was the added ingredient. Miss Faye conceded that it was
harder working in these pictures because the lights generated
more heat while filming in color. There seemed to be a direct
corollary between that greater heat and the greater rewards at the
box office.

Not many critics noticed at the time, but Ty's next portrayal, in
Alexander's Ragtime Band, was as fine a piece of work as he'd
ever done. The chipper high tones and eager grin of Dion O'Leary
in his previous picture were replaced with quiet determination, re-
strained gestures, and the lower voice register of a jazz bandleader
with hopes of respectability. He waved his baton as if he'd done it
all his life. He'd even spent three months learning how to play a
violin. At the end of the time, he was visually convincing, although all he could play was a number on one string.

There was little acting in the picture, whose chief function was
to race through a cavalcade of twenty-six Irving Berlin songs,
making them tell the story of American jazz and social life from
1911 to 1938. The stars, again Ty, Alice Faye, and Don Ameche,
don't add a wrinkle or a gray hair during the period. Thanks to
the meshing skills of director King, screenwriter Trotti, and
producer Zanuck, the show flowed smoothly, songs either advanc-

ing the story or allowing the story to be advanced by the way, time, or place they were performed. Thus, the music and the plot —simple as it was—didn't step on each other's toes, as so many other movie musicals of the period did. It was a triumph for all concerned, and they knew it would be as they shot *Alexander's Ragtime Band*.

It was to be the first of the "Coney Island plot" pictures, as studio wag Nunnally Johnson put it, invariably starring Tyrone Power and Jack Oakie, though the two never worked together. Its story revolved around one line: "What do you mean, you're going to break up the act?"

Behind the scenes, the stars were doing their best to break up each others' act. Henry King ran a tight ship, but the stars still performed a lot of juvenile hijinks. Ty and Ameche treated Alice Faye to a variety of indignities, all in the name of good fun. They overturned a can of garbage in her luxuriously appointed dressing room. They pulled away the steps of her portable dressing room, so that when she walked out of it one day she nearly fell on her extremely valuable face. They put a very realistic porcelain frog in the bottom of her coffee cup. Ethel Merman, brought out from Broadway to sing seven numbers, joined in the pranks by hiding Ty's temporary upper caps, which he slipped on for dazzling closeups. Ty, in retaliation, wrapped the gown she would be wearing for her next scene onto a clothes tree, then drove nails into it. With his trusty hammer, he also slipped into Ameche's dressing room and nailed his shoes to the floor. When the other actor slipped into them and tried to walk, he nearly toppled over.

These were the capers of close friends, who seemed to appreciate roughhouse humor better than subtle wit. In larger matters, their behavior toward each other was profoundly thoughtful. Since Ty and Alice Faye shared the same birthday, she being one year younger, they exchanged birthday telegrams every year until Ty's death. Don Ameche would be the best man at Ty's wedding to Annabella. They weren't intentional scene stealers, not from each other, at least. They were extremely good friends, and encouraged each other's successes.

That year, 1938, was to be the most impressive thus far for Twentieth at the box office. Four of its stars were among the top ten. Shirley Temple remained in first place, Sonja Henie was third, Alice Faye was ninth and Ty was tenth. His salary went up accordingly.

As soon as he was able to buy a house, Ty asked his mother to come live with him. Patia would later claim her moving in with her son changed her entire attitude toward their relationship. Ty was now a man, and this would be his house. His would be the final decision on all matters. It would be her responsibility to see that the house ran smoothly.

Patia decided never to entertain while Ty was filming, and she would make herself scarce whenever he wanted to entertain a group of contemporaries. Such selflessness, given her domineering ways, didn't last for long.

Wil Wright, who still slightly feared her, found Ty's mother to be a damper on any party. She'd revert to her schoolmarm ways if she felt the liquor flowed too freely, instructing the guests, "Now don't have another drink."

When early in 1938 Norma Shearer asked Metro to borrow Tyrone Power to play Swedish Count Axel Fersen opposite her as *Marie Antoinette,* Darryl Zanuck was delighted. MGM claimed to have more stars than in the heavens, but apparently a very important one was lacking. To get Ty, Metro agreed to loan Twentieth two stars for 1939 productions: Spencer Tracy for *Stanley and Livingstone* and Myrna Loy for *The Rains Came.* Both were among the top-ten money-making stars in films.

Walter Scott, who was Twentieth's supervising set decorator at the time, recalled that a friend went to Ty and asked, "Do you know what kind of deal this is?"

Ty didn't. The economic facts of life were explained. His contract at the time called for a salary of from five to six hundred dollars a week. The MGM stars were each making nearly ten times as much.

Rather humbly, Ty went to see Darryl Zanuck. "If I'm okay enough for you to loan me out in exchange for those high-paying people, why am I only making this kind of money?"

His logic was irrefutable. A new contract was drawn up, and

from that point on, Ty received the salary and perquisites of a star.

The sumptuous showcase for Miss Shearer, Irving Thalberg's recent widow, would run two hours and four minutes, cost almost two million dollars to produce, and take more than two months to shoot. Its window dressing of ninety-eight sets, including the Grand Ballroom at Versailles, several feet longer than the original, was complemented by more than 1,250 gowns custom-designed by Adrian. *Time* found the finished product "far superior to the revolution from which it was derived."

Ty was in the middle of filming when Evie Abbott, at his invitation, arrived in California to visit him and his family. His sister Anne, who had married at nineteen, was divorcing her husband and also living at the hilltop house in Bel-Air. Ty apparently needed and wanted his female relatives to come home to every night. "How many movie stars would have their mother and sister living with them?" Evie Johnson asked.

She had stayed in New York looking for work in the theater, and the two had corresponded during the two years they'd been apart. Ty sent her many thoughtful gifts. The first, picked because it was from department store located at the famous intersection of Hollywood and Vine, was an ostrich leather purse with a watch on the outside.

By this time, Eve was being seriously courted by Keenan Wynn, whose grandfather, Frank Keenan, had often appeared on the stage with Ty's father. Every day, at the house on Perugio Way, a bouquet of flowers would arrive from the New York actor.

"That's what's known as keeping your oar in," Ty noted drily.

Aware of the competition, he asked Eve to marry him. His grandmother Mudgie, visiting from Cincinnati, was even more insistent about pressing the matter. She highly approved of Eve.

"We'll spend our happy old age together," Ty explained to Mudgie.

Eve felt uncomfortable among Ty's female friends. "I felt they disliked me, and resented my staying with him," she said. "I saw too many women falling down over him. He was too attractive to too many people."

When she returned East, Eve wrote Ty and said she couldn't

marry him. "I'd be much too jealous of all those women," she explained. She agreed to marry Wynn instead.

Ty wouldn't accept that. He told Eve they were destined to wind up together. "I can see us now when we're nice and old and complacent," he told her.

Eve hadn't wanted to share the public spotlight with Ty. Ironically, the studio he was currently on loan-out to, seemed to be trying to eliminate the spotlight altogether.

The simply costumed Ty was overshadowed by the opulence of *Marie Antoinette* and made little impression. The film itself reflected a wit and intelligence that far exceeded the leaden epics of Ty's home studio, lending character to its opulence and irony to its artifice. Critic Otis Ferguson said that Robert Morley as Louis XVI "makes a grand figure," Norma Shearer "carries the main pattern," Joseph Schildkraut and John Barrymore "are good" and Tyrone Power "is in it."

Zanuck was so angered at MGM's cavalier treatment of his top star, which could diminish Ty's drawing power, that he refused to loan him out again. When he finished filming at MGM, Louella Parsons reported that Ty was the only one being considered for the role of Ashley Wilkes in *Gone With the Wind.* Director George Cukor, who prepared that Selznick-MGM film before he was fired, said Ty might have been considered among other actors, but he was never seriously in the running for the part. Even if he had been, Zanuck would not have permitted it. He refused to loan out Ty to Columbia for *Golden Boy,* which made a star of William Holden, and Warner Brothers for *King's Row,* in the role played by Robert Cummings.

Never again would he let his major male star be misused in this way. Louis B. Mayer had shrewdly realized that his players, given the showy star vehicles Twentieth wanted them for, couldn't be minimized. Yet, in downgrading Ty's role in *Marie Antoinette,* he proved that it wasn't Zanuck who was the biggest Twentieth Century fox of them all, but Louis B. Mayer himself.

It was a continual affront to Zanuck that movie moguls such as Mayer hadn't taken him seriously up to now. "You with your trick moustache," Metro's studio head had once said in dismissal.

Zanuck wasn't one of them, being neither Jewish nor of their generation.

He still hadn't proven himself as a filmmaker. Despite the rapid growth of Twentieth, few of the pictures he'd produced were distinguished ones. The blame rested directly on him. He was the moving force, a former screenwriter who controlled all scripts and insisted on final cut of the films. Zanuck was unable to delegate authority to others, as his competitors had learned to do.

Even his pastimes were found to be affected. He may have cut a dashing figure playing the rich man's sport of polo, but to his peers—there were perhaps half a dozen in the world—he was a ludicrous one. Zanuck had yet to prove he was crème de la crème to rise to the top of Hollywood society. It was an ambition his wife Virginia, a former Mack Sennett bathing beauty, wanted as much as he. His upbringing had probably been more privileged than that of such uneducated Jews as Mayer, Goldwyn, and Zukor. Yet, those men had grown considerably. Their products showed an innate taste and subtlety that Zanuck's lacked.

It was particularly galling that some of his underlings were more socially acceptable than he. Ty was welcome in distinguished homes and Zanuck was not. Bill and Edie Goetz were also on a higher social level. Her then brother-in-law, David O. Selznick, was involved with John Hay Whitney in the production of *Gone With the Wind,* and Whitney had leased a house next to the Goetzes in Bel-Air. When his sister, Joan Payson, was visiting, Whitney invited the Goetzes for dinner. Bill and Edie repaid the social obligation by having a party of their own, asking Joan Payson to put together a guest list of the people she'd like to see while in California. The Zanucks were pointedly omitted, and the Goetzes, through no fault of their own, were never forgiven.

Bill and Edie Goetz were Ty's closest friends. Under their protective eyes, he had grown from a shy and inhibited young man into a confident one well aware of his devastating effect on women.

Because it was expected of him, Edie Goetz recalled, "Ty became a terrible flirt. He made light of it, but he even flirted with me. He knew there was no chance, because I loved my husband."

Whenever he ran into him on the lot, Ty would ask Goetz,

"How's our wife?" Ty was one of the few allowed to call Edie by her nickname: Snoodgie.

Their closeness was misunderstood by the daughter of another studio mogul, who said Edie and Ty were having an affair. "How dare you?" Edie said when she confronted her. "He's Bill's and my friend. And *where* would I be having an affair? On top of a roof? I have too many servants. I wouldn't know where to have it." What the woman didn't understand was how Ty could be such close friends with Edie Goetz, being seen in public with her without her husband, without their being lovers. But that was indicative of Ty's closeness with the Goetzes, as well as other first families of Hollywood. He was accepted in a way Zanuck never could have been. He never argued. He never gossiped. He never insistently took over the conversation at dinner parties, like some studio heads Edie Goetz would prefer not to mention.

As a result, Ty was caught in the middle. Although Edie Goetz's social standing was on a higher level and, by extension, so was her husband's, Zanuck wielded the greater authority at the studio. It took all of Ty's diplomatic skills to cope with the situation.

CHAPTER

6

T<small>Y HAD NEVER KNOWN A WOMAN LIKE</small> A<small>NNABELLA</small>. T<small>RUE, SHE</small> was older than he, as Janet Gaynor had been, but the American actress had been the perpetual ingenue, while his new costar in *Suez* was worldly and cultured. He had found Sonja Henie's accent fascinating, but she was basically uncomplicated, and the ideas this new French actress could expound on were considerably more involved with the intellect.

Annabella was pertly beautiful, witty, and endowed with an enormous amount of charm. The house she'd rented at Sunset Boulevard and Beverly Glen was the scene of a delightful social life, usually Sunday brunches by the pool. That she could afford to live in such luxury showed she was already comfortably fixed. Her guests weren't the great stars who usually spent weekends at San Simeon or dined with royalty at Pickfair. Those who came to be captivated by the hostess were the younger group, a mixture of American and European creative people, not nearly so well established, but much more fun.

She was athletic, home-oriented, and luxury-loving, emotionally warm, unselfish, and generous. If she were Spanish she would have expressed the adage, "Mi casa es su casa." She certainly lived it.

Ty's sister Anne, who remains devoted to her former sister-in-law, finds great depth in Annabella. "She's always been extremely vital, with a beautiful nature, filled with heart and compassion. She's understanding and loyal."

Her real name was Suzanne Georgette Charpentier, and the date of her birth, as it does with most actors, became so obfuscated that film historians find it difficult to document that she was born at all. Most standard reference works place the date as July 17, 1909, which means she would have been a rather mature sixteen when she was cast as Josephine by French director Abel Gance, who began filming his silent classic, *Napoleon,* innovative because it was triptych in form, in 1925—this at a time when Tyrone Power was approaching puberty. Her greatest successes in France had been in the René Clair films, *Le Million* and *La Quatorze Juillet.*

Annabella arrived in Hollywood from her native France in 1934 with four other French actors. They were met at the plane by a transplanted countryman who had already established a solid reputation in American films: Charles Boyer. The newcomers were in the United States to act in French language versions of American pictures. It was a common practice to bring in foreign casts to work on American sets, thus creating original films for foreign markets. But it would soon be ending, for the procedure was too costly. Dubbing by foreign actors and use of subtitles followed. American actors, thus showcased, had even greater assurance of international stardom.

She'd stayed on in the United States to film other French language pictures before going to England in 1937 to appear opposite a rising Twentieth actor in *Wings of the Morning,* the first British production in Technicolor, and also her first English-language picture, in which she masqueraded quite convincingly and charmingly as a boy. Her costar was Henry Fonda.

Whatever her age, Annabella was a glamorous sophisticate when she bumped into twenty-four-year-old Tyrone Power in the hallway of the artists' building at the studio. A wardrobe woman introduced the star of *Suez,* in which Annabella was to be third billed after Loretta Young.

The French actress's father had been a magazine editor, and she'd been exposed to the minds of Europe's greatest intellects.

Annabella had already been widowed by the death of her first husband, French writer Albert Sorre, and was currently separated from her second, French actor Jean Murat, who was considerably older. Their daughter, Anne, was eight. (She would later marry Austrian actor Oskar Werner.)

The powers at the studio, who had arranged previous "romances" for Ty, had no intention of throwing him and Annabella together when they were cast with Loretta Young in the quasi-historical film about the building of the Suez Canal.

The French actress had played androgynous roles successfully. There was a prevalent supposition that she brought true-life credentials to her characterizations. A common conception during the thirties was that actresses with foreign accents were usually disposed toward overly intense relationships with other women. Not that it was of great importance in a society where homosexuality was looked on not so much as an aberration but as an idiosyncrasy to be handled with discretion. It was vitally important, however, that in the pairing of the studio's golden boy, his girl be as youthfully beautiful, sincere, and wholesome as he.

If others found Annabella in some ways lacking, they couldn't prove it by Ty. She didn't spare herself. While Loretta Young coddled herself in her dressing room at the Pico Boulevard studio, she was caught in the middle of a studio-manufactured sandstorm. Three thousand truckloads of sand were spread on a twenty-acre prop desert, created on the lot at a cost of $250,000, to create a *zobah-hab,* a cyclonic dust storm. One of the pivotal scenes had the tiny urchin of the desert tie de Lesseps to a large pole stuck in the sand, saving him while she was blown away to a certain death. It took seventeen days to shoot the scene, and Annabella proved the definitive trouper. It's gratuitous to carp that her makeup was so improbably overdone as to be as masklike as that of her friend, Marlene Dietrich.

Within Annabella was the commitment of an intensely dedicated actress. If the fates were kind, she would one day emerge as an international star. Ty admired her drive. If she aggressively pursued him—this was the pattern of his relationships with women all his life—it wouldn't hurt her career to have her name romantically linked with America's most handsome and sought-after actor.

Loretta Young was a total contrast to Annabella, having settled for being merely popular, demanding recognition of her star eminence. Whether she was an accomplished actress was totally irrelevant. In her way she was the unconscious catalyst who brought Ty and Annabella together.

Ty also was a star, although he hadn't yet come to realize the extent of his influence, and rarely would exercise it, but he wanted to grow as an actor. He needed to be inspired by Annabella's strength and dedication, for she had enough of those qualities for the two of them. He also related to her old-world manners, the same ones Patia Power had drilled into him.

His role of Ferdinand de Lesseps, the builder of the Suez Canal, was again more important than Loretta Young's, who was playing the Empress Eugenie.

Despite a shrewdly negotiated salary calling for four thousand dollars a week, Loretta Young was never a top box-office star at Twentieth—or elsewhere for that matter—and the way she was being downgraded greatly rankled her.

There were reports of her using many scene-stealing tricks during the filming, such as gesturing with a lace handkerchief in the middle of another actor's important lines or continually putting her hands to her face to show off her distractingly long fingernails.

Director Allan Dwan denied that this was so. "I didn't allow her to get away with anything that detracted from the picture," he said. "She fitted the part of Eugenie like a glove . . . an ambitious woman who took advantage of the situation and married the king. Will to succeed took precedence over love. She understood that. Loretta was always above everything, you know. And she used that quality in Eugenie, of having complete control over her situation and being vastly superior to everybody."

Her early scenes with Ty were a romp, the goings-on at the French court having a liveliness and spontaneity that promised more fun than the film ultimately delivered. The buoyant enthusiasm of its opening changed to portentous destiny. Loretta Young's frivolous part couldn't compare dramatically to the Annabella character giving up her life for the man she loves.

Suez asked the audience to accept the idea that the inspiration to build the canal came to de Lesseps one afternoon in the middle of a desert ride. As he envisioned a dry gully with water running through it, Ty was required to proclaim, "I could make this spot that we're standing on the crossroads of the earth!" Then later, "I was looking for a way to serve France, and I think I've found a way to serve the world!"

He could read the absurd lines quietly, intimately, and be pleasantly convincing, so that the moments didn't look as ridiculous on the screen as they sounded on paper. With him, his fans *wanted* to believe, not just to suspend disbelief. It was such moments—quiet and self-effacing—that illustrated his indispensability to Zanuck and the studio. And it was his character—also quiet and self-effacing—that proved how substantial his talent truly was. With better writers, Twentieth Century-Fox could have gotten by with less accomplished players than he.

One of them, however, was doing her best to more than get by elsewhere. Zanuck wanted Loretta Young to stay on, for he thought she was a decorative addition to any picture. Her sense of self-worth, however, wouldn't permit her to stay much longer.

When it came time to discuss an extension of her contract, she met with Joe Schenck and Darryl Zanuck.

"It seems like I've been here 150 years," Miss Young told the two men and their subordinates. Turning to Zanuck she said, "I'll work for Mr. Schenck but not you. In all the years I've been here, you've never once sent me flowers or given me a bonus or even a raise. Ty Power has been on the lot one year and he's been raised twice."

There were very substantial reasons for the studio's favoring Tyrone Power. He was already the studio's top male star, and three actresses—Shirley Temple, Sonja Henie, and Alice Faye—ranked as greater female box-office stars than Loretta Young. Ty was on the verge of becoming Twentieth's top box-office star, whereas her standing had stood noticeably still during the same period. Ty tried to treat the situation with his typical thoughtfulness and good grace, but he was frustrated by his costar's not-so-veiled resentments. Hoping they could remain friends, he decided to give her a wide berth until matters cooled.

What wasn't cooling, however, was his appeal to the public. Of the studio's four top-grossing films during the year of 1938, three Tyrone Power pictures—*In Old Chicago, Alexander's Ragtime Band,* and *Suez*—ranked first, second, and fourth. *Film Daily,* in its list of ten best pictures for the year, listed *Alexander's Ragtime Band, In Old Chicago,* and *Marie Antoinette* among them. *The Motion Picture Herald* had already placed Ty on its list of top ten box-office attractions for the year, and he was moving up fast.

Zanuck and his cohorts heeded the public groundswell. Ty would be the first actor considered for major studio productions, with Henry Fonda and John Payne getting second choice of roles. Students of film considered Fonda a better actor than Power, but he had yet to prove his box-office appeal, and monetary returns were what made—and still make—successful film careers.

One of the first perquisites of his stardom was the dressing-room suite assigned to him in the Stars Building across from the studio commissary. It was located on the southeast corner of the building, on the second floor, and designed specifically for him. From that point on it would be the most prestigious star suite on the lot.

When Walter Scott informed Ty that the suite was being decorated for him, the actor said, "If that's what I'm supposed to get, fine."

All the appurtenances were of the highest quality, yet Ty hadn't demanded this. Neither did he express a taste for any particular type of decor.

The dressing-room suite was paneled in oak and used plaid fabrics on the built-in settees. Leather club chairs and hunting prints on the wall gave the suite a prosperous, masculine look. The same motif was carried over to his portable dressing room, which was kept on the soundstage for his convenience while he was filming.

When Ty first looked at what Walter Scott accomplished and what his stellar name entitled him to, he simply remarked, "This is fine."

Although Scott didn't find him "clubby," neither was Ty aloof with workers on the set. He didn't sequester himself in his dressing room between takes, choosing instead to share small talk with the crew. If there was a barrier between him and the workers, it was due to his slightly formal manner with them and their awareness of Ty as a legitimate star.

Neither was he a primper, seeming totally unaware of his good looks. He would be made up, then go about his work as usual. "He didn't need a mirror," a male lover said. "He had one by just looking at other people. He saw their desire and admiration. The expressions on their faces became his mirror."

That Ty was one of the few actors allowed to use Darryl Zanuck's private steam room was a more immediate indication of his emergence as a major star. He once left the sauna and dived into the adjacent pool, which was usually kept at fifty-two degrees. But not on this day. Zanuck had instructed the pool to be filled with ice. Ty scrambled out of the pool almost as quickly as he'd dived in. He was now in the rarefied circle, one of Zanuck's guys. He had totally arrived.

With Ty's drawing power now among the greatest in films, less established players could be given greater exposure by casting them in his pictures.

One of the first to benefit by this arrangement was another actor whose talents Zanuck was tepid about, as he had been just three years previously about Ty's. The studio head, in fact, was unenthused about the upcoming project altogether.

He'd approached Henry King about directing *Stanley and Livingstone*. The director was agreeable provided the script had a story line and wasn't merely another African travelogue. Despite the dramatic conflict in the script that was delivered to him, King didn't like it. He asked Zanuck if he could do a film on Jesse James instead. His boss became infuriated.

"All right!" he angrily said. "Go ahead. You want to do *Jesse James?* Do *Jesse James*. That's fine. You've been doing these big pictures that are box-office attractions all over the world. *Jesse James* will be good in Tennessee and southern Illinois and Arkansas and Missouri . . . a few places like that. Go right ahead."

Despite his sarcasm Zanuck didn't intrude as King began preparing the picture. Among all the studio moguls, he was the most amenable to being proven wrong. By casting himself as the devil's advocate, he could determine if a filmmaker believed strongly enough in a project. If he developed an overriding passion for it, the final product would reflect this enthusiasm.

Screenwriter Nunnally Johnson was assigned to write a script. A droll Southerner, he told King he was writing the laconic, sod-kicking Frank James part for himself. He also brought to the studio, which had previously depicted the construction of the Suez Canal as one of the most momentous events since the birth of Christ, an unusually liberal anti-big-business sentiment.

When King told Zanuck he was thinking of Henry Fonda for the pivotal part of Frank James, he again met with resistance from his boss. "That guy has no business playing that kind of part," Zanuck said. "He's a lousy actor." King, knowing the studio head well, let the idea simmer for a few days.

Fonda, nearly ten years older than Ty, had been knocking around for years. Though he'd already starred in a dozen pictures, getting good critical notices in many of them, his boyish appeal hadn't registered strongly with the ticket-buying public.

He'd been brought to Hollywood and signed to a personal contract with Paramount producer Walter Wanger, and was borrowed by the old Fox studio in 1935 to repeat his stage success in *The Farmer Takes a Wife*. Fox again borrowed him that same year for *Way Down East,* intending to reteam him with Janet Gaynor, the costar of his first film. She withdrew from that picture because of "illness," and Rochelle Hudson replaced her. It was not a success. In the interim he'd been loaned out for two films at Warner Brothers at the request of their major movie queen, Bette Davis; she'd had a crush on Fonda during their summer stock days, which she later admitted was unrequited. He played virtual dress dummies to her imperious roles, and his reputation hadn't been appreciably enhanced.

Now King wanted to cast Fonda in a pivotal part at Twentieth Century-Fox, although the actor was still under contract to Wanger and would have to be borrowed. This was one reason why Zanuck was opposed to the move. Surely there must be a contract player who could play the role.

In looking at his contract list, Zanuck came to realize that King might be right about Fonda. At a later production meeting, Zanuck said, "Henry, I think you have something there. Find out if Fonda is available."

He was, to the mild disappointment of Nunnally Johnson, who'd been semi-serious about being cast in the part. The Jesse James title role, which Ty was to play, was conventionally written as an open-faced and likeable young man, circumstances beyond his control turning him into an outlaw, the righter of grievous wrongs. According to some reviewers, the part would be conventionally acted by Ty. His was a movie-star portrayal. When others remark, "He's crazy with wildness," not a hair on that beautiful head is out of place. The director planted the emotion one should feel about the character more in the audience's mind than before its eyes. Ty's actions were neither more nor less than they should have been.

Many directors feel actors don't steal pictures. It's the material they're given, coupled with their arresting presence, that creates the impact. Henry Fonda's portrayal came to be considered one of the classic ones in Western films, and much of its success was due to Nunnally Johnson's writing the Frank James character for himself, giving him the best lines and bits of business.

Fonda's imminent impact was apparent to those who went to the Ozarks to film the Technicolor picture. King decided to film on location around Pineville, Missouri, because the area wasn't teeming with such modern eyesores as telephone poles and hadn't changed much since the end of the Civil War. He and Ty flew to the location together in King's private plane. Since Ty was taking flying instructions, he was allowed to pilot two-thirds of the way from California to Joplin, Missouri.

The filming took many weeks, and it was Ty's first extended separation from Annabella since they'd begun seeing each other. In his case, the absence made his heart grow fonder, as actor Brian Donlevy, who shared a house with him during the filming, could testify.

King once told an interviewer, "I have never seen a star that was big enough to carry a bad story and a bad part." Fortunately for Ty, he hadn't as yet been so tested, though he soon would be; his role in *Jesse James* was an immediate test of his character, nonetheless.

Ty was either too gentlemanly to voice resentment over the way he had been surreptitiously downgraded or too obtuse to discern that this was actually happening. In striving for profits, Zanuck was taking the risk of too quickly turning his peacock of today into the feather duster of tomorrow. Yet, to Zanuck's credit, Henry Fonda at last captured the public's imagination.

Jesse James wound up being Twentieth's most profitable picture for 1939, but it was another film that year, *The Grapes of Wrath,* that was conceded to be the best film the studio had thus far produced. Directed by John Ford, and starring Fonda, it further increased the actor's stature and assured him a place beside his friend Ty as a fellow leading man, if not as big a moneymaker. Zanuck quickly bought out Fonda's contract and put him on the studio's star roster. He was next teamed with Don Ameche and Alice Faye in *Lillian Russell*—a surrogate Tyrone Power—and his total stardom was assured later in 1940 when a film was specifically put together for him, *The Return of Frank James.* He remained among the studio's top stars until 1947.

Ty's work on *Jesse James* was completed when, on October 31, 1938, Annabella announced plans to divorce Jean Murat. Reporters asked if Ty was the reason for her action. "Tyrone Power?" she asked. "He is a nice boy, but that is all."

Yet, over the next few months, they happened to be in several cities at the same time. In late November, when he arrived in Rio de Janeiro, Ty said it was a happy coincidence that Annabella was already in the Brazilian city. A month later, he expressed surprise and delight to reporters when they pointed out that he and Annabella were both staying at the Hotel Pierre in New York.

Whatever agreement the two came to, given his more than passing interest in sex with other men, Ty was seriously in love with Annabella. He felt he could sublimate his wayward desires if married to her. This wasn't a marriage of convenience to authenticate his masculinity. He was only twenty-five and it would have been of greater professional benefit for him to stay single for a few more years. If he insisted on marrying, there were several young women others would find vastly preferable. Annabella was a totally unsuitable choice in both the minds of the studio and

Ty's collective public, the large part of which was adoring and female.

When studio executives insisted on discussing the issue, Ty abruptly cut them off. "This woman," he told them, "has helped me discover more in myself than I've ever been able to find alone."

At that time in his life, Annabella was apparently the woman he needed. He hadn't had much experience with the opposite sex, and the French actress bowled him over. Kurt Kasznar said she was "a natural. She was elegant and French and wore clothes wonderfully. She became his mother image."

Expectedly, this didn't sit well with Ty's true mother, who was still living with him. Anne, trying to make a life on her own after her divorce, had moved into her own apartment. Patia was heavy-set and stolid and represented duty, whereas Annabella was slim, fun-loving, and exciting. His mother was a practicing Catholic and Annabella, through her several marriages, was not a true member of the church. The woman was also years older than her son, and had a daughter. There were many impediments to the marriage, and Patia was both surprised and disappointed that Ty overlooked them all. Ty's mother seemed to be the only human Annabella couldn't charm. Although she remained outwardly polite to her future daughter-in-law, both women knew they could never be close. They were both fighting for the devotion of the same man.

Ty and Annabella stopped playing coy with the press when they applied for a marriage license in Los Angeles on April 18, 1939. They were married five days later in the garden of the home of Charles Boyer and his actress wife Pat Paterson. Mrs. Boyer was the matron of honor; Don Ameche was Ty's best man. Millions of hearts were broken, most of them female.

The newly marrieds were on a Roman honeymoon while Patia Power began making arrangements to live elsewhere after their return. Ty said he would continue to support her in whatever apartment she chose to live in. Over the last few years, his mother had aged considerably. The continuing deterioration of her health coincided with her son's making a new life for himself.

When they returned to California, the new Mr. and Mrs. Power decided to buy a house in Brentwood formerly owned by the opera star Grace Moore. The small Bel-Air house where Ty had been living with his mother was leased to an acting couple newly arrived in Hollywood—Robert Walker and Jennifer Jones—who soon moved in with their two sons.

While Annabella was decorating the new house with her usual smashing good taste, Ty could reflect on how his marriage had affected his career. The just-released *Rose of Washington Square,* which he'd completed before his marriage, was the first test.

This was his third picture opposite Alice Faye and the first film to take dramatic license with the life of Fanny Brice, Ty being cast in the unsympathetic Nicky Arnstein-type role. As *Time* commented on the usual disclaimer about similarities between characters and living people being purely coincidental, "this legal formula has never rung more hollowly." Miss Brice sued the studio at this invasion of her privacy and received an out-of-court settlement.

Ty was cast as a worthless con man, sent to five years in prison for a stock swindle, the character showing none of the redeeming traits of the repentant rascal he played in *In Old Chicago.* Twentieth, in its casting of Ty, was copying MGM's attempts to toughen its pretty boy, Robert Taylor, but was not as successful.

Her love for the crook he was portraying gave Alice Faye a chance to sing a rather glamorous version of "My Man," a song Fanny Brice had performed more plaintively and dramatically years before. Ty was a disreputable character in the film and a very married man in real life. Would the public still buy him? Of course, although the third picture with Alice Faye wasn't as financially successful as their first two, and Al Jolson was said to have stolen the picture.

It could only have been his widespread appeal, as well as an unparalleled number of five pictures released in 1939, that made Ty number two at the box office behind Mickey Rooney. The MGM actor, still the boyish adolescent, might be the Prince Errant of the Movies, but he as yet couldn't assume the title of King, given annually by theater exhibitors, that year. The slightly older Ty got the honor by default, sharing it with Jeanette MacDonald as Queen of the Movies for 1939. Within a few years, because he'd won the title of King so often, Clark Gable retired the annually awarded accolade.

The sum total of Ty's output in 1939, however, despite his continuing enormous popularity, should have been dispiriting. Rarely had so many movie dollars been generated by so lackluster a series of performances. In one picture, opposite Sonja Henie, in which she was top billed, he played the title role in *Second Fiddle.*

In another, *The Rains Came,* Twentieth, which had borrowed Myrna Loy from MGM, gave the impression that it was deliberately answering the insult of Ty's minor casting in *Marie Antoinette* by proving they could do the same on his own lot. Ty was playing an Indian doctor chosen by the Maharani of Ranchipur to follow in her example of public service, but he was neglected for the bulk of the footage. Its budget of $2,500,000 gave *The Rains Came* a sumptuous look more associated with Metro's products. It sparkled in its dazzling, dappled light and shadow, in its exotic Indian atmosphere, and in a spectacular earthquake, dam burst, and flood. What it lacked was the scope of Louis Bromfield's bestselling novel.

In what was later termed one of Hollywood's most absurd moments by one film buff, the Maharani of Ranchipur, played by Maria Ouspenskaya, took Lady Eskith, or Myrna Loy, by the arm. "Listen, mine dear," she said in Yiddish tones about the role Ty was playing, "dott is Ind-yuss most prummising young *docterr.*"

Frank S. Nugent of *The New York Times* again took Ty's performance to task, saying his Major Safti "suggests none of the intellectual austerity, the strength of character, and wisdom of Mr. Bromfield's 'copper Apollo.' He is still Mr. Power—young, impetuous, and charming—with all the depth of a coat of skin-dye."

The sole distinction of Ty's fifth picture in 1939, *Daytime Wife,* was that it effectively ended his teaming with Loretta Young. She balked at being second-billed in that bit of comic fluff, and left the studio soon after. Linda Darnell, a recent high school graduate, was cast in her place.

Ty was a young man, and he had the energy to handle Zanuck's nonstop assignments, as well as the overriding desire. As a future male lover was to describe Ty, "He was 70 percent work; 10 percent women, which was involved with work; and 20 percent men." That percentage would be somewhat altered depending on what friend one talked to, and many would dispute the opinion that Ty courted and bedded women only because the studio expected it of him. What everyone agreed upon was that Ty seemed to take a sort of sexual pleasure in his work and from the veneration of fans. It isn't uncommon among actors. He loved being a movie star, and he wanted to prove he was a better actor than his current roles indicated. His career would always come first.

On the long-term basis, however, Zanuck's indiscriminate casting of him in so many pictures a year could considerably shorten his career. He was in danger of being overexposed. True, Ty's pictures were making money, but some students of film found his talent a hollow golden egg.

Already, his given name had crept into Hollywood lingo as a term of derision. To call any young actor Tyrone was to mean he was a pretty boy of little aptitude and much affectation. This was unfair, for the real article had more talent than that and was less assuming than most of his namesakes.

Simply put, anyone that popular couldn't be good. Frank Nugent of the *Times* continued being caustic, and clever. When *The Story of Alexander Graham Bell,* starring Don Ameche and Loretta Young, had been released the previous April, he wrote, "If only because it omitted Tyrone Power, the Twentieth Century-Fox production . . . at the Roxy, must be considered one of that company's more sober and meritorious contributions to the historical drama."

Such a gratuitous slam, far beyond the bounds of fair comment, forced a reaction from both Fox and the Roxy. Both canceled all advertising in the *Times* for almost a year, a loss of revenue to the newspaper of over $50,000.

Ty never voiced any resentment over these and other snipes. As always, he held any hurt he might have felt within himself. That's the way Patia had raised him, to take the good and bad with the same stoical grace.

It may have been consolation enough that nobody loved him but the public. His effect was as mesmerizing with crowds of thousands when he appeared in public as in a one-to-one confrontation.

Either way, he reacted to the adulation with humility and shyness. Almost apologetically, he told Rock Hudson of once driving near Alhambra and on a whim deciding to motor past the house in which he'd lived. He stopped and rang the bell. The woman who came to the door was speechless.

"How do you do?" Ty said. "My name is Tyrone Power."

It was the most unnecessary of self-introductions. The woman's mouth was open, but she still wasn't speaking.

"I was raised in this house," Ty continued. "May I come in and look?"

She stepped aside and let him in. As Ty looked around, the house seemed so much smaller than he'd remembered. The short tour over, he thanked the woman and excused himself. She nodded, never having uttered a word.

Ty's sister Anne remarried in January of 1940, and when her second husband, Elmer Hardenbergh, went into the service at the outset of World War II, she followed him East. As a result, Anne no longer saw her brother as much as she had in the past. Her husband, by whom she had a daughter, remained a career officer after the war, rising to the rank of general.

She wasn't in California to attend a celebration at which Ty was being feted as Twentieth's top box-office star. The studio's female stars had been carrying the studio over the last few years, but now the order was reversed. Ty's second-place ranking at the box office was followed by Shirley Temple at fifth; Alice Faye, seventh; and Sonja Henie, tenth. None of their films was called art by Eastern intellectuals. Their assignments were specifically geared to Midwestern audiences. These were the days when movie studios owned and operated their own theaters, and the bulk of Twentieth's 538 theaters were in the Midwestern states of Wisconsin, Illinois, Missouri, Kansas, and Colorado. The studio owned only one theater in New York, had a few in Washington state, and 205 in California. Because of mass migrations from the Midwest, California during that period was being called Western Iowa.

Consequently, despite what Eastern critics said, there was a very sound financial reason in Ty's retaining his Midwestern accent, even in period pictures. "Many actors," Kurt Kasznar said, "especially if they're intellectual, try to make a concession by adopting a mid-Atlantic accent. Ty never did this. He remained strictly American, and a very proud one."

For the present, Ty was equally proud of his salary, although it hadn't caught up with his new box-office standing. Neither had Alice Faye's—she in the coming year would become the studio's top money-making actress. She received $140,291 in 1939, compared to Ty's $151,250, plus a $15,000 bonus. The top studio salary that year, however, went to Sonja Henie, a shrewd negotiator who received $244,156, plus a $5,000 bonus. The year of 1939, however, would be her last successful year, as it would prove to be for Shirley Temple, and her salary was adjusted accordingly.

Alice Faye was at the party that honored Ty. He expressed appreciation not only to her for her past encouragement and support, but also to Louella Parsons' millions of readers, for the Hollywood columnist was also in the group. She reported later that Ty stood up before the gathering and said, "I've got one person to thank for where I am today, and that's Alice Faye."

Of course, the blonde actress-singer always had an abiding faith in his ability. "I thought he was a great actor," she said. "I couldn't find any fault in his work. He had no limitations. Because he died so young, he didn't have a chance to carry on. If he were living today, he would be one of the greats."

She never found any signs of the tormented man Ty was later described as being. "He was a fun person. He didn't carry himself tragically. Maybe there were problems in his private life, but he wasn't the kind to burden others with them. A tormented man? Never!"

Certainly, with a happy new marriage and a booming career, there was no present cause for anguish in Ty. He had timorously exercised his script-choosing prerogative, having expressed dissatisfaction in the cardboard lovers he had played in recent pictures, and Zanuck agreed to develop deeper roles for him.

In the meantime, he and Annabella were off to New York for the opening of *My Dear Children* at the Belasco Theatre. The advance sale for John Barrymore's last starring Broadway role was one of the biggest in theatrical history. Scalpers were getting as much as one hundred dollars a ticket.

The production was being staged only two blocks from the Harris Theatre where Barrymore had starred in *Hamlet* less than twenty years previously. In the audience opening night were Gladys Swarthout, Constance Collier, Ernst Lubitsch, Elsa Maxwell, and Jack Warner. Diana Barrymore sat between her two half-brothers, Leonard and Robin Thomas.

After the opening, Ty joined the Barrymores at Robin's apartment for a private party. It was a morose evening. The Great Profile brought his current wife, Elaine Barrie, with him, and seemed totally out of control. It was as if he'd fallen into a premature senility, and Ty was amazed that he had been able to get through the performance. Robin's appearance was equally shocking. He was grotesquely fat, bearing no resemblance to the beautiful young man who had once been Ty's lover.

Sobered by the deterioration of the two men, Ty couldn't get back to California quickly enough. He was due to start filming *Johnny Apollo* in the next few days.

In the new picture, Ty was cast as the college-educated son of a white-collar criminal who fell into the underworld and turned mobster. *The Brooklyn Daily Eagle,* for one, would praise his performance: "For the first time in his career, the pride of the Zanuck lot has shown traces of the dramatic skill that has been a family tradition for more than a century." But the *Eagle* wasn't *The New York Times,* and in finding merit in Ty's self-conscious and artificial portrayal, it mistook his loss of natural ease and conviction with a-c-t-i-n-g. Being cast against type may have made Ty work harder, but the odds were heavily against his creating a convincing screen portrayal. He didn't overcome them, getting little help from his director.

Henry King had shrewdly deployed Ty's looks, holding down his expressiveness and creating a personality of quiet strength. His director on the new picture, Henry Hathaway, wasn't nearly as gifted, he being a routine and fairly characterless craftsman who'd worked his way up from two-reel Westerns. His career had vacilated from passably good pictures to inexcusably bad ones. He generally depended on the strongest person—actor, producer, or novelist—involved in the production. Zanuck was executive producer on the film, as he'd been on most of Ty's earlier ones, but perhaps his attentions were diverted elsewhere. Maybe he thought Ty could get his artistic pretensions out of his system. Let him have a clinker or two and he'd once again be malleable and content to remain a popular actor of limited resources but with enormous commercial appeal. Ty had been moldable putty in the hands of an accomplished director like King. In *Johnny Apollo,* however, both star and director floundered.

Hathaway and his associates attempted to inject a comic air into the shady dealings, but this was the firm touch on the wrong note. Cary Grant could have gotten away with being disreputable and charming, but Ty didn't possess the same raffish quality. The audience could identify with the righteous outrage that turned *Jesse James* into an outlaw, but the motivations in *Johnny Apollo* made the character's turning to a life of crime an act of spoiled petulance. Perhaps the film allowed Ty to extend his acting range, but its effects required a style that would not materialize until his mature years. The public didn't buy this nice young man in the role, nor did it buy tickets for the picture.

Ty and Hathaway, however, had already started work on a second film before the first one was released, and there was no way Zanuck wanted this one to fail. He might let his top actor experiment with his "art" in low-budget pictures which could be released on the lower half of a double bill, but this he would not permit in *Brigham Young—Frontiersman,* a picture Zanuck personally conceived. He assigned novelist Louis Bromfield to write a story, which Lamar Trotti would then fashion into a screenplay. Zanuck didn't particularly want to delve into Mormonism, seeing the film instead as an epic tale about the suffering and privation twenty thousand people were forced to endure during their two-year journey from Illinois to Salt Lake in order to found a western empire. Young's story was envisioned as the American equivalent of the wanderings of the children of Israel.

In recreating the eighteen-hundred-mile pilgrimage, the filmmakers would have to approximate the original, in which the Mormons traveled in three thousand prairie schooners and took along 30,000 cattle, mules, horses, and sheep. Many of the women walked the entire way, since their wagons were piled with furniture and other possessions.

Bromfield spent four months in Utah, researching with the co-operation of the Church of Jesus Christ of Latter Day Saints. When he returned to Hollywood to work with Trotti, they mulled over the problem of how to tastefully handle Young's plural marriages. Their solution was to reduce the number of his wives from twelve to four, and their rationale was that this would make the dramatic threads of the story easier to understand.

Spencer Tracy had already turned down the title role in the $2.7 million production, feeling he'd played too many priests in the past to portray another religious figure. A stage actor from New York, Dean Jagger, was then recruited.

Tyrone Power was the star of the picture, cast in a nonstar role of a Mormon scout who falls in love with a non-Mormon girl, played by Linda Darnell. Twentieth, which three years previously had tried to build Ty and Loretta Young as a love team, was now attempting the same thing with his current costar. Announcement had already been made that the two would be romantically teamed in Ty's next picture, *The Californian*. Thousands of fans had written the studio to complain that there weren't enough love scenes in Ty's movies. Ten were written into the current script, averaging one every 180 miles.

The shooting of *Brigham Young—Frontiersman* took 133 days, the longest since *Gone With the Wind*. It would be the last superspectacular film until the foreign market lost to Hitler and World War II was regained. Five complete towns and settlements were built, to represent prairie outposts of the 1840s. Hathaway, a big believer in location shooting, took an enormous troupe to the Utah desert, to the Sierra Nevada Mountains, to Big Bear Lake, and to the Agoura hillside. Second unit director Otto Bower, who had done the desert scenes in *Suez* and horse chases in *Jesse James,* shot for six weeks in Utah, using Hollywood extras and actual Mormons. Inquiries to neighboring chambers of commerce finally hit the jackpot in Elko, Nevada, where cast and crew worked a week in the middle of an actual plague of locusts.

In spite of the panoramic spectacle, some beautiful location scenes, excellent camerawork, and grand release prints made in the then popular sepia tone, the picture faltered when it asked the audience to get passionately involved in the hardships faced by a religion it never even bothered to explain. For censorship and other reasons, the subject of multiple wives was brought up just enough to be mystifying. Not even mass migrations and miracles could save a film that, despite its original intent, was more interested in preaching to the audience than in engrossing it. Given the world situation in 1940, with Europe beset by war and the likelihood that the United States would soon be drawn into the fray, the film about Brigham Young and his followers seemed irrelevant and marginal to most Americans. Zanuck and the studio were stuck with their most expensive failure. Ty had been his engaging self in the picture, but he couldn't save it from its ambitions and pretensions.

Neither of the pictures he'd starred in thus far in 1940 had been released, yet word was out that they would be duds. Ty had survived poor pictures and poor notices before, but the stakes were now much greater, for both him and the studio. He didn't know if the fickle public would turn away from him, especially since his smallish role, no matter how stellar his billing, might lead the public to believe Twentieth was downgrading him. He had many anxious moments, plagued by the insecurity inherent in all actors.

Ty had been riding the crest of the wave only a short while before, but he knew of many examples where the good fortunes of other actors had abruptly turned around. He'd seen it in his own father. Ty didn't know how Twentieth would react. Despite Zanuck's many assurances, he knew how quickly the studio head had disassociated himself from such huge stars as Janet Gaynor and Loretta Young once their popularity started to slip.

Ty and Annabella went to New York in July. They did a Screen Guild Production of *Seventh Heaven* on radio, after which she said she was retiring as an actress to become a full-time housewife. She knew how desperately Ty wanted a son, and she was determined to give him one. As for Ty, he began telling interviewers he was thinking of returning to the stage. With his plans thus announced, he wouldn't lose as much face if the poor reception to the two pictures necessitated a switch in career plans. He'd long given lip service to his ambition of becoming a great stage actor. He might be forced to prove himself sooner than anticipated.

This, however, wasn't as yet to be. Zanuck decided to continue with his plans to produce *The Californian*. It would soon be renamed *The Mark of Zorro,* and coming at this time, it hadn't come a moment too soon.

Rouben Mamoulian, the director, had first established his innovative reputation in the early days of sound pictures, when it was theory and practice to use stationary cameras. Cinematography of silent films had been remarkably fluid, but movement had been forfeited because microphones weren't as portable and adaptable.

He directed Helen Morgan in *Applause,* and that 1929 picture had as dazzling a set of visual techniques as any silent film. Mamoulian was a rarity among directors, a mechanic and an aesthete. When he directed Greta Garbo in *Queen Christina,* he told her, "I want your face to be a blank sheet of paper. I want the writing to be done by every member of the audience." Henry King, among the directors at Twentieth, had used Ty in the same way. It appeared that the actor and the Russian-born director were made for each other.

Both *Zorro* and *Blood and Sand,* Ty's next film, were remakes of very successful silent movies featuring exceptionally charismatic silent stars (Douglas Fairbanks and Rudolph Valentino respectively), based on even more successful novels, Johnston McCulley's *The Curse of Capistrano* and *Sangre y Arena* by Vicente Blasco Ibáñez.

Though Mamoulian was a greater director than Fred Niblo, who directed both silent pictures, Ty was neither a Fairbanks nor a Valentino. He was less flatteringly compared in the first picture, for Ty could never match Fairbanks's acrobatic skill and physical comedy.

"Mr. Fairbanks, we can tell you, was really something to see," Bosley Crowther would later write in *The New York Times.* "A swashbuckler who swashed with magnificent arrogance and swished, when required, with great élan. Mr. Power rather overdoes the swishing, and his swash is more beautiful than bold. Neither does he vault about with the athletic ease of a proper Zorro.

And a Zorro, without at least one leap from a balcony to the back of a running horse, is gravely suspected by us."

Zorro was Ty's first swashbuckling role, as it had been for Fairbanks, who'd been an acrobatic comedian before, and he brought his individual qualities to the portrayal, which Crowther grudgingly conceded.

Mamoulian tapped Ty's comedic talents more fully than any of his previous roles had done. He was required to play an everyday fop who is transformed into a Spanish Superman at night to exact vengeance on the villainous Basil Rathbone and J. Edward Bromberg, the oppressors of the local peons.

With his characteristic adaptability, Ty wore both guises so naturally and with such subtle changes in gestures and body carriage that his masquerade allayed suspicion far longer than it should have. Ty took fencing lessons from Fred Cavens, who'd also coached Fairbanks in the silent version. The studio put out the fiction that Patia Power had also taught her son, saying she'd been women's fencing champion of Ohio from 1907 to 1912. His fencing scenes were natural and convincing, looking more like someone trying to kill an opponent with a sword than someone flailing a prop for a Hollywood camera. Cavens gave Ty the sword he used in the picture, the same one Fairbanks had earlier used. That seemed to be about all the two actors had in common.

The Tyrone Power interpretation proved to be hugely successful, catapulting him to number five at the box office for the year of 1940. His two other pictures that year had little to do with his continuing high ranking. It also spurred a fad among young boys to affect black capes and black masks, slashing swords into the air, some imaginary, with the letter *Z*. On a more global scale, the film made Ty an idol in Latin America. The picture was dubbed into six different Spanish dialects. For the rest of his career and to the rest of the world, Ty was now counted the preeminent swashbuckler.

By the time that *The Mark of Zorro* was released and Ty's lot as a film star was firmly reestablished, he had been married to Annabella about a year and a half.

Fan magazines described their unpretentious existence, picturing Annabella as just another housewife who weeded her own garden while her husband worked in his photographic darkroom. At night, the pipe-smoking Ty, his two dogs at his feet, played backgammon with Annabella. Or they might read to each other from French and English classics. Or so the columnists wrote.

Annabella's strongly accented English had been learned only three years previously for a film role, and her vocabulary was still quite limited, while Ty had picked up enough French to understand a smattering of the chatter whenever his wife's friend Claudette Colbert came calling.

They had taken separate bedrooms in their modern Georgian house. Ty's was papered in Chinese grass cloth, its beige color repeated in the shaggy rug. The furniture was Japanese Oak, the bleached wood rubbed down with a steel brush. Annabella chose the chintz for draperies and chairs. On his bedside table was a picture of his mother. Put away in a locked closet was a collection of prints of his father's old films. Set in plain sight was his collection of model railroad trains. The overall effect was highly spartan, and suggestively boyish.

Annabella's room, in celadon green and faded rose, was appropriately French provincial. The draperies and bedspread were of a quilted fabric, also used to upholster the headboard.

The house itself, despite its large size and its celebrated inhabitants, was not ornate. The only addition they made to the Paul Williams architecture was a rear staircase on the back of the house so that they could go directly from their bedrooms to the swimming pool.

It was furnished with Annabella's distinct chic, but to Ty's specifications for great comfort. Its overall effect was casual—upholstered seats on the window bays of every downstairs room—yet it was also furnished with several signed antique pieces from France.

During the past year, despite the distractions of problems at the studio, Ty had been listening to Annabella talk about her plans for the still unfinished living room. She told him what specific pieces of furniture she wanted and the fabrics that should be used on the upholstered pieces. When she descended from her bedroom that Christmas morning, Annabella discovered that Ty had instructed their decorator, John F. Luccareni, to refurbish the room according to her tastes. The transformation had been completed overnight while the couple slept.

Although he was publicly painted the master of his own house, Ty actually bowed to most of Annabella's wishes. If in his costume pictures he wore tights at the studio, his wife wore the pants at home, except when asked to pose for fashion layouts, to which she'd respond, "I get the clothes for nothing, yes?" And yes, she got the designer clothes for nothing.

Annabella continued to think of Ty as just a boy, and treated him as one. Her behavior wasn't markedly different from that of his mother's. Patia Power had sacrificed all her life to raise her children. Ty saw in Annabella, despite her many indulgences, a practical Frenchwoman his mother should have appreciated if she hadn't been so jealous of her. The two women were also alike in that they were very private and possessed great dignity.

Evie Abbott was now married to Keenan Wynn, and the couple were neighbors of Ty and Annabella in Brentwood. "After I was married," Evie Johnson recalled, "Ty couldn't send me gifts like before. Once, he brought me a book with pictures of Keenan's grandfather and Tyrone Power, Sr.

"I don't know if I have any regrets that Ty and I didn't marry. Sometimes if you don't the love continues stronger. As long as we didn't marry we remained steadfast, just like we did when we met."

The Wynns were included in parties that revolved around the Powers' pool. Keenan and Evie didn't have a pool of their own. Sunday afternoons were extremely casual, consisting of swimming parties and playing croquet. If guests stayed on for dinner, they would play charades and other games.

Annabella, however, preferred to entertain more formally. "She was a very accomplished hostess," Evic Johnson said, "and always had wonderful food. She knew how to mix people and the right ingredients for a good party."

To all outward appearances, she was a credit to her husband.

Darryl Zanuck wanted to borrow Jane Russell from Howard Hughes for the role of the temptress Doña Sol in *Blood and Sand* and even offered to pay $35,000 a week for her services. Hughes, however, wanted to harness and introduce the talents of his contract player in *The Outlaw,* and he refused the offer. More than thirty other actresses were tested before director Rouben Mamoulian decided to borrow Rita Hayworth from Columbia.

She'd made her first impression as Margarita Cansino, dancing in Mexican border towns with her Spanish father, Eduardo. Yet her mother, Volga Haworth, was descended from an English theatrical heritage going back two hundred years. Ty's father, in fact, had at one time worked with the Joseph Haworth company.

Contrary to her public impression as an effortless sex symbol, Rita Hayworth was extraordinarily dedicated and had worked hard to perfect her craft. Anything she decided to do, she did well. Harry Cohn at Columbia hadn't known how to cast her in the past, nor did he want to go to any expense to further train her as an actress. She was happy to be loaned out, for she could serve her apprenticeship elsewhere. *Blood and Sand* was to be her thirty-first picture, the bulk of her previous credits such programmers as *Charlie Chan* and *Blondie,* and with this assignment at Twentieth she would be acting in her third loan-out in a row.

Once, while I was a guest in her home, Rita told me of the time in 1940 when director George Cukor borrowed her to play a supporting part in *Susan and God* at MGM. Two years previously, when Cukor was at Columbia to direct *Holiday* with Cary Grant and Katharine Hepburn, studio head Harry Cohn suggested Rita be cast as Hepburn's younger sister.

"I didn't have enough experience to do that," she said. "I was terrified. George called and told me he was going to test me for the part. I was nineteen and so nervous! He had me come to his office every day to read the script."

Cukor, after extensive testing, told her, "This isn't the right role for you. But that doesn't matter. You'll do other things. You have a quality. It's extraordinary."

"I think he meant sex," Rita said, "but he didn't say that. George recommended that I be given voice lessons and French lessons. Cohn paid for them for about two months, and then stopped it. I had to continue paying for them myself. George said he would use me in a picture someday. I was very happy when he asked for me for *Susan and God.*

"I didn't have much to do, but this was the first time I'd been in an A picture. They put me in a lot of program things before. The shooting went on for a long time. I was at MGM for six weeks. I didn't have a call every day, but I'd go anyway. I'd sit and watch Freddie March and Joan Crawford and George. I wanted very much to learn from them."

Now, a year later, she and her proud Spanish genes, which lent so much to her haughty carriage in the film, were ready.

Because Mamoulian had a concept for the picture, in which his colors would borrow from such Spanish masters as El Greco, Goya, Velasquez, and Murillo, he suggested Rita change the color of her brunette hair to the coppery red tones which remained throughout most of her career. Mamoulian didn't intend to photograph the story; he wanted to paint it.

Somber burgundy, chocolate, and olive colors melded moodily into the balanced light and eerie shadows of the images modeled after Spanish painters, but the color red emerged the most dominant, splashing across the screen with a startling effect that only early Technicolor could provide. Mamoulian considered red as much an actor in the film as any of the players, and it suggested more emotions than some critics found in the live actors—passion, love, and hate, as well as death.

Mamoulian brilliantly built the drama with color, starting the early scenes with subdued shades and progressing through brighter and brighter hues until the violent red climax of death.

The overall effect was studied, stately, lurid, and gorgeous. *Blood and Sand* was lushly mounted romantic hokum, failing as tragedy, but succeeding as melodrama.

The recurrent Christ imagery, so overused by others, was appropriate here. Large crucifixes abounded in the time and place of the story. The bloodthirsty crowd that cannot be pleased and ultimately destroys the matador is as reinforced by the metaphor of the crucifixion as is the concept of the messiah who is destroyed by his admirers.

Mamoulian was handicapped by an actor who couldn't fight bulls, a censor who wouldn't allow him to stab them on camera, and a script that dallied in the bedroom instead of moving to the arena. His pyrotechnics were ingenious. To suggest the killing of

With Gene Tierney in
Son of Fury

On marine duty on
Saipan, 1945

A scene from *The Razor's Edge,* Tyrone Power's first postwar movie. Seated are Gene Tierney, Clifton Webb, Anne Baxter, and Power. Standing are Herbert Marshall and John Payne.

A new discovery teamed with Ty Power in *Captain from Castile* was an Ohio coed named Jean Peters, who was later to marry Howard Hughes

With Orson Welles in a scene from *The Prince of Foxes*

Ty visits his wife Linda Christian and her co-star Richard Conte on the set of the Columbia Pictures film *Slaves of Babylon*.

A party at home—Linda Christian with her daughter Taryn Power

Ty Power with daughter Romina and Peter Shaw, Angela Lansbury's husband

The principals in the stage companies of *Mr. Roberts* and *John Brown's Body* meet with their movie counterparts. Standing are Lloyd Nolan, Ty Power, Raymond Massey (head bowed), and John Hodiak. Seated are Charles Laughton, Anne Baxter (Hodiak's wife), Dick Powell, and Henry Fonda.

Made up as an old man for *The Long Gray Line,* the Columbia film directed by John Ford

With Victoria Shaw and Kim Novak in a publicity shot from *The Eddy Duchin Story*

As Eddy Duchin

With Mai Zetterling in
Abandon Ship

With Ava Gardner in
The Sun Also Rises

A courtroom scene with
Charles Laughton in
Tyrone Power's last
film, *Witness for the
Prosecution*

the bull, he had a bullfight fan repeatedly stab a sausage with a knife as the torero presumably thrusts the sword into the bull off camera. Then to suggest the bull's death, the same fan inadvertently stabs his own flagon, pouring out the bloodlike wine on the arena.

Ty, in repeating a role which made a star of Rudolph Valentino, to whom he'd been compared, could not bring the same smolder to the role of the matador Juan Gallardo. It is in his portrayal that Mamoulian showed least imagination. He lazily settled for cinematic shorthand by giving Ty greasy hair, to indicate Spanish birth; a cigar clenched in his teeth, to indicate a desire for success; a habit of snapping his fingers at the camera, to show the bravado within.

He was required to learn the capework, but Ty was never allowed to go near a bull. Footage of the great Spanish bullfighter Armillitas was spliced in to represent the fights of Gallardo. A crowd of over 30,000, the largest ever to watch the filming of a movie scene, took in the simulated action at the Plaza de Toros in Mexico City.

If the *corridas* had a taped together look, they weren't as obviously spliced as in the Valentino version nineteen years previously. Ty in his *traje de luces* looked a touch paunchy, but with its embroidery and beading, it added forty-five pounds to his weight. He looked more the handsome modern dress idol in his scenes with his wife, Linda Darnell, and the heartless Rita Hayworth. Scenes showing him as an innocent illiterate being seduced by the other women well reflected Ty's true ingenuousness and suggestibility. He remained the nice movie star, and as popular as ever.

Critics faulted Rita's sultry interpretation, but the public made her a star in the role. Coupled with the famous picture that same year in *Life* magazine, showing her in a satin negligee kneeling on a bed, she emerged as America's love goddess, and Ty had been instrumental in launching another new star.

CHAPTER

7

IF IN LATER YEARS, HYPERBOLE HAD IT THAT JOHN WAYNE WON the war, Darryl Zanuck could point to Tyrone Power as the man who put America in a fighting mood in the first place.

Strength*Quality*Leadership. So ran the studio proclamation when Zanuck came into his own there. A questionable aspect of Fox's motto was its second word. In a marginal fashion, the studio began its involvement in World War II as early as 1932, and on the same side as Hitler. Millions of Germans would not have heard his hypnotic oratory if Fox's German subsidiary, Fox-Tönende-Wochenschau, a weekly newsreel, hadn't disseminated propaganda favorable to Hitler in such short films as *Der Fuehrer* (*The Leader*) and *Hitler's Kampf um Deutschland* (*Hitler's Fight for Germany*). The Fox subsidiary also loaned sound trucks to the Nazis, so that Hitler could speak to the increasing multitudes. The films were screened throughout Germany right before the national elections which led to Hitler's becoming a national factor and which ultimately resulted in his being named German Chancellor in January of 1933.

Foreign profits of American motion-picture companies often were frozen in the countries in which they were made, and the studios often didn't know to what use their subsidiaries put the money. It was nevertheless appalling to Zanuck that his company could have been even indirectly involved in bringing Hitler to power, and little matter that he wasn't affiliated with Fox at the time.

Zanuck was a bantam, feisty, combative man. No one had accused Twentieth of giving aid and comfort to the future enemy. Certainly, he wasn't Hearst driving the United States into an unnecessary Spanish-American War. Yet, he felt he must do something. The honor of his studio was at stake.

Already, two major films had been made that would set the tone for future war films: Alfred Hitchcock's British production of *The Lady Vanishes* in 1938 and *Confessions of a Nazi Spy,* produced by Warner Brothers the following year.

In 1940, Zanuck began to mount his own offensive. Two films, *Four Sons* and *The Man I Married,* were released almost simultaneously that year, in which German refugees defamed the Fuehrer. In the latter, Lloyd Nolan as an American newspaper correspondent in Germany represented Zanuck's hawkish thinking when he spoke a line about war as "one way, perhaps the only way, to make an end to these lunatics who spread fear and hatred over the world."

Neither picture, however, drummed up a fighting spirit for the Forces of Democracy, or revenue for Twentieth Century-Fox. The American movie-going public didn't seem interested in the war in Europe as a subject for films.

Undeterred, Zanuck persevered in 1941 by inserting a warlike production number—"It Won't Be Fun, but It's Gotta Be Done" —in a listless comedy, *Cadet Girl.* The idea of militarization was even broached in Laurel and Hardy's *Great Guns.* Then, he permitted German expatriate Fritz Lang to expound on his anti-Nazi wrath in *Manhunt.* Still the public didn't buy.

Such complacency had to be eliminated once and forever. Zanuck unleashed his ultimate weapons, his human embodiments of the atomic bomb which would end the war four years later—a war that for America was yet to begin. The double whammy was Tyrone Power and Betty Grable, and the picture Zanuck began preparing in October of 1940 was *A Yank in the R.A.F.*

Zanuck originally called it *The Eagle Squadron,* and it would revolve around an American test pilot played by Ty who enlisted in the British Royal Air Force, "a cocksure know-it-all, a breezy, brash young guy." To bring the lessons of war tragically home, Ty would be killed in the first German air raid over England.

British government officials, who were cooperating in the production, requested that the American be allowed to live. It was then that the final title was settled on, and the screenwriter went to work. His name was Melville Crossman, also known as Darryl Zanuck.

There was no question that Ty would play the central role. Twenty years later, the director of Twentieth's New Talent Program would still be claiming, "They've got a Tyrone Power tradition at this studio and that's what we're looking for." They wouldn't find it in such rough facsimiles imminently coming along as John Sutton, John Payne, William Eythe, and Dana Andrews, but they still hadn't stopped looking for their new Tyrone Power well into the 1960s.

For the big films, however, it would always be the original. And in this film, as was de rigueur for every Tyrone Power picture, a girl would be introduced into the proceedings, one the pilot would fight with and fight for. And what a girl.

Almost as quickly as Alice Faye was conceded to be Twentieth's top box-office star, another blonde had come along to steal away the title. In her three previous films—*Down Argentina Way, Tin Pan Alley,* and *Moon Over Miami*—Betty Grable's peaches-and-cream appeal in the sunny musicals totally captivated America, particularly the male half. GIs would later equate their reasons for fighting with apple pie and motherhood, but she, who would become the greatest pin-up of World War II, was in another way what the war was all about.

King saw great dramatic potential in his female star. "I've been directing pictures for twenty-seven years," he told an interviewer, "and have seen many stars come and go, and I feel certain that Betty Grable has talents for straight dramas. Give her three dramatic roles in a row and she will surprise Hollywood. She can do what Ginger Rogers, Myrna Loy, Joan Crawford, and many other stars who began as dancers have done."

Ty had only one week of rest after finishing *Blood and Sand* before he started work on the new picture. It wasn't the physically taxing aspect of the part that gave him so much difficulty. It was the requirement of the ingratiating but rude character he would be portraying. The role called for a young James Cagney. But in the interests of the war effort, Ty would do his best.

The screenplay Crossman/Zanuck wrote was about a brash American, going to the rescue of England, standing up night club entertainer Betty Grable on one date after another, not being truly charming, because the audience was to find him both amusing and obnoxious until he learned the lessons of military discipline. Thrown in was an ungainly love triangle involving another suitor of Grable's.

In mounting one of the biggest Hollywood productions of the year, which included a $250,000 sequence filmed up the California coast, which ran fifteen minutes and represented the evacuation of Dunkirk only months after the actual events, Twentieth had the full cooperation, of the governments of the United States, Canada, and Great Britain.

The effort was a symphony of coordination, and the characters in the picture spoke earnestly of the virtues of self-discipline. Yet, like *Crash Dive,* which Ty was to make in 1943 just before going into the marines, and also incorporating a love triangle, *A Yank in the R.A.F.* lacked both. It was a jumble of insipid love scenes; rabble-rousing speeches; frequent logistical montages of roaring airplanes, imposing maps, and the patter of marching feet; and smashing battle scenes. In retrospect, it's of interest to note in these antiviolent days that several critics complained that the intimate scenes got in the way of the spectacular aerial battles filmed over Germany, France, and England—the actual ones. They were put together by an unsung special effects man, Fred Sersen, who also created the sandstorm in *Suez,* the various disasters in *The Rains Came,* and the fires of *In Old Chicago.*

During the preparation of the movie, the participants seemed to take on the mocking attitudes of real warriors going into battle. They were sharing a common, ennobling experience to be conducted with the eat-drink-and-be-merry credo that had come down through the ages.

Henry King joked that Ty spent so much time in the land-bound Spitfire built on a soundstage that he could qualify for a commercial license.

Ty began shooting his own film between takes, a slapstick production called *How the Mighty Have Fallen.* Shot with a sixteen-millimeter camera, the scenes were a series of practical jokes. One showed Betty Grable's reaction to finding sawdust all over her dressing room. Another had Alice Faye falling through a breakaway chair. Other visitors to the set involved in the escapades were Linda Darnell and Brenda Joyce.

The cast and crew got their revenge on Ty by presenting him with a goat, which he found at home one evening, tied to the foot of his bed. It was added to the menagerie at the Power house of four dogs, two cats, three ducks, and a guinea pig.

One of the biggest laughs came from Zanuck himself. He was so pleased with the way the picture was progressing, that he was considering a sequel about an American woman soldier in England. The title, it was suggested, would be *A W.A.F. in the R.A.F.* But, no, Zanuck was serious. Then he changed his mind, thinking he might make it a reverse situation. *A Tommy in the U.S.A.* Neither came to pass, but he would be involved in other war pictures, to be sure.

Ty's work on the picture ended in time for him to begin the scheduled rehearsals for *Liliom,* in which he and Annabella would perform at the Westport Playhouse in Connecticut. The couple announced in June that they would tour in twenty cities that summer, but the itinerary was shortened when the studio informed Ty he'd be needed to start filming *Benjamin Blake* in early September.

He had spoken of his first love, the stage, and of his plans to alternate films with theater work. Annabella totally supported that ambition, since she had similar ones. No matter how many specialists she'd seen, she hadn't succeeded in getting pregnant, and it was increasingly doubtful that she would ever give birth to another child. Her return to the theater was a welcome distraction from her continuing frustration.

Ty envisioned the Powers becoming a younger, if less distinguished version, of Lunt and Fontanne. He knew he still had much to learn. His disreputable but fascinating role of the carnival show barker might not have been the most suitable to his temperament and personality. Neither was Annabella's Julie. But their joint star debut was not being made on Broadway, and they could experiment with the shadings of the roles throughout the two-week run. He'd been required to hold back on the pyrotechnics in films, but now he could let go and give vent to the larger theatrical gestures and mannerisms that his parents at separate times had instilled in him. As for Annabella, she could broaden her range and in a foreign language at that.

On the Friday before *Liliom's* Monday opening at Westport, the studio called Ty back to Hollywood. Retakes were needed on *A Yank in the R.A.F.* Ty protested. He was due to open in a show, he explained. The studio was insistent.

Ty went to the founder of the Westport Repertory Company, and explained the situation. Lawrence Langner said he would act as an intermediary. He called the studio and was connected with a company attorney.

"Why are you demanding his immediate return?" he asked. "You gave Ty permission to sign an Equity contract to play with us."

"That was only a gentleman's agreement," the lawyer replied. The answer totally bewildered Langner who, being a gentleman, thought that should have been binding enough. He in turn went to his own lawyer, and discovered that an old state law still in existence provided that a man could be enjoined from leaving the state if by doing so he broke a contract. Langner called the sheriff in Bridgeport, who came to serve notice on Ty.

"You cannot leave the state of Connecticut without breaking your contract," the sheriff said.

Ty, grinning happily, responded, "You mean I am *forced* by law to stay in Connecticut until I open in the play?"

That was exactly right. Ty called the studio, and explained his dilemma. He was allowed to open as scheduled, play for a week, then return to California for a few days of shooting. His work was urgently needed to help win the war that hadn't yet been declared.

Once the few days of shooting were completed, Ty was allowed to complete the final week's run. The show wasn't extensively reviewed by the New York press, other than to give passing notice

to another movie star experimenting on stage. Yet it wasn't an opportunity that automatically came to every one of them.

Jean-Pierre Aumont, who escorted Simone Simon to Westport,
recalled the opening in his autobiography. "Annabella and
Tyrone Power were an incredibly handsome couple. How they
loved each other! And how I envied them for being on a stage
. . . Acting was like opium to me, and I needed it badly."

Ty was back working at the studio on *Son of Fury*, as *Benjamin
Blake* had been retitled, when *A Yank in the R.A.F.* was released
in September.

The predictability of the film's plot was overlooked by most of
the public and some of the critics. War fever had gripped the
country, and movies had little to do with it. The atrocities in
Europe were finally striking home in the minds and hearts of
Americans. "It is neither imaginative nor conventionally captivat-
ing," Howard Barnes wrote in the *New York Herald-Tribune*.
"What makes *A Yank in the R.A.F.* a rather stunning entertainment is the fact that it keys right in to the memorable events
which constitute the present chapter in history . . . *A Yank in the
R.A.F.* may be warmongering. That is what makes it worthwhile
screen entertainment."

America and the world agreed. The picture was a solid commercial success, Twentieth's second highest-grossing film of the
year, behind *How Green Was My Valley,* which won the Academy Award for Best Picture of the Year.

Ty's 1941 salary of $203,125 was the highest he'd ever re-
ceived. Yet he dropped out of the top ten at the box office that
year. Both *Blood and Sand* and *A Yank in the R.A.F.* were highly
successful pictures, but those were the only films he made that
year; he'd been making as many as six in previous years. His star
power hadn't dimmed, but Ty was aware that it could if it didn't
shift into a different orbit.

He called on Zanuck. It wasn't the first time he'd had the same
complaint. "I need another formula," Ty told him, "a change of
pace. I come in here and talk to you and it's like talking down a
rainspout."

Zanuck assured him that he had Ty's best interests at heart. He did agree, however, that future pictures would be more selectively chosen. Just incidentally, the newer crop of actors would be used in the lesser pictures, in hopes of also building them up into stars.

Evidence of Zanuck's faith in his top male star was an announcement that Ty would be making four pictures over the next two years, budgeted at an impressive $9,000,000. He was currently playing Benjamin Blake in *Son of Fury;* he'd portray a whaler in *Down to the Sea in Ships,* a pirate in *The Black Swan,* and would star in an as yet unspecified part in *Brooklyn Bridge.* In addition, Ty announced plans to also film *The King's Secret,* a swashbuckling story written by the original Tyrone Power, his great-grandfather, set in eighteenth-century England.

There could be no doubt that Ty, even though his top box-office standing was slipping, would always be a major factor as a film star, and that he was reaching his peak as a movie actor. His refined features, once considered vapid by some, were solidifying and allowing him to broaden his range. His eyebrows, of their own accord, no longer met over his nose, and it was no longer necessary to shave or pluck them. The space between his front teeth was closed as his wisdom teeth grew in.

Given good scripts, good productions, and good directors, he could deliver solid entertainment and capable craftsmanship. His next three pictures would prove his great competence.

Twentieth announced plans to alternate his roles, first in a costume epic, then in a modern dress picture. Studio spokesmen said Ty had taken his cue from the public, which wanted to see him in both kinds of roles. He no doubt also took his cue from Zanuck, who saw a way which would allow Ty to still make two movies a year, one monumentally expensive with a long shooting schedule and the other commercially popular yet made on a low budget. The first in this series, which would take sixteen shooting weeks, the production wrapping less than a month before the United States went to war, was *Son of Fury*.

Ty was directed by the solemn John Cromwell, whose most notable previous achievement had been the Bette Davis film, *Of Human Bondage. Son of Fury* cast Ty as an English Gauguin, cheated out of his birthright by a cruel English plutocrat and transplanting himself to the idyllic South Seas with an Eve played by a new Fox player, Gene Tierney. The film got in some vicious digs at a villainous social system before putting everything to rights in the end. Ty, who'd been inordinately coddled in his previous action roles, and had come off looking neither menacing nor tough, insisted on letting his naturally heavy beard grow. This would have been fine for the sake of verisimilitude, but director Cromwell knew that the audience still didn't want that handsome face disguised in any way. They worked out a compromise. He would wear a beard in all the scenes at sea, but be shaven while on land. Ty also insisted on doing his own deep-sea diving. He was rewarded with a case of the sniffles and a three-inch gash in his left foot. He and George Sanders had previously been rivals in *Lloyds of London* and *Love Is News*. Their fisticuff royal this time out was, in Ty's case, performed by a double, who apparently had become a much better fighter since his last stand-in duty. "Mr. Power, especially, displays a vigor . . . that is quite a surprise," *The New Yorker* emphatically but wrongly stated. "Some of the meanest fist fights I have run upon in a long time happen here, and Mr. Power does well by himself in a couple of nasty scuffles."

For his first modern dress picture in the new cycle, Ty was cast opposite Joan Fontaine in *This Above All,* directed by Anatole Litvak, another filmmaker with a reputation for effectively handling actresses. Joan Fontaine, having won that year an Academy Award for Best Actress in *Suspicion,* also had two other immediate spectacular successes in *The Women* and *Rebecca*. Although young, she was formidable. Her costar gave her a wide berth.

"Ty Power was very much under the thumb of his wife, French actress Annabella, several years older than he," she wrote in her autobiography. "I gather he got a bit of flack over his leading lady each night when he arrived home from work. Therefore, he was circumspect, fairly distant, but would play endless games of gin rummy with me in my stage dressing room."

In his own dressing room, however, the games he was playing were with a younger actor who might someday replace him as Twentieth's male star. As much as he had tried, Ty realized that he could not give up having sex with other men, noble as his ambitions had been when he married Annabella. The least he could do, for her sake and that of the studio, was to handle these entanglements with extreme discretion.

If his unaware leading lady found Ty not one to dally with because of his wife's jealousy and possessiveness, it left time for Ty to indulge in this extracurricular homosexual affair. Since he was serving as an air-raid warden in Brentwood for three hours every Sunday between midnight and six in the morning, he was permitted to come in late for work on Monday mornings. Time was stolen to continue meeting his male lover.

Though the casually involved might consider Annabella dominating and Ty henpecked, they weren't aware she was used as both a wife and a "beard." Yet, the disillusionment was Ty's, perhaps in himself, and he brought it to his role in *This Above All*. He portrayed a lower-class Britisher—although with an all-American accent—who attacks the British social system, wondering why he should risk his life in brutalities like Dunkirk and the Battle of Flanders to preserve a way of life that victimized him. Joan Fontaine was the upper-class daughter of a doctor who tries to straighten out his muddled thinking. Ty's mother Patia, through the use of her portrait in one scene, "played" Fontaine's mother.

The finished product came across more satisfyingly as a tale of romance amid suffering than the dramatic social document that was originally intended.

"Although Tyrone Power gives the performance of his cinematic career as the embittered young deserter, it is not good enough," *Time* concluded. "His handsome, unlined face contradicts the profound words he is asked to utter. He does not for a moment look as if he either thought or lived them." It was the last time any critic found his face not weathered enough for the part.

Before starting his second costume picture of 1942, Ty took a quick trip to Chicago to visit Annabella, who was appearing on the stage in *Blithe Spirit*. Any passion he had for her was gradually flagging. He might have remained more constant if Annabella had only given him a son.

He returned to California in April to start work on *The Black Swan,* based on the Rafael Sabatini novel, which was to be Twentieth's last extravaganza until after the war. This time out, Henry King insisted that Ty should have a beard for the part of a pirate, and received no front-office opposition. Ty's romantic interest, playing an Irish wildcat for the first time, but certainly not the last, was Maureen O'Hara. They'd been scheduled to appear together in *Son of Fury,* she in the role of an icy Englishwoman, but illness forced her to drop out of the picture.

The new film, with witty input from Ben Hecht, was a romp, Ty performing, as *The New York Times* put it, "as if to the hokum born."

His nemesis was again George Sanders, who had shaped up as the quintessential heavy of Tyrone Power pictures, embodying everything—stuffiness, obnoxiousness, old-world gentility—that Ty was not.

Ty was twenty-eight when he enlisted in the United States Marine Corps in August of 1942. Zanuck had entered the army as a full colonel the previous January and was sent to London to coordinate training films. He offered to get Ty a commission. "Why should I ask for a commission?" Ty asked. "What do I know about being an officer?" Ty, however, did agree to Zanuck's petition that he be placed on inactive status until he finished a film directly connected with the war effort, *Crash Dive*. It was the same love triangle as *A Yank in the R.A.F.,* this time involving two men in a submarine, Ty and Dana Andrews, with Anne Baxter. The teenage actress, a granddaughter of the famed architect Frank Lloyd Wright, was one of several new contract players to be signed by Spyros Skouras, who succeeded Sidney Kent as president at Twentieth. Others would include Gregory Peck, Clifton Webb, Paul Douglas, and Dan Dailey.

The picture took on the look of a navy recruiting film and ended with a patriotic montage of all the impressive military hardware that could be borrowed by Twentieth. Its plot appropriated from *A Yank in the R.A.F.* the narrative absurdity of taking two men in love with the same girl, having them go off into battle together, yet refusing to give them any significant interplay—selfless rescues, selfish reprisals, inspirational teamwork—that would create any drama from their basic rivalry. What resulted was such a romanticized view that it prompted Bosley Crowther of *The*

New York Times to remark, "It leaves one wondering blankly whether Hollywood knows we're at war."

Movie audiences wondered the same thing. Since the United States was now in the war for real, families with boys overseas were beginning to resent the sugar-plum fantasies they had turned to Hollywood for all through the Depression. But Power, before the picture was released, left Hollywood and his male lover with anything but fantasy on his mind. The studio would have to look elsewhere for his successor. John Payne was left behind to play one facet of Ty's screen persona, the heel with a heart. But the swashbuckler and the gentle romantic and the light comedian— those three other characters—were gone in the one body of Tyrone Power for the duration.

Ty was now on active duty, and he received no special consideration during basic training at Camp Elliott outside San Diego. Because he was a movie star, he did receive special treatment, however. It was of the most grueling sort, a far cry from his physical conditioning in the luxurious studio gymnasium, followed by the loving ministrations, with perfumed unguents, of the studio masseur. When later asked if he'd had a rough time in boot camp, Ty replied, "In a way. They made me do everything twice. I guess they never believed me the first time." He welcomed the opportunity to prove he was as tough as his swashbuckling image. Ty didn't back down when, during basic training, another recruit said, "You're the prettiest marine I've ever seen." He went in swinging, knocking the other man down. As he stood over him, he said, "You started this, and I don't want any more of it."

"Okay," the guy said. "You're just a marine."

The two men shook hands.

It was the first time in his life, as it was for millions of others, that Ty was being so tested. He withstood the rigors and the pressures admirably.

When he and a buddy spent New Year's Eve at the Goetzes' beach house, it was tacitly understood that his marriage to Annabella was ending. Bill Goetz, whenever the Powers had explained their differences to him, would sit behind a desk in their library and act as their mediator. That time had passed, and Ty began seeing other women. The continental Annabella must have been aware of this, but she chose to ignore the ongoing flirtations while preparing herself for the eventual culmination of their marriage. The difference in their ages was becoming increasingly apparent. Ty would never outgrow the sophistication and the intellect which was his first wife's. The problem was that she would out-age him, becoming more matronly in his eyes, as younger and more exciting competitors came along.

The first of these romances which came to public knowledge was with Judy Garland, then twenty years old and separated from David Rose, her first husband, which occurred while Ty was on furlough. He was due to go on to Officers Candidate School in the spring of 1943 to be commissioned a second lieutenant.

"Judy got around," her close friend Chuck Walters said. "She had the frustration of not being a Lana Turner or Elizabeth Taylor. She tried to make people fall in love with her, and she was quite successful at it." She may not have been conventionally beautiful, but Judy Garland was enormously appealing.

Now it was Ty's turn, as it had been Annabella's in the past, to be considered a totally unsuitable match. Because he was already married, MGM tried to keep the affair secret, to protect Judy's wholesome image, while studio executives tried to convince her that she had fallen in love with "the cover of *Photoplay*." She wouldn't listen. Like Ty, she was the incurable romantic, in love with love.

He often took Edie Goetz into his confidence about such matters. "I think I loved him more than Annabella," she said, "because I loved him despite all the problems." Mrs. Goetz may have guessed that Ty was sexually involved with another actor, a known homosexual, but this was an area they never delved into. "When he was mad about a woman, he couldn't wait to have her. He talked to me about his romances. When he was in love, he was totally in love. He wanted Judy."

Before leaving for Quantico, Virginia, for OCS, Ty gave Judy a copy of a novel, *Forever,* which told of a boy and girl vowing to love each other forever, their death in an automobile accident indeed making their love eternal. Ty said he wanted to make it as a film with Judy after the war.

He wrote her many letters from Quantico. When a mutual

friend told her that Ty had been reading her letters to his buddies, she bitterly ended the affair. Ty was incapable of such insensitivity. It went against his whole grain. He insisted on preserving his privacy.

Judy Garland went on to have an affair with screenwriter Joe Mankiewicz before marrying Vincente Minnelli, her director in *Meet Me in St. Louis.*

As for Ty, he went on to Corpus Christi, Texas, having been commissioned a second lieutenant, for flight training. Annabella, in the meantime, had achieved Broadway stardom in *Jacobowsky and the Colonel.* The Brentwood house was closed up until both could return home.

During the show's run, Ty went to New York in May of 1944 to see his wife perform at the Martin Beck Theatre. "You should have seen how happy he was to be in a theater again," Annabella told the press. "The first evening he saw the play from the front, and the next he was backstage with us. The whole company told him if he stayed longer he would walk right out on the stage and start acting. He looked around my dressing room and said he remembered coming into it to talk to Katharine Cornell when he was in her company. He came to tell her he had a chance to go into pictures. He did not know if it would be a good thing for him, but he would like to try."

Over the next six months, Ty logged 635 hours of flight training at Corpus Christi; Cherry Point, North Carolina; and other bases. He was stationed in San Diego, waiting for his overseas assignment, when, on a weekend pass, a friend introduced him to Smitty Hanson.

Today, Hanson is a Hollywood character, hired by many of the movie industry's social lights to tend bar at parties, then often staying after the guests have gone to sexually service the host, the hostess, or both. A nondrinker and nonsmoker, he keeps himself immaculately clean and in top physical shape. He is a rarity, for there must be very few men in their fifties who can still sell their sexual favors, considering the competition from much younger hustlers.

At the time he met Ty, Hanson was eighteen and training to become a paratrooper. "I spent the night with Ty," he said. "He was a sweetheart, a gentleman. We were friendly and saw each other until he died. Sometimes I wouldn't see him for a couple of years, if he was away or something but when he returned we got together. He was always a trick." Hanson was impressed that Ty never openly handed money to him, putting it in his shirt pocket while he slept.

Those who buy his favors have always been assured of Hanson's utmost discretion. Many of his clients are among the most sexually desirable in the world, but it's safer for them to employ people like Smitty Hanson for sexual release than to risk their reputations in more blatant ways. That was no doubt Ty's reason.

Today's middle-aged hustler talked about his relations with Ty because he resented the statement in the European edition of Kenneth Anger's *Hollywood Babylon* that the actor was involved in coprolagnia. "Ty was never way out in what he wanted to do. If there's such a thing as normal gay sex, that's what he was interested in."

Hanson had no doubts that Ty was basically a homosexual who "found himself married with girls from time to time."

This doesn't explain his extramarital affairs with other women. If Ty were exclusively homosexual, it would be an enormous strain to prove his manhood time and again, and an unnecessary one, for with the security of a marriage society wouldn't expect him to.

In February of 1945, the Navy Department announced that he was now a lieutenant-pilot in the Aerial Transport Service and ready for overseas assignment. Annabella at the time was in Europe, traveling with a U.S.O. troupe.

Ty had come up through the marines the hard way, refusing to join the "Culver City Commandoes," a special services unit based at the Hal Roach Studios, consisting of filmmakers and actors whose sole contribution to the war was the making of training films.

Now, he would be assigned to fly supplies under fire to Kwajalein, Saipan, and Okinawa. He never talked later about his flying through enemy gunfire, but some of his buddies, stationed at El Toro after the war, did.

They described a time when Ty was flying an R5C from Chimu Airstrip, Okinawa, with thirty squadron mates in the back. He was taking them back to Guam because Japanese kamikazes had left Okinawa in flames. As he gunned the ship down a coral strip and lifted it into the sky, he froze. Diving straight through a cloud toward him was a Japanese bomber. Ty hoped to dodge the dive bomber, to somehow get back on the ground. As he banked steeply, the oil cap flew off his left engine, and black oil sputtered out.

Within the plane, his passengers began to razz him.

"Look who forgot to preflight this bucket of bolts!" one called out.

"Lights! Camera! Action!" another shouted. "This ain't no rehearsal, Power. It's a take."

Ty somehow avoided the Japanese bomber, getting back to the final approach. But he badly undershot it. The plane slammed through a sand hill, Ty fighting the controls and bringing it to a stop. Only then did his passengers realize the danger they'd faced.

On another flight back from Le Shima, he was the second to land behind a Commando. Suddenly, the Giretsus, the deadly superkamikazes, were coming in. One belly-landed on the airstrip and a dozen Japanese jumped out and raced for his airplane. Ty grabbed a machine gun and started shooting. The Japanese, however, got to his plane, the *Blithe Spirit,* which was parked in a hangar. Suddenly, there was a bright orange explosion and Ty's ship went up in flames.

Sixty-nine men were killed in the raid. The tears Ty had been holding back for all his thirty years poured forth and wouldn't stop. For one of the rare times in his life, the more conventionally oriented might understand how Ty could find comfort in the embrace of another man.

CHAPTER

8

TYRONE POWER, HAVING LOGGED ELEVEN HUNDRED HOURS OF flying time since he'd entered the marines, a considerable part of it under enemy fire, left Japan early in November of 1945 after being released from occupational duty, two months after the hostilities ended. Annabella, whom he hadn't seen in over a year, met the U.S.S. *Marvin McIntyre* when it docked on November 22 in Portland, and the press reported a spontaneous love scene between husband and wife before a shipload of cheering servicemen. It also noted that Ty would soon report to San Diego Marine Separation Center for discharge.

Ty and Annabella flew to Los Angeles the following day to spend Thanksgiving at home. Patia Power met them at the airport. Waiting to join them was Annabella's mother, who, after a four-year fight waged by her daughter, and a six-thousand-mile journey, was safely settled in the United States. Her husband, Paul Charpentier, had died in Bordeaux during the war, and her older son Pierre had also died in France from the effects of injuries received in a Nazi concentration camp. Annabella's older brother, Jean, was safe in Paris.

Other American veterans were returning to a land of far greater opportunities, made possible by a grateful nation. The GI Bill enabled them to finance college educations, which they hadn't been able to afford before the war, and to procure low-interest, low-down payment loans for new homes under guidelines established by the Veterans Administration.

His fellow servicemen were returning to a better life, while Ty was continuing to question the validity of his own. His personal circumstances were the main cause for his increasing restlessness. He would seem to be ideally cast as the searching idealist of *The Razor's Edge,* which Zanuck had been preparing since shortly after he was deactivated from military service in May of 1943.

Zanuck had returned to Twentieth to discover that Betty Grable, in his absence, had been virtually carrying the studio. She would remain a top box-office star well into the 1950s. Her gaudy, hugely profitable Technicolor spectacles allowed Zanuck to indulge his new attitude, the desire to make more daring and provocative films. Their success, within a few years, was responsible for Twentieth's supplanting Metro as the quality studio.

At the moment, Zanuck had a void in leading male actors. None of the Tyrone Power lookalikes—one of whom had been Ty's lover—had captured the public imagination. Only one actor created an impact in a Twentieth film during the period Ty was in the marines. He was a free-lancer, Gregory Peck, who made a great critical and commercial success in his role of a priest in *The Keys of the Kingdom,* a 1944 production, for which he also received an Academy nomination for Best Actor. Peck, not being under contract, went on to create equally great impressions at other studios in *Spellbound, The Yearling,* and *Duel in the Sun.* Of course, Zanuck planned to borrow Peck in the future, should his major male star for some reason not be available. For the moment, however, he would start looking for another leading man to play Larry Darrell in *The Razor's Edge.*

The novel, by W. Somerset Maugham, was bought while still in galley form for $250,000, and Zanuck began looking around for a director. He approached George Cukor, a close friend of Maugham's, and asked if he'd be interested. Cukor said he might.

Cukor was a guest at a party one night, and he heard Orson Welles say, "You can't imagine what a thrill it is to read the *Odyssey* in the original. It makes you feel as if you only had to get on tiptoe and stretch out your hands to touch the stars."

The fanciful talk sounded familiar. Eventually, Cukor remembered its source, a speech of Larry Darrell's in *The Razor's Edge*. It was then that Cukor realized Maugham's literary agent had virtually papered the town with the galleys of the book. Nevertheless, Cukor indicated to Zanuck that he was seriously interested in directing the film version.

Lamar Trotti in the meantime was writing a screenplay, while Zanuck and Cukor looked for a leading man. They still hadn't found a suitable actor when Trotti delivered the script.

"There was a long, silly entrance at a big ball," Cukor said. "Everything important was squeezed in between the dances. I didn't understand the style of the thing."

Cukor went to Zanuck. "I'll do the picture only if you can get Maugham to write the script himself."

"I don't think we can afford him," Zanuck said.

"Let's try anyway," Cukor replied. He called his friend, who happened to be in New York. Maugham not only agreed to take on the assignment, he would do it for nothing. He considered it to be his last major novel, and his most philosophical. Thus he wanted it to be translated to the film medium with its message intact.

Maugham arrived in California and stayed as Cukor's houseguest while he worked on the script. "I recall," the director said, "that Willie started it with a car driving up to a house and a man getting out, just like in the book." Maugham saw the work as a human comedy. Trotti, who'd written the first draft, found the hero's turning his back on convention and marriage as basically antiheterosexual.

After weeks of work, Maugham's script was delivered to Zanuck. He found it totally unacceptable, being too verbose and lacking visual appeal. Maugham hadn't fully succeeded in illustrating the premise that the road to salvation is as difficult to walk as the sharp edge of a razor. Zanuck suspected Trotti's attitude might be right, and he decided to rely on his version and vision. The book's simplistic philosophy was muddled.

"It was a disappointment to Maugham," Cukor said, "and to me. I had a commitment at Metro for another picture, so I too dropped out."

Zanuck was now convinced only one actor could play the part: Tyrone Power. He waited eight months for his once and future star to complete his military obligation.

In January of 1946, Ty was discharged as a first lieutenant and became an active member of the Marine Corps Reserve. The war had released him from the burden of recycled scripts and repetitious roles. He was thoroughly enthused with the new order at Twentieth, of which he was to be an integral part. The new film excited and challenged him. He'd read *The Razor's Edge* early in 1944 while sunning by the poolside at the Piedmont Driving Club in Atlanta. He related to Maugham's premise. Ty even thought he and Larry had many things in common. Ty happily signed a new seven-year contract with Twentieth Century-Fox. He would continue to be offered the most choice roles of the studio. He would have complete access to Zanuck personally, who usually had few direct dealings with his actors. Others at the studio whom the boss cultivated were Clifton Webb and Reginald Gardiner. What the three actors had in common with the other distinguished people Zanuck and his wife courted at their palatial Ric-Su-Dar estate in Palm Springs was a civilized urbanity. Perhaps the studio head aspired to achieve that in himself.

His greatest male star was well aware that his name on a picture might no longer carry the automatic clout it once did. The war had seen to that, and Ty would have to be proving himself all over again. He was eager to do so, particularly in a role he so identified with and which seemed specifically written for him.

Ty had never been outwardly religious, not even as a child. Not even his sister Anne could confirm the existence of God in his life. Olive Behrendt didn't recall any religious discussions the two ever had. "If he was devout, I couldn't say. Because his parents were divorced, there might have been some conflict there. Yet I don't ever recall seeing Ty on Sundays. He could have been in church."

Parishioners at a Brentwood Catholic church were surprised to see Ty occasionally pass the collection plate at Sunday mass, despite his marriage to the divorced Annabella. It was as if he were serving notice that he didn't consider himself married.

Jacque Mapes, today the producing partner of Ross Hunter, who became a close friend of Ty's when both were in the military, found him to be extremely religious and sensitive. "I didn't talk too much about it to him," Mapes said, "but I know that he retained a lot more of his religious training than he'd want people to know. He didn't wear his religion on his sleeve, but it was of great importance to him, even if he'd fallen away from the church."

Years of luxury and indulgence hadn't erased the memory of his childhood privations. Austerity had been forced on him, and its memory was never far from his mind. Ty related greatly to Larry Darrell. He returned from the war more secure in his own person. He was now a man who refused to let his wife treat him like a boy. As a result, he questioned more, seeking answers that were as elusive to him as they were to the character he was portraying.

If Ty felt his career was progressing and he was growing as an actor, he was well aware that his personal life was at a standstill.

Living around their Saltair Avenue home in Brentwood were several people with whom Ty and Annabella often socialized. They included Keenan Wynn and his wife Evie, before their subsequent divorce and her second marriage to Van Johnson; James Aubrey and his actress wife, Phyllis Thaxter; Cesar Romero; and a well-connected Easterner named J. Watson Webb, who was working under the supervision of Twentieth's head cutter, Barbara McLean, and would be the film editor of credit on *The Razor's Edge*.

They formed a core of about twenty-five people who met at the Powers' every Sunday for an early supper before playing The Game. This was an elaborate form of charades, highly competitive, in which two teams of players would try to guess a phrase or saying. Most of the group were actors, drawn from the English, French, and upper strata American colonies. They could be demanding and autocratic on the set, but they reverted to being warm and impish children during The Game. At one time or another, such actors as Humphrey Bogart, Clark Gable, James Stewart, Henry Fonda, and Jennifer Jones joined the group to grimace, gesture, and contort the evening away. Since most of the guests had early morning Monday calls at their respective studios, the parties ended around ten or eleven at night.

Ty and Annabella, because of his six-day-a-week work schedule, had only that one day to themselves, and yet they crowded it with as many people as possible. Cordial and expansive, Ty and Annabella seemed to have time for everyone but each other. They were consciously avoiding the inevitable.

Olive Ponitz had been married for some time to George Behrendt, an insurance man whose family-owned company had written the first motion picture insurance policies. Hers was a refined world of music—Heifetz, Piatagorsky, Rubenstein—far removed from the international set in which Ty and Annabella traveled.

One day, while she was driving in Beverly Hills, somebody honked his horn at Olive Behrendt. It was Ty.

She flew out of her car, leaving it on the street, as did Ty, who rushed to hug her. Their reunion had been so exuberant and spontaneous that their cars blocked traffic. The two never saw each other socially, yet they would always consider themselves the closest of friends.

After they parted, Olive Behrendt tried to fathom what there was in Ty that disturbed her. She concluded he wasn't as happy as he should have been.

With Edmund Goulding directing, the picture started filming in March of 1946. *The Razor's Edge* was a multi-character, all-star extravaganza, a *Grand Hotel* with soul. The cast Zanuck put together in support of Ty included Clifton Webb, Gene Tierney, John Payne, and Herbert Marshall. He wanted to cast Alice Faye as the dipsomaniacal Sophie, but she retired—perhaps wisely—on him. Next he thought of Betty Grable, but she knew her limitations. Anne Baxter got the role by default and, subsequently, an Academy Award for Best Supporting Actress.

The studio boasted that a record one hundred shooting days were spent on the production; its budget was $4,000,000, including $250,000 for the screen rights to Maugham's book. It built eighty-nine sets costing $641,800, and gathered $800,000 worth of props to be used, including so much silver for a wedding scene that two Pinkerton men were hired to guard it during the filming. A single love scene between Ty and Gene Tierney cost $121,000, the studio proudly proclaimed. For the first time since the days of silent films, an orchestra was engaged to play on the set during re-hearsals, to get the stars into the proper mood. The love scene was accompanied by Strauss waltzes; Clifton Webb died to funeral airs.

Overlooked was the contradiction in all this, the concerns for sumptuous settings in a film about the irrelevance of materialism. Indeed, as the film flows on, the camera roaming restlessly and meaninglessly in gargantuan single takes, characters have a habit of gliding by like proud galleons passing such equally proud ships as the candelabra, fountains, and chandeliers. The audience is given longing views of the opulence which, in respect for the hero, it should be turning its back on.

Perhaps, through the mass deployment of cast, props, and scenery, the movie audience wouldn't notice the vacuum that was Larry Darrell's character. It was a difficult, beatific role, and Ty was performing it with great sincerity. His long speeches about eventual redemption had to be delivered with a genuine sense of inspiration, since the camera held him mercilessly in its close-up gaze. He delivered the lines with great conviction, his voice mellowing and his eyes scanning distant horizons. His range was being extended as never before.

However, this was a basically hollow and self-indulgent character, striking introspective poses and speaking poetically about the meaning of life, parading his sensitivity nearly to the point of insufferability. Yet, rarely in the film was he seen to commit a selfless, altruistic act. Many would find this the picture's greatest flaw.

Time would say the film "dawdles away several million dollars trying to make a greater philosopher of W. Somerset Maugham and a great actress out of Gene Tierney."

Filming proceeded on schedule. Any reflection and introspection would be limited to the Darrell character and not to the business-as-usual crew behind the camera. The four-month shooting schedule was at the halfway point toward late May when Ty and Annabella had another of their Sunday gatherings, this time to welcome David Niven's wife to Hollywood. Keenan and Evie Wynn left after the outdoor barbecue by the pool, and the rest of the guests moved inside.

An alternate game the group played, equally childlike, was Sardines, in which the lights in the house were turned off and everybody would hide, except for one person who had to find the others. There were many suppressed giggles as groups clustered together in a closet, as the name of the game suggested, like sardines. The last person to be found, however, would be the true sardine, the winner of the game.

David Niven, before the war, had been a standing member of the group. His twenty-eight-year-old English wife, Primula Rollo, hadn't as yet met many of the regulars at the Powers. "Primmie" was the mother of two boys, one three and the second six months of age. Unfamiliar with the layout of the house, she opened a door in the dark, thinking it was a coat closet. It was instead a door to the cellar. She fell down the steps, landing on the stone floor below.

Her husband was hiding under a bed upstairs when Ty came looking for him. "Come down, quick, Primmie's had a fall!"

Niven found his wife lying unconscious on the cellar floor. Her forehead was dabbed with a damp cloth and a doctor was called. She appeared to be only knocked out.

Ty thought she would be all right. "Come on," he told the group. "There's no sense standing around. It'll only frighten her when she wakes up. Let's keep on playing."

Soon after, the doctor arrived. Within a few moments, Niven and the doctor were carrying Primmie to a car to take her to a hospital. Her injury was diagnosed as a concussion by the doctor, but not serious. Niven, relieved, returned to Ty and Annabella's.

The group had been listlessly playing The Game until news came of Primmie's condition. "It's nothing," Niven told them. "Just a mild concussion. She'll have to stay in the hospital for a few days. Then I can bring her home. Now, I need a drink."

The group—which that evening included Cesar Romero, Miss Tierney and Oleg Cassini, Richard Greene and Patricia Medina, Rex Harrison and Lilli Palmer, and Major and Mrs. Arthur Little (he'd flown with Ty in the marines)—broke up soon after.

The next morning, Niven was called at his studio by the hospital. A blood clot had formed on his wife's brain and an operation was immediately needed. He gave his consent. An hour later, the doctors came out to the waiting room where Niven had been anxiously sitting. His wife, who was a WAAF officer who had gone through the war unharmed, had been in the United States only six weeks, and now she was dead.

The group was devastated, Ty in particular. He hadn't been aware of the seriousness of Primmie's injury, yet in insisting that the group continue playing The Game as if nothing had happened, he'd been guilty of the greatest insensitivity. To him, it was unforgiveable.

That Sunday was the last one for the group at the Powers. The clique, because of the tragedy, disbanded. Ty had seen in the war how fragile a person's hold on life could be, and Primmie's death further underscored this. Instead of bringing him and Annabella closer together, the tragedy created a different effect. Circumstances could change with the snap of a finger. The tragedy in effect spurred Ty to end his marriage, to be truer to himself and to his nature.

From Damon and Pythias to Butch Cassidy and the Sundance Kid, the male animal has strongly related to the devotion and, indeed, love that one man can have for another. There is a certain point, however, beyond which that love does not go, and that is in its sexual manifestation. Most males have absolutely no interest, to the point of aversion, in pursuing their love for each other to the ultimate.

During my days as a newspaper reporter, I had occasion to interview Gore Vidal. When during my questioning I referred to him as one of the most vocal exponents of bisexuality, he declined the "honor." "It's like being called a spokesman for blue eyes," he protested. "It doesn't mean anything. Everyone is bisexual. Period. Not that everyone practices it."

The generalization struck me as excessive at the time. I'd forgotten the conclusion by Alfred Kinsey and his associates in *Sexual Behavior in the Human Male* that several of the so-called perversions are so common as to be considered normal. Bisexuality is one of them.

Judging from the baiting humor in locker rooms, many men must be joking on the level when they cast aspersions on each others' masculinity and declare their rapacious intents on each other. Generally, it's a harmless safety valve. All can laugh off their vague curiosity about having sex with another male and can then turn to more socially approved avenues of sex. To most, sex with another man is nearly as repulsive a taboo as incest.

What happens, however, when that curiosity turns into a desire that won't go away? In this self-indulgent age, more men seem to be living out the Oscar Wilde aphorism, "The only way to get rid of a temptation is to yield to it." Another saying from the same Wilde work, *The Picture of Dorian Gray,* declares, "The only difference between a caprice and a lifelong passion is that the caprice lasts a little longer."

If homosexuality was a caprice in Ty's life and his love for women his lifelong passion, the usual momentary impulse was indeed lasting a long time. There was no dearth of partners offering themselves to him, seductively laboring to make up Ty's mind as to where his primary desires lay. His personal charm and his major star standing permitted him to indulge all the desires which the common man would ordinarily suppress. He took no joy in them, cursing the beauty that had made him famous, if not yet rich.

"For anyone truly interested in the theater," he told Elia Kazan, "it's a tragedy to be born handsome."

Kazan, directing several films at the studio during that period, replied, "It's a greater tragedy to be born homely." Reflecting on that, he added, "The greatest tragedy is to be born at all."

Ty agreed. Because he was too intense to take matters lightly, his internal conflicts ate away at him. His wife described herself as pink-seeing and Ty as black-seeing. That Irish sense of foreboding and doom was too much with him. His enormous guilts were beginning to show on his face. He was a man of thirty-two, but no one had called him bright-eyed in years.

At a time when Ty started making a concerted effort to come to grips with his psyche, the publication of Kinsey's monumental myth-shattering study was still two years in the future. Ty's only guide was the Judaeo-Christian tradition dating back thousands of years, specifying that the only permissible sex act is the one that results in procreation.

Recent studies have suggested that a chemical imbalance within the fetus may be a cause of homosexuality. Yet, by all psychological criteria of the time, which are still widely accepted today, Ty's upbringing was such that it shouldn't be surprising if he were exclusively homosexual. As early as 1905, Sigmund Freud was suggesting that many men with weak or absent fathers and domineering, frustrating mothers were apt to become homosexual.

Why, then, was Ty a bisexual? Patia Power was decidedly ambivalent about her husband. She could denigrate Ty Power, Sr., as a man while encouraging Ty to emulate his father as an artist. He was an absent, flawed individual, but appreciation of his acting genius was drilled into the son. Ty felt awkward and fearful with his father at the same time he looked on him with veneration and awe. He was a mama's boy who yearned to be known as a chip off the old block. In his bisexuality, he was, in a way, both.

During the summer of 1946, Ty got into the habit of stopping off at the house of Ann Stewart, a studio contract player, for a drink or two before going home. She lived near Twentieth, and the vivacious actress's house was a stopping-off place for the likes of Ann Sheridan, Cesar Romero, and Jacque Mapes.

Ty was also seen at social gatherings in the company of one handsome man after another. Those who knew that he and his wife were having differences, though they might not have known the reasons, felt Ty was too much the gentleman to be seen with another woman. It was generally known at the studio, however, that a young singer named Doris Day was spending a lot of time in his dressing room.

Others surmised that the men he was being seen with, some of them known homosexuals, might be the reason for his apparent troubles at home. Hollywood, however, chose not to pay notice. Ty was so well liked that the scandal mill busybodied itself elsewhere.

Filming on *The Razor's Edge* was completed on July 23, a week under the four-month shooting schedule. It was a bloated picture, running almost two-and-a-half hours, apparently suffering from a glandular condition. Despite its elephantine size, it proved to be an immediate blockbuster, and would ultimately earn

$5,000,000 for Twentieth, the most successful studio picture of the year.

As part of the big ballyhoo, the studio worked out an advertising tie-in with a cigarette company, in which the picture's stars endorsed the product in ads which were run in many national magazines at the same time the movie was released late in the year.

Jacque Mapes was surprised that Ty would be a party to this. His feeling had nothing to do with a possible connection between smoking and cancer. Mapes felt that endorsing a cigarette wasn't dignified, particularly since the role Ty was playing simply crawled with dignity.

"I have no control over it," Ty told him. "The studio told me to do it. I'm not getting much money for it."

Why a star of Ty's caliber should be so blindly cooperative, and so unaware of the value of his name, was a mystery to Mapes. "But then," he added, "I don't remember hearing Ty object to anything. Maybe he didn't want to make waves."

Praise for his performance was lukewarm. "Power is intense— for Power," Philip K. Scheuer wrote in *The Los Angeles Times.* "I do not consider him up to the requirements of the role, but in all fairness it might have thrown anybody."

Nevertheless, Ty was still awash in truth and beauty. He began making plans for a personal search of his own. This was an odyssey on a movie-star scale, Ty flying a twin-motor, 450-horsepower Beechcraft, the *Saludos Amigos,* which the studio put at his disposal. It was a planned journey of twenty-two thousand miles throughout Latin America. Cesar Romero, Ty's best friend, was recruited to go along as companion and interpreter. Also on the trip were Bill Gallagher, Ty's secretary; studio publicist Jim Denton; and John Jeffries, Jr., the copilot.

Annabella was about to make a trip of her own, going to New York to play the lesbian in Sartre's *No Exit.* Ty wasn't happy about her choice of roles.

The morning of their departure, Ty called Romero and asked him to pick him up for the drive to the airport. Annabella invited their friend in for coffee. Ty casually kissed her good-bye, then they were off.

During their ten-week tour, the two were met by thousands of people at each stop. Studio functionaries in each country advertised their arrival at different airports, then hired guards to keep the exuberant crowds at bay. The studio considered this a goodwill tour, and Ty and Romero were greeted as conquering heroes, which in fact they were. Some of the people who met Ty were disappointed that he spoke little Spanish, as they had expected he was fluent in the language. His voice was dubbed in Spanish by other actors when his pictures were released in Latin America. Romero, during the press conferences they held in the hotel suites he and Ty shared during the trip, smoothed it over. The two paraded through eighteen capitals, making front-page news wherever they went. They met nine presidents of Latin American countries, some of whom feted them at state banquets.

Their most fascinating evening occurred in Buenos Aires, when the two men dined with Juan and Evita Peron. The Argentine dictator, who spoke no English, remained relatively quiet during the dinner. His wife, however, was vital and animated, leading the conversation.

"You could see the wheels going around and you could easily visualize that she was running the whole bloody country," Romero recalled.

She tried to include her husband in the conversation by periodically asking him, after she made some astute remark, "Isn't that so, Juan?" Peron would nod his head.

"I don't understand how you people continually think of my husband as a dictator," she continued. "He is no dictator. He is a great patriot! Isn't that so, Juan?"

Modesty forbade an answer.

Their last stop before returning to the United States was Havana. The two men had shared ten weeks of travel together, probably the greatest test of any friendship. They had talked about matters sundry and particular, so that Romero felt there were few things about Ty he didn't know.

The night before they were due to fly back to California, Ty asked Romero, "Do you mind if we go to New York in the morning? I want to see Annabella."

They arrived in New York on October 23. Ty spent the evening with his wife, while Romero was elsewhere occupied.

The next morning, the Latin actor picked up a newspaper that had been delivered to his hotel room. In it, Louella Parsons announced that the seven-year marriage of Ty and Annabella Power was at an end. They had confirmed the fact to her in a joint statement.

Ty had told Romero nothing of these plans. His friend was dumbfounded. Just then the phone rang.

"Have you had breakfast yet?" Ty asked.

"No," Romero replied.

"Well, come on over and have breakfast with Annabella and me."

When he joined them, the two acted as if nothing had happened. After breakfast, Ty kissed Annabella good-bye, as he had ten weeks previously, and the two men flew back to California. Ty never mentioned that he and Annabella had parted, and this was with his closest friend.

Ty's role in *The Razor's Edge* had affected him deeply. Some found it had made him merely affected. One was screenwriter Philip Dunne, who recalled, "Ty, who was an extremely normal, virile fellow, took to wearing white clothes and got a white shepherd dog and used to go around the lot looking dreamy. But then he took up with Lana Turner, and that was the end of that phase."

The dog, Olaf, was a gift from Gene Tierney, and Ty did take it everywhere. The end of his spiritual phase, however, was caused by several concerns. Through conversations with friends more intellectual than he, Ty had come to wonder whether *The Razor's Edge* was pretentious, simplistic claptrap. He also heard the advance praise that Gregory Peck was receiving for a role in *Gentlemen's Agreement,* a no-nonsense look at anti-Semitism, a hard fact as opposed to the gauze-screened moonbeams of his own picture. Ty might have played the Peck role, but he chose to do the Maugham picture instead. His dreamy period abruptly ended. Lana Turner had a lot to do with it.

Ty could switch from a homosexual to a heterosexual affair

with considerably more ease than when he left a woman for another man. He was not one to face drawn-out unpleasantness. In trying not to hurt the people he was involved with, he abruptly withdrew, leaving a larger hurt in his women than if he'd left them with assuring and consoling words. It was cruel to treat them this way, yet Ty couldn't bear the confrontations and recriminations. For a man of such famous breeding and kindness, this was a Tyrone Power at his most thoughtless.

Most of the men in his life didn't expect great protestations of love, although they did come to believe that he would prefer to have sex with males than with women. Women in his life felt the opposite. He had the capacity of approaching each encounter with the same degree of tender passion. Only he knew which he truly preferred, and he was too private about himself to confide this information in others. He and the men he turned to used each other to satisfy particular desires, then went on to other males. If chance or opportunity threw them together again, each knew the other had had additional homosexual adventures in the interim. Not since the days with Robin Thomas had Ty even hinted at a permanent emotional commitment to another man. His homosexual affairs were purely physical.

Despite her reputation as a sex symbol and despite her two unsuccessful marriages thus far, the Lana Turner of these early years was not a hardened creature. She'd had many previous affairs. Yet, she was more victimized by the men who coveted her than she was the heartless vamp.

There was a sweet acquiescence about her, and she embarked on her affairs with a generosity of spirit the men who flocked around her could well emulate.

One of her closest friends in those days was Sara Hamilton, a fan-magazine writer. "Lana was not a bit like they said she was," she stated. "I was much older than she, but she was very sweet and thoughtful with me. She had a lot of beaux, and I think they exploited her."

Jacque Mapes agreed. "Lana had a sweet vulnerability about her. The early Lana was entirely different from the one that finally emerged."

Later, neither Ty nor Lana could recall how they'd met. They'd been aware of each other for a long time but, being stars at different studios, their paths hadn't crossed. Socially, they circulated in entirely different groups. They may have met at a party thrown by Gene Tierney. Hedda Hopper chose to believe that Lana was sitting alone in a booth at Romanoff's when Ty walked in. She was supposed to have smiled and patted the empty seat beside her. Ty sat next to Lana and, as Hopper described it, "combustion set in."

The old dictum that a man should treat a duchess like a whore and a whore like a lady was never practiced by Ty. He treated all women, including famous sex symbols, as if they were at the manor born. "If Ty hired a whore for the night," his third wife, Debbie, told Rock Hudson, "he'd send her flowers the next morning."

In 1971, a quickie biography, *Lana,* was published. Its authors, Joe Morella and Edward L. Epstein, maintained Ty liked his women "glamorous, sensual, and aggressive." Lana at twenty-six, they claimed, was all three. As in most very definite statements, this was only partly true.

There was substance in Lana Turner's character that only Ty appeared to see. "No man except Tyrone Power took the time to find out that I was a human being," she later said, "not just a pretty, shapely little thing. That could have been my fault . . . I didn't know myself."

People gasped at their beauty whenever they walked into a restaurant or a night club. Each was a certifiable star, Lana having reached the peak of her sexual appeal in her most recent picture, *The Postman Always Rings Twice,* and Ty again a proven draw at the box office with the *The Razor's Edge.* Lana, to most men, was the embodiment of profane love; Ty, to many women, represented its sacred incarnation. Yet, their teaming seemed right in the public's mind. They were tremendously drawn to each other, and they called it love.

Ty was the most sensitive and gentle man she'd ever known. He found in Lana a childlike innocence that had endured despite the tragic unsolved murder of her father when she was still a young girl and her resulting unhappy childhood.

Because of her many affairs, much of Hollywood didn't find

Lana quite respectable. Ty protested to Hedda Hopper that Lana had been badly treated and cruelly judged. If others didn't as yet see the true lady in her, he was the Pygmalion who would mold her in that image. "You don't know the real Lana," Ty told the columnist. "I'll bring her to your house and show you."

They spent all their free time together, Ty gladly including Lana's small daughter, Cheryl Crane, in many of their outings.

When questioned by columnists, Lana replied, "Ty Power's the only man I've ever loved."

Hedda Hopper asked Ty, "Is it love?"

"If it's not," he replied, "it's the nearest I've ever come to it."

Lana, yearning to be considered seriously as an actress, had been given the starring assignment in *Green Dolphin Street,* which had originally been intended for Katharine Hepburn. Most of the picture, with a New Zealand setting, was shot on the Klamath River, seven hundred miles north of Hollywood. When the company returned to shoot interiors at Metro's Culver City studio, Ty often visited Lana on the set.

Playing Lana's maid was a Dutch-Mexican actress named Linda Christian. She and Ty were casually introduced.

Ty was scheduled to leave soon for Mexico, to begin shooting his next picture, *Captain from Castile,* under his favorite director, Henry King. The separation, he and Lana vowed, would not end their affair.

A caravan of eight railroad cars containing a company of 130 left California in mid-November for the three-and-a-half months of filming in Mexico. It included a dry-cleaning plant and refrigerator units to preserve the Technicolor film. Shooting would take place at two other Mexican locations, and Ty volunteered to pilot a shuttle plane for fifty members of the cast and crew.

Filming started the week before Thanksgiving. *Captain from Castile,* as written, was a curiously muted film with a few exciting moments thrown in. The script introduced subjects with great dramatic potential, then dropped them as if they were red-hot ingots. It became quickly apparent that the energy and drive that go into the preparation of any film weren't coming through. Ty looked his age, and he wasn't convincing as the naive young man with a twelve-year-old sister, still living in the home of his Spanish nobleman father. King's stratagem of showing Ty to be *shorter* than all the men he acted with didn't succeed in convincing the audience that he was *younger*.

King, who worked with Ty more than any other director, expounded on what makes a star in a 1959 interview with *Film Daily:* "There's a very good reason for stars and that's because stars are pretty good actors. I don't know of anyone who became a star accidentally. I look upon the art of acting just the same as if a person was going to become a doctor or a lawyer. Hard work and study. One must have the know-how and the can-do. An actor can be the victim of a bad story, but as a general rule, the actor is a pretty capable person when it comes to knowing his job. That's why he is a star."

The director was a patient and analytical craftsman, who would work with his players at a leisurely, understanding pace. He could show flashes of cruelty, but King hid very well the bulk of his frustrations, particularly when Zanuck saddled him with untested actors.

He later said that if he'd worked with Ty exclusively, his directing career would have lasted ten years longer. "Ty was a very sweet, wonderful person . . . always just a simple, honest person. He wanted to be a good actor more than anybody I ever saw in my life." Ty's enthusiasm continued despite the reservations he was feeling about the picture.

The hero in Samuel Shellabarger's romantic novel had red hair. Ty adamantly refused to dye his dark brown hair for the part. He'd been accused too many times of trading on his looks, and anything at this stage to augment them or draw attention to them courted disastrous snipes. Nevertheless, Ty should have been in his element, for the picture being directed by Henry King was in the same swashbuckling style as two of Ty's previous ones, *The Mark of Zorro* and *The Black Swan,* and allowed him another exciting sword-fighting scene, in which he dispatched the evil John Sutton.

Captain from Castile was one of the first post-war films to make extensive use of location shooting, which in Ty's career hadn't been possible since *Brigham Young—Frontiersman.* King habitually scouted locations by plane. As far back as 1933, he'd discovered Morelia 350 miles southeast of Mexico City, which could do double duty as Mexico and fatherland Spain. Only now, in the story about one of Cortez's lieutenants, was he able to make use of the locale.

Yet, what King thought was its biggest asset was turning out to be its greatest liability. The smoldering volcano in the area was colorful to film, yet the threat of its eruption was a continual worry. Ty's leading lady, Jean Peters, was a twenty-year-old coed signed off the Ohio State campus. The test King shot of her, a dramatic scene from the picture, revealed an earthy appeal and a natural acting talent . . . or so studio executives thought. It had necessitated many takes and much editing to create that impact. When she was assigned to star opposite Ty in the picture, King didn't protest. He'd worked with more famous and less talented people in the past.

Yet, Jean Peters' limitations didn't cause the greatest delays. It was the bad weather, which pushed filming from a scheduled 89 days to 112, and the $2,000,000 budget to $4,500,000, the second most expensive picture Twentieth had ever made. It would be the first time a Henry King film went over the budget. Also costing considerably more, turning out to be the studio's most expensive picture to date, was *Forever Amber,* which was being filmed at the same time.

Movie-making is a boring business and the principals often have to wait for hours and sometimes days until the camera and microphones are set up for them. This film was being found even more deadly than usual, since its progress was so slow.

Henry King wasn't noted for being a gregarious man, but he realized that the morale of the company was dangerously low. Already, he'd organized a Thanksgiving dinner, and invited everyone to a Christmas Eve party. Ty offered to host a New Year's Day breakfast. He also organized a softball team, playing first base, the money raised from games with local teams going to Mexican charities. Then he'd be off with a few friends for a spin around the countryside. In the cast were two actors with whom Ty had had sexual affairs, so presumably he had additional distractions to take up his time.

Lana was still making *Green Dolphin Street* at Metro. As the new year approached, she decided to fly down to join Ty. When she arrived, he was eighty miles away from Mexico City on location. He sent a plane for her, and the two drank to the happiness that 1947 would bring.

Back in New York, Annabella was awakened by a reporter who asked her to comment on her husband's affair with Lana. "We are separate," she was quoted as saying. "You wake me up to tell me about heem weekending in Mexico with thees Lana Turner? Why don't you ask heem how ees thees with Lana Turner?"

Lana planned to be back in California in time for her early morning studio call on Monday, January 6. A heavy storm struck the area, and she was advised not to risk flying to the Mexico City airport in the light plane available to her. The rain came down so heavily that the road to Mexico City was washed out. She was stranded until the storm ended.

Lana was distraught. She'd desperately wanted the part in the film, feeling it would prove her capabilities as an actress, and now she'd be missing two working days. The studio would continue to think of her an an unprofessional dilettante. Ty got on the phone with her when she called the studio to explain the delay.

She went straight from the Los Angeles airport to the studio. Her absence had already cost the company thirty-five thousand dollars. She shook while being made up, dreading the reception she'd get from her coworkers. Thinking she'd brazen it out, she picked up the serape she'd brought back from Mexico, put a red rose between her teeth, and walked out to the set.

It was dark and empty. She was wondering if the director, Victor Saville, had canceled the week's shooting because of her absence. Suddenly there was a blaze of lights. The whole cast was in serapes and sombreros. Somebody started strumming a guitar, and they all began to sign, "South of the Border."

* * *

Ty's company continued filming in Mexico well into the new year. On January 13, Annabella announced in Hollywood that she wouldn't institute divorce proceedings against Ty until she returned from France in the fall.

Later in the month, Ty received word that Evic Wynn had married Van Johnson. He wired the bride: AWFULLY GLAD YOU DIDN'T MARRY A MOVIE STAR.

Although she felt threatened by Hollywood when Ty asked her to marry him, Evie Johnson's thinking had changed. "I was better able to cope with it years later with Van," she said. "I was one of them now. I was secure, and I knew who I was."

Ty was back in Hollywood, the principal location filming completed, at the beginning of March. Lana had finished *Green Dolphin Street* and was currently starring opposite Spencer Tracy in *Cass Timberlane*. Ty resumed his visits to the Metro sets.

As the affair with Lana resumed, Annabella was cast as the villainess-wife standing in the way of true love. She finally felt compelled to make a statement to the press. As printed, it implied that her English had appreciably improved since she'd been awakened by a previous reporter to comment on the affair. "I hear from all sides that I am refusing to divorce Tyrone," she said. "The truth is I had to ask him several times to get a lawyer of his own—as I had done myself—to arrange our divorce. Does this seem that I'm behaving like the dog in the manger?"

She and her mother left for Paris in the middle of the month, where Annabella was to star in a new film, *The Eternal Conflict*. In no way did the title reflect any feelings of rivalry she might have felt against Lana Turner. She didn't consider herself a runner in a matrimonial relay race, unwilling to pass on the baton in the form of Ty to Lana, the runner of the next lap around the track. Her parting from Ty was amicable. He, in fact, helped her pack for the trip.

"Tyrone is a closed chapter," she amplified in another statement. "Although we were married seven years, Tyrone was away for four of those years in the marine corps and it is inevitable that the attitudes of people, who are separated for long periods of time, change. Tyrone changed considerably, and I did, too, I suppose. We decided that we had come to the parting of the ways and the separation, by mutual agreement, was a very amicable one. We are still very good friends, and I am happy that it is this way."

Studio executives decided to delay the release of *Captain from Castile* so that they could concentrate their promotional efforts on their more expensive blockbuster, *Forever Amber,* starring Linda Darnell. Ty was able to film a modestly budgeted picture, his first B production since the war which would be released two months before the epic he'd made in Mexico.

Why did Ty want to make *Nightmare Alley?* "Stan Carlisle fascinated me," he said. "He was such an unmitigated heel. I've played other disreputable fellows . . . but never one like Carlisle. Here was a chance to create a character different from any I had ever played before. But aside from Carlise himself, the story had the tough realism and the dramatic impact that many modern novels lack."

The film opened on a seamy backstage carnival, with Ty as the opportunistic heel who steals the phony spiritualist act of a drunken carnival worker married to a blowsy Joan Blondell. He rises to triumph—if success as a night-club star can be considered the zenith—before his inevitable comeuppance occurs. He returns to the carnival, the geek in the sideshow who eats live chickens. It was an ugly little picture, but indicative of Ty's desire to broaden his range.

His romance with Lana continued. As desirable as he found her, however, he was gradually being choked by her possessiveness and her great insecurity. Her beauty was her stock in trade. An imaginary wrinkle or skin blemish was cause for disaster.

"Ty had so much charm it was illegal," Morella and Epstein quoted a friend of Ty's. "But his tastes were varied. He could never be happy with just one person . . . not even Lana . . . He had an insatiable desire to be like the wind. He wanted to go everywhere and do everything."

The writers cryptically alluded to Ty's varied sexual tastes without revealing them, leaving it to the cognoscenti to know what they were referring to.

Ty had to get away. The solution came in another goodwill trip for the studio, which he would begin on September 1.

Lana wanted to announce their engagement before he left. Ty balked. He wasn't even divorced from Annabella, and this was an unseemly thing to do.

He did, however, agree to be honored at a going-away party

which Lana gave. Its theme was love. Decorations and favors included hearts and flowers entwined. Guests coming to hear an engagement announcement were disappointed if not surprised.

Accompanied by studio spokesman James Denton, his secretary Bill Gallagher, and three others, Ty took off in his reconverted DC-3 from Howard Hughes Airport. Lana was there to see him off. She said she would meet him halfway through the trip, as soon as the filming on her current picture was completed.

The men flew from Los Angeles to Miami, then on to Brazil before hitting the African continent. As in his previous flight, national leaders welcomed him everywhere.

He was still in Africa when word reached Ty that his notices on *Nightmare Alley* were among the best he'd ever received. At last, the waspish critics had begun to take him seriously as an actor. Ty envisioned enormous opportunities opening up for him. He *would* become a singular actor.

Even his director, Edmund Goulding, felt impelled to call Ty "the greatest actor of this generation." Neither Spencer Tracy nor Laurence Olivier demanded equal time.

Paeans from the reviewers were not as excessive as Goulding's, but they were nevertheless highly positive.

"Mr. Power has a juicy role and sinks his teeth into it," Tom Pryor wrote in *The New York Times,* "performing with considerable versatility and persuasiveness." *Time* said, "Tyrone Power —who asked to be cast in the picture—steps into a new class as an actor." On the West Coast, his performance was equally praised. "Power is much more convincing as a phony spiritualist than he was as the real thing in *The Razor's Edge.*" So wrote Philip K. Scheuer in *The Los Angeles Times.* "His is a surprisingly incisive performance surrounded by incisive performances."

He looked forward to sharing his good notices with Lana when they met in Casablanca, possibly to live out their own version of the famous film that had been based there.

Then it happened. Gossipy Hollywood let him know that Lana was having a mild affair with Frank Sinatra in his absence. One reason why he'd made the twelve-week trip was to get away from her possessive clutches, to give himself time to think out their relationship. Also in the back of his mind was the doubt that

Lana could remain faithful. With the realization that her constancy had been rather early tested and found wanting, his mind was made up for him. There could be no future for them together. He sent word to her that he couldn't meet her as planned.

"Ty caught on to it," Edie Goetz said, "and that ended it. He never liked that, to be cuckolded, at all." It was an affront to him as a man, not to mention a spoiler of his movie-star image.

Lana arrived in New York in October, the first leg of her trip, to join Ty. By this time he was spending two weeks in Rome and had already had a private audience with Pope Pius XII. She wired and phoned him. He refused to speak to her.

Staying in the same hotel was Linda Christian, who ostensibly had brought her sister to Europe from Mexico in order to place her in a private school. Ty invited her to join him for cocktails.

She was in his room when the phone rang. Lana Turner's shrill voice could be heard across the room. "Tell me you love me," she insisted.

Ty, unemotionally, replied, "I love you."

She insisted that he meet her in New York. Ty half-heartedly agreed. Soon after, he heard that Lana had been seen touring the night spots of Harlem with a musician.

From Rome, Ty and his friends flew on to London and Dublin. While in Ireland he shot some exteriors for his next picture. As they flew across the North Atlantic Ocean, they ran into weather eighteen degrees below zero, and they were forced to fly nonstop from Iceland to Newfoundland. They landed there with only three hundred gallons of gasoline left and no de-icing fluid.

Ty flew back to the United States, bypassing Lana in New York and landing in Kansas City instead. From there, they flew on to California.

Ty set down at Howard Hughes Airport on November 29, twelve weeks after his global tour of eighteen countries and four continents had started. Annabella greeted his return with a statement to columnist Harrison Carroll. She said if Ty wanted a quick divorce so that he could remarry, she would gladly go to Nevada to get it. The rumors about his breakup with Lana may have reached Annabella by this time, and Ty wondered if there wasn't a touch of malice in her statement to Carroll.

Ty reported to his chief of state, Darryl Zanuck, at his Palm Springs home. From there, he told reporters, "I'm glad to be back in a democracy. From what I saw in Europe, the United States should adopt universal military training at once and be prepared for anything. I'm more convinced than ever before that America should be eternally prepared and vigilant."

It wasn't clear who was writing Ty's material, for he'd never expressed a political thought in his life. Lana, further forcing the issue, flew to Palm Springs from New York. When he emphatically told her the affair was over, she became resigned to it.

The reason for his political statement became quickly evident when, a few days later, Lana confirmed to Hedda Hopper that the romance was over.

"We never discussed marriage," she told the columnist, "but the press did, and that put us out on a limb."

When Hopper expressed regret over the ending of the romance, Lana replied, "So have I. I've had a wonderful year. Ty's a great guy . . . From now on I will carry my chin a little higher and work harder."

Joint statements from Metro and Twentieth confirmed Hopper's scoop. It was diplomatically hinted that Ty would have no time for romance and marriage in the near future because he was dedicated in his fight against the Communist menace, as if love and work were mutually exclusive.

He quickly discovered that his anticipated career triumphs had come to naught.

At no other time in his career were his character and his image typified as in the three films he'd made since returning from the war. *The Razor's Edge* represented his ascetic nature, which was a considerable component of his being. *Captain from Castile* was the public's image of him, and its appeal was wearing as thin as his performance. Within a short period, *Time* would be stating, "Tyrone Power keeps a medium-tight rein on his passionate Spanish nature." *Nightmare Alley* was the degradation and the humiliation which his inordinate sense of guilt called for, and which would be lived out in somewhat modified fashion later in his life.

The public bought the emptiness of the Larry Darrell character.

Ty had come to look on the picture and his role as a fraud and a deception, however, no matter how high the grosses.

Despite his great notices, *Nightmare Alley,* which was next released, was a commercial failure, notwithstanding its low budget. It took another actor to analyze the reason why. Rock Hudson, later to become one of Ty's closest friends, said, "A man who looked like Ty would never be reduced to eating a live chicken. If I were producing a film I would never have cast him in *Nightmare Alley."* If that debasing role were an essential aspect of his makeup, the public preferred not to know.

The studio was banking on *Captain from Castile* to thoroughly reestablish Ty in the postwar era. The public spoke here too, for the picture's domestic gross, because of the runaway budget, did not make back its cost. It was the most monumental failure in Ty's career.

Whether *Captain from Castile* justified its expense to the studio is an issue involving labyrinthine studio economics. The larger the actual budget of a film, the greater is the percentage of studio overhead that is tacked onto it. It was required to be a phenomenal hit before it could be said to break even. *Captain from Castile* would make $6,000,000 worldwide. It still lost, according to studio bookkeeping, $1,500,000. This is a consideration that needs to be understood when estimating the success of nearly all the Tyrone Power epics of the future which were called modest successes and quasi-failures. The sliding financial formula applied equally to *Forever Amber,* which had approximately the same $6,000,000 gross. It wound up being a more expensive film, and was said to have lost even more than Ty's film. It failed to establish Linda Darnell as a sex symbol and didn't establish Cornel Wilde as a swashbuckling rival to Tyrone Power.

Wilde was competing for a near-meaningless title. The genre Ty came to prominence in was losing its popularity with postwar audiences. Twentieth's most successful film of 1947 was *Boomerang,* a semi-documentary study of small-town politics that marked the film debut of director Elia Kazan. The public's taste for froth abruptly shifted and solidified into a desire for something with more substance. Zanuck took the cue and started a neorealism wave at Twentieth Century-Fox which was roughly comparable to what was happening in Italy at the same time, and which saw the international rise of such directors as De Sica and Rossellini.

What then of Ty himself? Zanuck didn't mince words. He was in a precarious position. If he was no longer right for the roles that were once his standard fare, and if his forays into the unconventional were too disturbing for his fans to accept, what was left? As his range was expanding, the roles the public most associated with him were diminishing.

Whom could he turn to for understanding and encouragement? There was always Linda Christian, who had followed him back to America from Rome.

CHAPTER

9

HOLLYWOOD COLUMNIST JAMES BACON, THEN A REPORTER FOR the Associated Press, recalled that when she appeared on the Hollywood scene, she was the most sensually beautiful girl he'd ever seen. As the daughter of Gerard Welter, an itinerant Dutch oil engineer, and Blanca Rosa Villalobos, whose family owned copper and silver mines in Mexico, she'd been exposed to a privileged international education and had acquired a five-language proficiency which other young actresses in Hollywood—Lana Turner, Ava Gardner, Marilyn Monroe—would never remotely approach. If her detractors refused to admit that she had quality and class—attributes Ty's estranged wife possessed in multiples—they had to admit that she had style and flash.

She was a Madame DuBarry born two hundred years too late. All her life she'd been trained in the arts of pleasing a man. Bright and shrewd, fevered with the desire to be somebody, the chief blind spot in her makeup was her inability to distinguish fame from notoriety.

Already her natural attributes—reddish-brown hair, catlike green eyes, a sensuous mouth, and a tall, voluptuous body—had earned her the press agent's title of The Anatomic Bomb.

When Ty met her, she was twenty-three, certainly no Colette

character, no Gigi trained to be a courtesan, who held out for marriage instead. There'd already been several men in her past.

One was Errol Flynn. Ironically, rumors had it that he and Ty also had a sexual affair. Had the three of them been mutually involved at the same time, it would have been a Noel Coward play, *Design for Living* come to life.

Flynn had played Fletcher Christian in an Australian film, *In the Wake of the Bounty,* and when he brought Blanca Rosa Welter to Hollywood under personal contract to him, he changed her name to Linda Christian. She was living with him at his house on Mulholland Drive at the time Flynn was being tried in Los Angeles Superior Court on a charge of statutory rape, his two accusers not much younger than Linda herself.

In his 1959 autobiography, *My Wicked, Wicked Ways,* published shortly before his death, Flynn told of sending Linda to his dentist to have the edge of a fanglike tooth filed down. He later got a bill for nine hundred dollars. She had also gotten all of her teeth capped.

The actor laughed off her "acquisitive" nature, adding "good for her . . . I started her on the road to fortune. She has more jewelry than Paulette Goddard—and that is like talking about Fort Knox."

As often happens in such "business" relationships, Linda Christian's contract with Errol Flynn was professionally unproductive. She next moved into a boarding house where six other aspiring actresses, one being Ruth Roman, lived. It was known as the House of the Seven Garbos.

Linda hadn't had much luck in films thus far. Her sole bit role was that of a WAC in the Danny Kaye picture, *Up in Arms,* at Samuel Goldwyn Studios.

Linda had to go through Ruth Roman's room to get to her own, and she was appalled at the brunette actress's sloppiness. Her bed was never made, whereas Linda's always had fresh perfumed sheets. She overlooked her distaste, however, when Ruth introduced her to the head of casting at RKO, and Linda was signed to a standard starlet contract at two hundred dollars a week. She was rechristened Linda van Loon, and spent six months there without any appreciable success.

When she returned to Mexico to visit her ailing mother—her parents had recently divorced and her father had returned to Holland—Linda was reintroduced to Miguel Aleman. He'd been the minister of state who arranged Mexican passports for the Welter family to escape Nazi occupation in Holland during the war. Now he was President of Mexico. The teenaged infatuation she'd had six years previously for her family's benefactor apparently became a mutual one.

Linda returned to Hollywood under contract to Metro-Goldwyn-Mayer, her friendship with Aleman instrumental in her being signed in accordance with the studio's good-neighbor policy. She reverted to the name of Linda Christian.

Suddenly, she was living in one of the more expensive apartment suites at the Bel-Air Hotel. Although the kitchenette was inadequate for her gourmet cooking talents, there was always room service.

Her first Metro picture was *Holiday in Mexico,* starring Walter Pidgeon, Jane Powell, and Xavier Cugat. She was at this point in her career doing slightly better than such other studio starlets as Ava Gardner, Cyd Charisse, and Gloria Grahame. In her personal life, she was proving as romantically accomplished as Flynn found her to be materially acquisitive. Linda had been cast as Lana Turner's maid in *Green Dolphin Street,* but she'd proven the movie queen's better in her ability to attract away her lovers, first Turhan Bey and currently Tyrone Power. There was no doubt in her mind that Ty was her route to celebrityhood and stardom. She was unaware how tenuous Ty's own career was at the time.

Linda and Ty saw in the New Year of 1948 in Acapulco while Lana, on the rebound, was involved in an affair with Bob Topping, a wealthy tinplate heir. He was to be her next husband.

In the same week that Lana was suspended by her studio, not because of her abruptly shifted affections from one man to another, but because of her refusal to play a lesser part in *The Three Musketeers,* another form of disunity was evident in Ty's life.

An unannounced property settlement had already been made when Annabella, on January 16, filed her long-expected divorce suit against Ty. They'd been separated sixteen months, and her husband had been involved in two highly publicized flings with other women in the interim, one of whom was arriving that very day from Mexico to be met by Ty at the airport.

In attempting to end the seven-year marriage, Annabella charged that Ty "willfully and without cause was guilty of extreme cruelty toward her, causing her grievous mental anguish and suffering and physical illness." She specified that Ty often left guests in their home to go to his room and sulk, and that he stayed away from home for long periods of time without explanation. Two days later, as a matter of form, Ty would deny the charges.

At the moment, however, his most immediate concern was in being reunited with Linda. She'd arrived from Mexico City carrying four fur coats and a trench coat, but was detained by immigration officials because her border-crossing card had expired and should have been renewed in Mexico City.

"I've traveled so much and gone so many places that I get confused with all the papers," she told the authorities during the hour and a half she spent with a three-man immigration board of inquiry. She was eventually released in the custody of Bill Gallagher, Ty's secretary, and instructed to return the following day to the immigration and naturalization office to straighten out the matter.

By that time, despite the pleadings of newspaper photographers who wanted to capture their reunion, Ty had long left the airport. When asked why he wouldn't wait to be photographed with Linda, he replied, "That would not be in good taste at this time."

Ty and Linda were reunited later at the house on Rockingham Road which he's bought from Henry Hathaway. She noticed how meticulously the house was kept. There was a place for everything. Ty's spartan upbringing and military schooling had molded him into a methodical, fastidious man. Now this beautiful girl had appeared, and his life would never be fully in order again.

Because of his two recent professional disasters, Ty was having to prove himself for a second time. He was an established star, but he submitted to a renewed studio buildup similar to that which would involve any tyro film actor. It was a necessary move, the studio insisted, and Ty bowed to the demands, although he was not as clear-eyed and idealistic as he'd been when he'd undergone the same promotional support almost a dozen years previously.

During this period, columnist Sidney Skolsky wrote what could have been an update of his first studio biography:

"Not temperamental, comes on set knowing his lines. Generally goes upstairs two at a time. Doesn't remember his own phone number—carries it with him.

"Plays piano well, speaks French, likes white carnations, swims, plays tennis, bowls, rides horseback. Ticklish. Best friend is Cesar Romero."

Another very good friend, however, didn't appear to be as outwardly constant, despite their continuing fondness for each other. On January 26, 1948, the same day that principal photography started on Ty's new picture, Annabella obtained her interlocutory divorce decree in Los Angeles Superior Court.

Under the terms of the property settlement, she would receive $50,000 a year, or 17 percent of his income over $310,000 annually, less her own earnings. Not included were earnings from her foreign films. She would also get the house on Saltair, benefits from $67,000 in insurance policies which Ty was to keep in force, and various bank accounts. He also agreed to pay $291 monthly support for her daughter Annie, now nineteen, whom Ty had adopted. The settlement was taking a considerable portion of his weekly $5,000 salary.

Annabella hadn't made a film in two years and, although she could command as much as $75,000 a picture, she wasn't known to be under consideration for any movie roles. She moved back to Europe shortly thereafter.

According to California law, Ty wouldn't be free to marry for at least a year. Linda was an extraordinarily desirable girl, and Ty was enthralled and excited by her. Yet, he was in no hurry to marry again. His fading star had to blaze again.

The studio didn't know what to do with Ty. It was well aware of his strong following abroad. He was still the favorite male star in Latin America. After his trip to Africa, there were three hundred bookings for his old pictures on that continent, seven films running simultaneously in Capetown, South Africa.

Yet, during this period, Twentieth's most consistent male box-office winner was the prissy Clifton Webb, starring in such frothy, unpretentious comedies as *Sitting Pretty* and *Mr. Belvedere Goes to College.*

Ty's maturing features, the bags under his eyes now quite noticeable, were at odds with the youthful swashbuckling capers he'd performed in the past. Perhaps, now that his delicate beauty had settled into a more rugged handsomeness, he would be more acceptable as a leading man of light comedies.

Not that Twentieth was extravagantly underwriting this new career. The recent United States Supreme Court ruling forcing studios to divest themselves of their theater divisions had eliminated the automatic market for Twentieth's pictures. They would have to compete on the open marketplace with the products of all other studios.

Where bold measures were called for if Ty's career was to be bolstered, they were not possible at the moment, neither at Twentieth nor at any other studio. Ty had to resign himself to whatever Zanuck would throw his way. *The Luck of the Irish* was a low-budget, nonmusical ripoff of *Finian's Rainbow,* in which Ty played his first Irish part—Irish-American actually—of a reporter on holiday in Ireland. His costar was Anne Baxter. To everyone's delight, Ty displayed an easy charm and a deft sense of comedy.

The studio was pleased enough with Ty's performance that it decided to cast him in the same light, albeit low-budget, vein, this time in a remake of his own picture, *Love Is News,* now called *That Wonderful Urge.* Mark Stevens was originally cast as Ty's reincarnation opposite Gene Tierney, but it was decided to use the genuine article instead. It was now up to the public to decide whether it would buy Tyrone Power as a Cary Grant imitation.

In the meantime, Linda Christian's contract at Metro was abruptly terminated, the studio explaining its action because of her refusal to do a picture. Most of Hollywood thought otherwise. Had her Mexican sponsor heard of her new romantic interest and withdrawn his patronage?

While Ty was attempting to again win the public, Linda was now free from all commitments to wage her own campaign: The Winning of Tyrone Power.

Ty never discussed his affairs with anybody. Consequently, Ray

Sebastian was surprised when he asked him, "What do you think of Linda?"

The reply of his makeup man was noncommittal. Ty persisted.

"I have no way of forming an opinion on her," Sebastian replied. "I think she's an attractive woman. She seems to be a lot of fun. She's built like nobody's business. She impresses me as being a very sexy woman."

"That she is, my boy," Ty answered in an Irish brogue he occasionally affected.

"What do *you* think of her?" Sebastian asked.

"I think she's wonderful!"

In June of 1948, Ty went to Florida to accept an Honorary Doctorate of Humanities at the University of Tampa. When he returned to California, he started making plans to leave later that month for Europe. Filming of his next picture, *Prince of Foxes,* was due to start in August.

Few of those close to Ty felt he was discerning about women. He was much less worldly than Linda and seemed totally under her spell. His friends assumed the two would marry. The couple had recently been in San Francisco, and Linda was proudly showing off an extravagant Chinese robe Ty had bought her at Gump's.

Cesar Romero gave a party in their honor that summer. Jacque Mapes, who escorted Ann Sheridan to the affair, said, "Everyone present was talking about their getting married. It was very apparent that Linda was pushing for it."

She was on the same plane with Ty to Italy, explaining to the Associated Press that she was on her way to Rome to attend her sister's wedding. Ty said his plans were to tour through Portugal, Spain, and southern France before reporting for his film assignment in Rome.

Over the next few weeks, an inquisitive press reported on Ty and Linda's activities. They were seen dining nightly at the Golden Dove Restaurant while in Venice, then retiring to their hotel, where Linda occupied the Louis XV room and Ty the Louis XIII room. No mention was made of who was in the Louis XIV room in between.

Announcement of their engagement was made in early August,

only to be vehemently denied within hours by a studio publicity man.

The "announcement" was followed two days later by a communication to Hedda Hopper from Linda's mother in Mexico City that Ty and Linda were marrying within a week in a Catholic church in Rome. Mrs. Alvarez Amezquita—she was now married to a doctor—followed up her wire to Hedda Hopper with a second one to Louella Parsons, in which she again stated that the two would imminently be married. Linda's sister Ariadne would be maid of honor and Darryl Zanuck would be Ty's best man, with four of Linda's former schoolmates in Florence acting as bridesmaids. Linda's mother added that the couple would have time for only a two-day honeymoon before Ty started work on his new picture.

Twentieth again issued a denial. Zanuck had his own reasons for opposing Ty's marriage to Linda. His star had been placid and compliant in the past. He would come around to Zanuck's thinking.

Some of the people who'd worked with him at the studio, however, knew there was a largely untapped angry and defiant streak in Ty. Walter Scott, for one, recalled the violent arguments Ty would have with his secretary-advisor, Bill Gallagher. They'd be walking on the lot, Ty almost a head shorter than the long and rangy Gallagher. He'd look up and shout about some point of contention, usually having to do with Ty's inability to budget his money. When he noticed that others overheard, he lowered his voice, but his anger remained apparent.

Ty wasn't a profane man, despite his marine-corps training. The extent of his swearing was a random "damn" or a "son-of-a-bitch." It was therefore a shock to the publicity woman whose daily habit it was to ask, "What did we do last night?" When she asked the same question one morning, Ty replied, "I fucked four broads last night. I was trying for the fifth, but they all ran out on me. I was quite a guy last night."

The woman couldn't get away from him fast enough. She'd always thought Ty was the only true gentleman on the lot.

Ray Sebastian thought Ty's behavior with her was more of a

gag than anything else. He halfway expected the woman to come back the next day and ask, "How many?"

"I'm still tired from the night before," Ty would reply. Then, they could all have a laugh. But the woman never approached him again. It was mildly upsetting to Ty.

Sebastian went to the publicity woman. "Ty wonders why you don't come to see him."

She replied, "I don't think I want to talk to Mr. Power any more."

Sebastian wouldn't leave the matter alone. "Why? Are you envious?"

The woman was incensed. "Envious of what? Where were you? Didn't you hear what he said?"

"There's nothing wrong with that," Sebastian said. "It happens all over Hollywood."

Even with that assurance, the woman avoided Ty from then on. He couldn't have been happy with his behavior. Ty might have thought of it as a joke at first, but he now realized he was passing on his frustration to somebody who couldn't cope with it. What he should have done was to talk directly to Zanuck.

Yet, Ty never expressed any great resentments about his treatment to the studio chief. For, at the same time that the studio head was urging him to get rid of Linda, Zanuck's other actions suggested that he was no longer interested in nurturing Ty's career. A double-edged rebellion was in the making.

Zanuck's insistence that *Prince of Foxes* be filmed in black and white, when Henry King protested that the picture screamed for color, was to Ty and the rest of Hollywood a sure sign of the studio head's faltering confidence in his most durable star. It couldn't have consoled Ty to notice that in his three pictures at Twentieth —*The Keys of the Kingdom, Gentlemen's Agreement,* and *Twelve O'Clock High*—Gregory Peck had garnered Academy nominations for Best Actor. Now the implication was obvious. Ty was no longer the biggest money-making machine, and Twentieth, being a capitalistic enterprise, wasn't about to risk huge sums on another career shift for Ty until the returns of his still unreleased light comedies were in.

"Over and over," he complained. "Swash and buckle, damn the torpedoes." He was ready to report for duty.

Orson Welles, always in need of money, desperately needed the second-billed role of Cesare Borgia. Henry King was almost as desperate in his desire to give him the job, despite some serious reservations.

Charles Feldman, Welles's agent, told King, "Listen, Orson wants to play this part. He wants to play this more than anything else. He's just playing hard to get."

"Well," King replied. "I'm playing hard to get too, and I *am* hard to get. I have somebody else. I'd rather have Welles, but I want to tell you something now. I understand from Gregory Ratoff . . . when they were doing *Black Magic* . . . that Orson doesn't start working until two o'clock in the afternoon, but then he'll work all night. I want him to know that I start at eight o'clock in the morning and I quit at six, whether there are actors there or not."

"He'll do anything you want," Feldman assured him.

"Well," King firmly said, "you'd better impress upon him that if he wants this part he is going to be on the set when I call him, or the next day the other guy will be playing it."

"I'll guarantee that because he wants to do it more than anything else in the world," Feldman replied. "Furthermore, he needs the money. I'll tell you what I'm doing. I'm not charging any commission, so you're getting him wholesale."

"Very good," King responded. "Then we can have that understood."

Welles reported to the wardrobe department. He had a noon call for his first day of filming.

King was surprised, therefore, to see Welles on the set at eight-thirty that morning, already in makeup and clothes, walking about the big reception hall where the shooting was taking place and, as was his custom, expounding and pontificating to his co-workers.

"What are you doing here?" King asked. "You don't work until noon."

"Henry, you know I just love to get the atmosphere and the feeling," Welles replied. "I want to see how you work. And I want to see how this goes."

King didn't feel threatened by this, despite Welles's already enormous stature as the director and star of *Citizen Kane.* "Why, that's wonderful!" he told his actor. "More power to you. But I just hoped somebody hadn't made a mistake and called you for nine this morning when you don't work until noon."

"Oh, no," Welles assured him. "I want to get into the clothes so they feel right on me. I want to get the feel and atmosphere of the room."

Significantly, Ty—a less gifted actor than Welles—didn't need that preparation, being able to slip into costume and period in a trice. Throughout the filming, Welles would appear on the set at least an hour before his call, while Ty would arrive promptly on time. One thing the two actors had in common: They were both equally prepared when it came to knowing their lines.

Ty had acted as Welles's sword bearer in the 1935 Katharine Cornell production of *Romeo and Juliet,* and was still somewhat awed by his friend and his subsequent achievements. Orson Welles was an artist, a claim Ty didn't presume to make about himself.

Italian women would come up to him and touch his arm, "Per un ricordo" . . . for remembrance . . . their awe-struck approaches proving that Ty was the far greater star. Yet you wouldn't have known it by his kowtowing to Welles. In a garden party scene, King had all the nobility in Florence welcoming Borgia, the military leader thought to be the model for Machiavelli's *The Prince.* The scene called for everyone to bow from the waist as Borgia walked by. King saw this as a slight bow, while Welles envisioned the Florentines bowing so low that their foreheads nearly scraped the ground.

The director was standing by the chief cameraman on an elevated platform when Ty came up to him. "Orson feels those people aren't bowing enough to him," he said.

"You get back over and play your part," King said, "and let him play his. Don't tell me how he should play his part."

"I'm just trying to tell you this is the way Orson feels," Ty quietly replied.

From the opposite end of the room came Welles's booming

voice. "I can't do anything unless these people bow to me and give me the respect that I deserve."

"You're getting a damned sight more than you deserve," King yelled back. "You just play the part. The people will do what I tell them."

From that point on, Welles was sweet cooperation itself. The members of the company were left wondering at the self-effacement in Ty which impelled him to act as Orson Welles's errand boy. Again, Ty's insecurity as an actor may have caused him to think he wasn't good enough to play anything other than a foil for the great Orson.

In the picture, Ty was portraying a peasant masquerading as a nobleman. He'd be convincing playing either. With his mispronunciations of "Che-*sa*-re" for "*Che*-sa-re" and "*See*-nior-ee" for "See-*nior*-ee," Ty was also an American masquerding as an Italian in 1500, and somehow he made *that* convincing. His character is described as having "the grace of a dancer, wrists of an assassin" who "must charm, as a snake charms a bird, yet he must make no friends." The part was as tailor-made for Ty as his costume. Boyish in his sophistication, earthy in his ethereality, genuine in his artificiality, he was both soft and rock solid, the chameleon and his backdrop at once, everyman and no man at all.

Ty could be considered the textbook example of the kind of actor Hollywood kept employing, a convenient stand-in for whatever emotion the director wanted to tap, while intellectuals and New York critics loudly stated their preference for "real actors." But time tested the movie mettle of stage actors like Clive Brook, Hume Cronyn, and Tallulah Bankhead, and they were found lacking. It was easy to prefer the "versatility" of a Laurence Olivier on stage, who could play Hamlet one week and Othello the next. It was less easy to see in the cold eye of the camera that Olivier was just as fully playing Olivier in the guise of Hamlet or Othello. Who, after all, could possibly play Othello in a full-screen close-up but a black man?

Ty was a purely filmic actor, like Clark Gable, Errol Flynn, and Greta Garbo. Theirs were different personalities appealing to a different kind of audience. Many if not most stage actors couldn't transfer their incandescence to the screen. When the Midwest public fell in love with Tyrone Power, its instinctive awareness of cinema aesthetics was far beyond that of more literate East Coast "superiors." Ty was never so busy acting that he ever stopped being himself. He considered this his greatest weakness. In fact, it was his greatest strength.

Nevertheless, Ty as a "cool" actor required the greatest effort from his audience. It was a cool that held its own with the hottest frenzies of his colleagues. When he shared the screen with such scenery-chewers as Orson Welles, the eye was continually drawn to him, the emotional center, and not to the more gestured and mannered player. It looked like effortless acting, particularly when contrasted with Welles's great histrionics, and to a large degree it was. Those who make it seem easy are the ones who can lay claim to their own kind of artistry. Tyrone Power never made such claims for himself. He, as well as most intellectual critics, greatly underestimated his gifts.

It was a lesson that had come down from the earliest days of the cinema. To test the powers of editing, shots of a well-known actor named Ivan Mozhukhin were intercut with shots of objects he was expected to relate to: hot soup, a cute kid, a cold tombstone. Mozhukhin's response appeared to vary with each new stimulant when, in fact, it was as frozen a visage as any on Mount Rushmore. The inner reaction of the audience supplied deeper emotions than any they could view, and Mozhukhin was seen as a performer of the most sensitive order. Ty had unconsciously arrived at the credo, under the tutelage of Henry King, that less is more.

Halfway through the four-month shooting, its budget inflated to a then astronomical $4,500,000—despite Zanuck's cost-cutting measures—Ty was about to get involved in a spectacular production of his own.

Word again reached Hollywood columnists that he and Linda would marry on November 6. Hedda Hopper quoted Linda as saying they couldn't get married on their previously scheduled August date because they couldn't get permission to be married in the Catholic Church. After a complete investigation, the church gave its consent, according to Linda.

Louella Parsons reported a somewhat different story. She quoted Linda as saying the two were marrying in a civil ceremony. Ty still hadn't confirmed the marriage plans. Parsons revealed how adamantly opposed to the wedding the studio was.

"Miss Christian is a very determined young lady," she wrote. "Her wedding dress is all made and ready, and she says her papers are all in order and there is nothing to stand in the way of the marriage in Rome now.

"She almost was married last August when the wedding date was set, but Ty's studio begged him to wait. So again I'll be surprised if they actually marry on November 6, but the lady is persuasive."

Was it rebellion against his studio, which had long exacted so many sacrifices from his private life? Was it to escape from a life of exclusive homosexuality, which filled him with dread apprehensions? Was it the resultant publicity, which could reestablish his romantic image and bolster his career? Was it the seductive Linda herself, one of the world's great beauties? Did he want to have a son to carry on the proud acting tradition of the Power family? Only Ty knew why he finally agreed to marry for the second time. Yet those who knew him best say it was probably the last factor that most greatly influenced him. He desperately wanted a son to carry on the family name. Annabella had failed to give him one. Now it would be up to Linda. The two decided to get married after he completed the current picture.

Elsa Maxwell, an old friend of Ty's who disapproved of Linda, asked him, "Why are you doing this?"

"Gee," Ty replied, "I never dreamed of having a wife so brilliant that she can speak seven languages. I have the same ambition that every normal young man has. I want a real home and a family."

Financially, Ty wondered if he could afford to marry again, given the generous alimony payments to Annabella and his personal high overhead. But there was a provision in the law which excluded those Americans working a minimum of eighteen months out of the country from having to pay income taxes. Ty agreed to stay outside the United States until late 1949, signing to star in two other pictures on location.

It all started with announcements to friends that Ty and Linda would be married in a Roman church on Thursday, January 27, 1949. Errol Flynn's reaction to the news was quoted all over Hollywood. "He's marrying *her?*"

It would take the assistants of one of Italy's top couturiers, Madame Fontana, fourteen weeks to work on Linda's white satin bridal gown, which was being hand-appliquéd with old lace, seed pearls, and sequins. The bride-to-be had obviously planned ahead, since the announcement of the upcoming marriage was made less than two weeks before the wedding.

Already, the engaged couple was involved in a hedonistic prenuptial social whirl. They'd met many of the European aristocracy at a party Elsa Maxwell gave for the Duke and Duchess of Windsor.

Ty, with Linda as his hostess, entertained later at Villa Madama, reported to be the most intact piece of Renaissance architecture, which he'd leased from the American-born Countess Dorothy di Frasso.

The day before the wedding, Ty made a statement to the press that Linda would give up her film career to raise a family. Shortly thereafter, Linda was bemoaning to the same reporters that because of the enormous publicity, she and Ty would probably not be married by Cardinal Federico Tedeschini, archpriest of St. Peter's Basilica, as she had hoped. Vatican sources said the Holy See did not feel the occasion warranted the presence of a prince of the church.

"You see what you have done?" Linda complained to reporters. "Because of all the publicity, it looks like the cardinal may not want to officiate."

None of the reporters pointed out that by being continually accessible to the press, Linda was contributing to the flood of publicity she claimed to abhor.

The ongoing festivities were further dampened when it was revealed that Ty's divorce from Annabella wouldn't be final until eight hours after the scheduled 10:30 A.M. ceremony. Should California officials choose to be sticky about it, they could consider Ty's marriage to Linda a bigamous one. Ty told reporters that he and Linda would get married again if the marriage was not recognized in California, but the religious ceremony would go on as scheduled.

So did the dinner dance thrown by Dorothy di Frasso at the Whip Club. It lasted until seven in the morning, giving the wedding guests a couple of hours to freshen up before the ceremony at the tiny Church of Santa Francesca Romana, built in the tenth century, less than one hundred yards from the Roman forum where Julius Caesar had been assassinated.

That party hadn't broken up before Italians by the thousands, predominantly glamor-starved women, began to gather, trying to push their way through the iron gates of the church. Over one thousand carabinieri would be called out to control the crowd, which would ultimately swell to over ten thousand people.

Inside the church, a purple floodlight shone over the altar, which had been especially built to give photographers a better shooting angle. White lilacs laced the kneeler on which Ty and Linda would kneel during the ceremony. Walls of lilies, carnations, camellias, and potted palms had been built up to hide the electric generator which powered the floodlights throughout the church. In this way, the photographers, who had mushroomed from an original sixteen to one hundred, wouldn't need to use disrupting flashbulbs. Heating facilities were installed in the church as well, because some of its windows had been broken over the years. A special electric organ was installed for the ceremony, to play Handel's "Largo" and Mendelssohn's "Wedding March," as well as to accompany the twenty-five choir boys who sang throughout the ceremony.

As the guests arrived, they had to push their way through the milling crowd, which became more frenzied when Ty appeared fifteen minutes before the ceremony. The thirty-four-year-old groom was in a severely cut morning coat. The press noted unkindly that he was wearing elevator shoes. He kept his composure as women pushed and jostled him. He managed to get into the church unharmed, the cries of the crowd—"Ty il Magnifico!" —ringing in his ears.

When his twenty-five-year-old bride arrived half an hour later, the crowd broke through the police lines, greeting her with a single roar, "Viva Linda!"

Several women fainted in the crush, and many were bruised by the mass buffeting about of bodies. One man suffered a broken finger. The mob hysteria would later be described as having caused the busiest day for Rome's policemen since the rioting that followed an attempt to assassinate Communist leader Palmiro Togliatti the previous July. Twice during the ceremony, girls charged the church doors, trying to get in. Three hundred *tifosi* (or bobbysoxers) did manage to break through before head usher Mike Frankovich clanged shut the church doors, leaving James Dunn, the ambassador to Italy, stranded outside. He managed to work his way inside the church, almost losing his overcoat in the process.

The double-ring ceremony, in English, was to be performed by the Reverend William Hemmick, a Pittsburgh-born monsignor who was a canon at St. Peter's Basilica. He'd been ill for three days, but consented the night before to officiate after Cardinal Tedeschini withdrew.

Ty asked George Ornstein, the Rome manager of United Artists who was married to Mary Pickford's niece, to be his best man. His witnesses were Prince Alessandro Ruspoli, Count Rudy Crespi, and Lieutenant Commander Victor Schrager, the assistant United States Naval Attaché in Rome.

Linda was given away by her former tutor, Leon Miglievitch, and was attended by his daughters Ada and Lilia, as well as her sister Ariadne.

As the rites started, the din from outside proved so great that the ceremony couldn't be heard past the fifth row. The guests inside—"frazzled nobility," as *Life* magazine called them—proved no better, buzzing aloud about the proceedings and moving into the aisles to get a better view. Ushers got involved in a shoving match with them, trying to get them to return to their seats.

During the proceedings, an enterprising cameraman rudely pushed Monsignor Hemmick aside to get a better shot of the bride and groom. After he declared Ty and Linda man and wife, the clergyman declined an invitation to join the newly married couple at a reception hosted by Ambassador and Mrs. Dunn, and returned to his sickbed.

As the new Mr. and Mrs. Power left the church, they braved the crowds again, who greeted them with joyous, near-violent, roars. The carabinieri protected them from the adoring masses while they cleared a way for them, so that they could go to the Vatican to receive Pope Pius XII's blessing during a special audience. The Pontiff gave the bride a rosary and a booklet of "Instructions about the Good Christian Family."

All in all, during the Roman circus, the Christians lost and the celebrity lions won. Church officials were incensed at the way the religious service had been demeaned and exploited.

Studio publicists, readying their press releases, were calling it The Wedding of the Twentieth Century. Back in Hollywood, however, in Darryl Zanuck's office, he was feeling no joy in the name of Twentieth Century-Fox.

Several hours after the Roman melee, Ty's attorneys appeared in Los Angeles Superior Court to ask that the interlocutory decree obtained by Annabella a year previously be made final. The California court didn't make an issue of the wedding in Rome prior to the granting of the decree and in effect recognized Ty's second marriage.

Ty and Linda planned to spend their honeymoon motoring through northern Italy, Switzerland, and Austria. They left the day after the ceremony, their first planned stop being Florence. On the road, their convertible crashed into a small Italian car, turning it over before it landed in a ditch. Its passengers suffered minor injuries, but the newlyweds were unharmed. Thus the collision course that was their marriage began.

Had Ty possessed foresight, he wouldn't have lingered abroad, returning immediately instead to the United States to bolster his faltering career.

He'd received good notices for The Luck of the Irish, which had been released the previous September, but the box-office returns were disappointing. His second light comedy in a row, released the week after his wedding, proved that all the world except the United States loved this particular lover. As far as the

American public was concerned, *That Wonderful Urge* was to stay home and watch television. Movie attendance in 1949 was to be affected for the first time by the new medium, starting a downward spiral from which theatrical films never recovered.

Ty and Linda were still on their honeymoon when they arrived in London in the middle of March, where the studio had arranged a press luncheon for them.

"I haven't heard from my studio lately," he commented, "but I think I still have my job." From California, studio spokesmen reacted by stating that not only was Ty a star in good standing at the Twentieth, he was about to start filming another epic called *The Black Rose*. It was originally cast with Cornel Wilde and Peggy Cummins, but was postponed two years previously because of mounting costs. Wilde wasn't considered a big enough draw to recover them. Now it was Ty coming to the rescue of a $4,500,000 white elephant.

Linda, preparing for the trip, brought home half a dozen evening dresses. Ty looked at them and asked, "Are you going to wear them in the Sahara Desert?"

"Of course," she recalled, "I returned the dresses immediately."

They were to be separated for the first time since their marriage soon after, since Linda was having passport difficulties and couldn't go with Ty to Africa. She joined him later in Casablanca.

By all standards, *The Black Rose* was a distinctly minor film, directed by Henry Hathaway, its sole source of excitement and danger the cloudburst that caused a flash flood in French Morocco, where location shooting was taking place. It came on a weekend, and costar Cecile Aubrey was missing for three days before she was found. Ty and Linda were driving from Mekness, 125 miles northeast of Casablanca, where the production had set up camp, to a desert Arab village where a second film unit was shooting, when they were trapped by the flood. Bill Gallagher was with them. They slept huddled together for two nights, dressed in their lightweight summer clothes, while freezing gales tore through the dirty native huts that had been made available to them. Ty, at the wheel of the car during the day, tried to drive back to higher ground. The three suffered terrifying moments when the water they were driving through proved deeper than anticipated, causing the car to float and water to rush in through the doors.

Then, out of nowhere, came a Russian innkeeper named Sacha, who took them to his home. When the crew found them, they were enjoying a dinner of filet mignon, baked Alaska, French pastry, and champagne.

The production company returned to England to finish filming. While there, the studio announced that Linda was expecting a baby the following January, and the Powers would return to California for its birth.

The Black Rose was completed in mid-August, and Ty and Linda stayed on in Europe to wait out two more months before they could return to the United States in accordance with the eighteen-month tax loophole.

It fit in well with both their desires, for they loved to travel. "I've traveled all over the world since I was a year old," Linda would say. "The only time I feel I'm living is when I'm going somewhere." They were in Paris on holiday when Linda suffered a miscarriage in late September. She and Ty stayed there for one more month, until it was time for them to return to the United States.

It was during this period that they ran into Errol Flynn. "I saw her abroad with her late husband, Tyrone Power, who had amazed me by marrying her," Flynn wrote in his autobiography. "He was a very soft, nice kind of man.

"Often, when Ty was about, she looked at me with those big oblique eyes of hers, smiling inwardly, I am sure, for Ty never knew the origin of our friendship.

"I would look at her and murmur, 'Smile, honey. I just want to see those choppers. They took their first bite out of me.'"

"She pretended not to hear."

Neither of the two films that he'd made while abroad had been released when Ty and Linda arrived in New York. Ty's sister Anne came down from her home in New England to meet her beautiful new sister-in law. She found Linda to have "infinite charm and extreme intelligence. Yet Linda and I were never very close, because after all I wasn't near them very much. I was living my own life elsewhere."

While in New York, the Powers accepted many invitations. At a cocktail party given by Josh and Nedda Logan, Ty's hostess asked him, "Why don't you do the London version of the show?" She was referring to *Mr. Roberts,* the smash play that a triumphant Henry Fonda had made his own.

Ty was intrigued. The careers of the two actors had leapfrogged for years. Ty had been in the original production which spawned *New Faces of 1934,* in which Fonda was starred. He had gone on to greater stardom at Fox, until Fonda stole *Jesse James* from him, and became almost as big at the box office. Fonda returned to the stage to create the definitive interpretation of what would become an American classic. What better way to prove he was Fonda's equal than by playing the same role? As part of the negotiations of his previous contract with Twentieth, Zanuck gave Ty six months off to do a stage play. The time was right.

"Can you wait until I do a picture in the Philippines?" he asked. Both Logans enthusiastically agreed.

Thus, it was desire and not necessity which prompted him to return to the theater. Within a month it would be considered a matter of both.

Prince of Foxes didn't prove any great shakes at the box office. Critics faintly praised Ty's performance. "Power handles cape and sword and euphemism with practiced ease," the notice in *Newsweek* read. Bosley Crowther of *The New York Times* said that Ty "as the bold adventurer swashes as much as he can, but the tempo and mood of the picture perceptibly hold him down."

On the other hand, Louella Parsons loved Ty *and* the film, for whatever that was worth. She had waged a one-woman vendetta against Orson Welles since *Citizen Kane,* his *roman à clef* film about her boss, William Randolph Hearst. Since she found *Prince of Foxes* to be estimable, she was hard-pressed to ignore Welles's portrayal. "Although Orson Welles is never my favorite actor," she wrote, "I must admit he doesn't overact too much as Borgia. This is the awesome Orson at his best, so if you like him at all, you won't find him too objectionable—although you can think of a dozen better actors Twentieth could have chosen."

In his absence, Twentieth perhaps chose a better actor to cast in roles Ty might have handled. The studio's pecking order was passing on from him to Clifton Webb to Gregory Peck. Henry King's two collaborations with the studio's newest major star—*Twelve O'Clock High* and *The Gunfighter*—were to be two of the most important pictures in the director's career. Peck gave even less of himself than Ty, thereby riveting the attention of the audience. *Twelve O'Clock High* was among the studio's top money-makers for the year, earning back $3,225,000, as did *Broken Arrow*. The studio's most prestigious picture of 1950, *All About Eve,* was also a big success, earning back $2,900,000. The most successful picture, however, was *Cheaper by the Dozen,* an innocuous Clifton Webb comedy, which earned $4,350,000. Neither of Ty's pictures that year was of great import to either him or his studio. While Peck was drawing raves from both critics and the public, the reception to Ty's second picture abroad, *The Black Rose,* would prove dispiriting. "Poor Mr. Power," a reviewer for *The New York Times* wrote, "looks like an actor, and when he reaches the court of Cathay and makes the bewildered inquiry, 'What am I doing here?' one might reasonably accept that as the ultimate comment on the film."

For Ty and Linda their stay in California was a three-month layover until they left to shoot another picture in the Philippines. It wasn't idle professional time, for during that period, Ty shot a quickie Western opposite Susan Hayward, *Rawhide,* its outdoor locations filmed at Lone Pine, California, a four-hour drive from the studio. His wardrobe on the two previous costume pictures had totaled almost ten thousand dollars. On this film, it was less than one hundred dollars. Ty was elated. "I don't have to worry about the crease in my pants when I sit down, because there isn't any crease."

Three weeks before the Powers were set to embark on the Lurline to Honolulu, the first lap of their journey to Manila, they announced that they would become parents in the fall of 1950. A newly made friend, Mario Lanza, accompanied them. Ty would fly from Honolulu to Manila, while Linda would take a more leisurely boat trip to join Ty and director Fritz Lang, while they shot *An American Guerilla in the Philippines.*

By this time, Ty's traveling habits were well instilled. Given the various studio toadies to meet him along the way, he could travel light, since most of his location shooting involved the wearing of costumes.

For Linda, however, it was a different matter. "She may start traveling light," Ty told Bob Thomas, "but she has a knack of finding places to buy things, no matter where we go."

Ty stayed over in Honolulu a few days after Linda sailed on the *President McKinley* for Manila. He then flew directly to Manila on March 31, to be met by a crowd of five thousand Filipinos at the airport, all demanding an autograph. He had to return to the plane, which taxied the length of the runway, where he was picked up by a limousine and whisked off to their hotel.

None of the principals had any great faith in the film they were making, particularly its venerable director, Fritz Lang, who explained his involvement by saying, "Even a director has to eat." Henry King had been originally set to direct and Fred MacMurray was going to star.

Shooting was scheduled to take place at a location in the hilly jungle region northwest of Manila. Because Linda was with him, Ty refused to travel by overland route, having heard that Hukbalahap guerillas had infiltrated almost to the suburbs of the city, and the roads were a perfect setup for an ambush. The Commander of United States Naval Forces in Manila lent Ty and eleven other members of the company his launch so that they could sail for Subic Bay, closer to the interior shooting location. Personnel and equipment were also shuttled by water.

Linda didn't stay long on location, choosing instead to take a few side trips to Bali and Hong Kong, returning shortly before the company folded up its tents.

The picture was a routine war drama, made on a relatively modest budget, depicting the ugliness of jungle warfare. Shooting was completed a week before the conflict in Korea broke out, giving it a timeliness and relevance to moviegoers, striking the right nerve at the right time for its audiences. Since he returned from the war, *The Razor's Edge* was the only unqualified success of the nine pictures Ty had starred in. A couple of the epic films had big grosses, but their budgets were even bigger. When he least expected and most needed it, Ty was about to enjoy a success. The studio, aware of the picture's timeliness, delayed release of *Rawhide* so that it could bring out *American Guerilla* earlier.

Ty didn't particularly expect a hero's welcome, but he thought that he might recoup the apparently dwindling respect held for him at Twentieth. Just as he and Linda were preparing to return to the United States, she had her second miscarriage. She flew to Bangkok, Cairo, and Rome to recuperate, while Ty returned to the United States with one of his costars, Micheline Presle. Patia Power met them at the Los Angeles Airport.

The Powers, by this time, had been married only a year and a half, but a pattern of separate travels was already being established. Each needed freedom, and perhaps license. If friends thought these separations were a visible crack in the foundation of their marriage, they kept their own counsel. Rumors of a rift had started soon after their marriage, and friends didn't expect it to last anyway.

They were reunited in London a month later as Ty began rehearsals for *Mr. Roberts*. He was working with two very distinct disadvantages. The pacing had to be more leisurely so that British audiences could understand the American slang-ridden dialogue. The set at the Coliseum Theatre, which had recently housed *Annie Get Your Gun,* was three times the size of the original production.

Patia Power made her first trip to Europe, as her son's guest, to see his opening. In a short time, she would be incapacitated by a series of small strokes, and Ty hired round-the-clock nursing care for her. She was rational enough at the moment, however, to enjoy her son's reception in the production. "This is the first time I've seen my son's name on a theatre," she said. "It looks good."

His performance looked as good to the reviewers, who were uncharacteristically generous, Ty being praised more for his ambition than his accomplishment. The London critic of the *Christian Science Monitor* found Ty's interpretation "beautifully quiet and well judged." John Barber of the *Herald Tribune* said Ty gave "the performance of his life as Mr. Roberts, his quietness redeeming the character from goody-goodiness." W. A. Darlington, correspondent for *The New York Times*, wrote "Personally I find Tyrone Power just a shade less right than Henry Fonda. In plays such as this, where accent is placed heavily on exact realism, it is high praise to say of a man that he never lets you remember that he is an actor. Mr. Fonda never let me remember. Mr. Power reminds me now and then. All the same, he gives a very pleasant performance as a very likeable character."

Ty's friend, Kurt Kasznar, was more realistic in his appraisal. He found that the sets dominated the story. "They built three decks instead of two. The production was so big, it could have been a major musical. I thought that Ty was absolutely ineffective."

Still, over that six-month period, Ty played before 250,000 people and hadn't disgraced himself. He'd also succeeded in getting the studio to rewrite his contract so that he could make what few pictures he owed them at a rate of one a year.

Linda had similarly enjoyed the stay in London. She met, along with her husband, such British notables as Lord and Lady Mountbatten, the Duchess of Kent, John and Mary Mills, the Richard Attenboroughs, Florence Desmond, and Jack Hawkins.

She was also seen around London in the company of several men while Ty trod the boards. Certainly, she couldn't be expected to hang around backstage every night. Her socializing could mean nothing . . . and everything.

When it became apparent that the show would soon close, Ty accepted a film assignment, *I'll Never Forget You,* a quite forgettable remake of *Berkeley Square,* recreating the part originally played by Leslie Howard, which was being shot in England.

While he prepared for the role, Linda posed for a semi-nude statue. Sculptor Peter Lambda had completed half the figure when Linda learned she was again pregnant. She told him she could no longer pose for him. Lambda decided to use a drape on the lower part of the statue, and thus completed the work.

Work on the picture, which costarred Ann Blyth, hadn't been

completed when Ty received an offer to make another film in South America. Because of her past miscarriages, he wanted to be near his wife. He was desperate to pass on the family name, as Linda well knew. This time, he was determined that she should carry the child for the full term.

The couple was touring the English countryside when they received a call from Scotland Yard. Their Mayfair apartment had been broken into, and all of Linda's jewels stolen. Also taken was a gold cigarette case given to Ty by Haile Selassie. Insurance covered the loss.

It was definitely time to return to the United States. Linda was already five months pregnant, and it would soon become hazardous for her to travel. One of the few acquisitions which they brought back from England was Mr. Roberts, a medium-sized black poodle. The Powers returned to California to discover that changes, few for the better, were occurring at Twentieth Century-Fox.

That spring, the financial problems of the studio resulted in all executives taking 50 percent pay cuts. Ty's salary was reduced from $5,000 a week to $3,500. He had an extravagant wife and a luxurious life-style. In addition, he and Linda were expecting a child in October, and they were planning to buy a larger house.

In June, he was assigned to yet another costume picture, *Lydia Bailey*. Such predictable casting didn't show any great faith in his growth as an actor. His career was regressing, artistically as well as financially. He was polite, but adamant. He wouldn't do the film.

Ty understood that, as an example to other contract players, he would have to be suspended. It was the first time he'd rebelled in his fifteen years there. The studio put him off salary for eight weeks.

He rather reasonably explained his action to Bob Thomas. "I've done five costume pictures in a row. That's too much for one actor. I think it's time I had a change of pace.

"You have to talk in a stilted kind of dialogue in costume pictures. I'd like to do a picture in which I can talk as normal people talk. I'd like to do a really smart comedy next—a regular parlor, bedroom, and bath sort of thing. It has been too many years since I had one.

"I hate to cause any trouble at times like these when the business is in such poor shape. But I look at it this way: There's no thrill left in the movie business any more. There's no more glory left, and it's silly to think that you can add anything to your bank account; it all goes to taxes. So I figure it's better to be doing something that you like to do."

Ty's life-style didn't become more modest during the suspension. He and Linda in fact bought a one-and-a-half-story Bermuda modern home on Copa del Oro Road in Bel-Air for the then extravagant price of eighty thousand dollars. They hoped to move in before the baby's birth.

They were staying at the Bel-Air Hotel, however, when a daughter was born on October 2. Ty was glad that Linda had been safely delivered. However, he still didn't have a son. The infant was named Romina Francesca, to commemorate Rome and the church in which her parents had been married.

Her birth coincided with the end of Ty's studio suspension. He reported back to Twentieth for *Diplomatic Courier,* a violent role in which he played a state department messenger. Ty had won a minor victory; it was a modern-dress picture.

During the filming, the Powers moved into their new house, having auctioned off the furniture from the Rockingham Road house beforehand. Ty also was promoted to captain in the marine reserve. Production of the film ended in late November, and Ty and Linda flew to New York for a three-week working vacation. They performed on three network radio shows together, while Linda starred alone on three television programs.

Any hopes that a modern-dress role would change his fortunes at the studio were dashed by the reaction to his performance. While not directly criticizing Henry Hathaway's competence as a director, Henry King noticed that Ty didn't convey his usual quiet strength in the picture. "Ty would get around with people," King said, "and they would have him overact. He had a tendency to sort of push on things a little bit. There were a lot of things I saw him in that he had overdone it completely." In this picture, King found that Ty was "trying, trying, trying all the time. It just took all the believability out of it."

His standing at Twentieth didn't improve with his next assignment, *Pony Soldier,* an arduous Western filmed in northern Arizona, his last commitment under his exclusive contract at the studio.

Ty still owed Twentieth two pictures, to be made in the next two years. It was expected that one, in 1953, would be *The Robe,* the first film to be produced in the new Cinemascope process.

Significantly, Ty told Linda he didn't want her joining him on location this time. She went to Mexico, leaving Romina with a nurse. While she was there, Ty wrote her a letter saying he wanted to get away from it all.

"Ty had a tremendous amount of unhappiness and frustration in his life," a bisexual friend of his said. "I'm sure he wasn't capable of satisfying Linda's emotional and sexual desires. Yet she stayed married to him. He was a name, and she was important for the first time. She'd think twice before giving all that up."

After the picture was completed and Ty returned to California, Twentieth wanted to make an adjustment. They weren't willing to include him in profit participation, yet they still wanted him to continue making pictures for them. Many of his films might not be money-winners, according to their curious way of bookkeeping, but they were still paying a great part of the studio's below-the-line costs.

There were too many unkept promises for Ty to show any great sense of gratitude now. During his last few pictures, he was assigned stories, directors, and costars that were indifferent in scope and ambition. The results were uniformly mediocre, even when the pictures turned a profit. Yet, if Twentieth was making money, Ty very apparently was not. He'd seen what Bill Goetz had accomplished at Universal-International.

Ty went to see his friend. "I'm broke," he confided. "Linda has just ruined me."

"What can you do about it?" Goetz asked.

"Do you think I could get the Jimmy Stewart treatment?"

"You've got yourself a deal," Goetz replied.

Ty would still make the Twentieth pictures he was committed

to, but as of now he was more committed to Bill Goetz. In late June of 1952, a moving van pulled up to the stars' building at Twentieth and removed his personal effects from his dressing room. One of the longest exclusive contracts in Hollywood history had come to an end.

CHAPTER

10

OCCASIONALLY IN INTERVIEWS, TY WOULD STRESS THAT HE WAS basically a man of spartan tastes who longed for the simple life. He wanted to keep the option open to return to a more ordered existence as life threatened to get away from him.

Ty had been thoroughly seduced by Hollywood, and he was an acquiescing, compliant victim. He loved being a movie star, with all its attendant idolatry and perquisites. His had been an open and beautiful young face, romantic and idealistic, seemingly without a care in the world.

As he returned from the war, he had turned into the embodiment of the Byronic hero, an image he at first fostered, then shied away from. It was uncomfortably close to his true core, Ty being a sad and melancholy man, brooding upon something mysterious and evil in his background which he could not—would not —explain.

Now, he was rapidly turning into the picture of Dorian Gray. Disillusionment and dissipation showed on his face. In moments of repose, there was a cynical, downward curl to his lips. The effort to be pleasant and convivial became a greater one. He was as trapped in a career going no place as he was by his material possessions.

In many ways his life wasn't ostentatious. He didn't have a

flashy wardrobe, but it was nevertheless an understated, expensive one. His collection of gold jewelry and cigarette cases bespoke quality and substance.

The collection of cars was his most visible self-indulgence. They included a Duesenberg, an Alfa Romeo, and a recently purchased twelve-thousand-dollar Bentley.

Twentieth had absorbed the costs of some of his indulgences. The apartment Ty and Linda had used in Rome actually belonged to the studio, but because the Powers loved the city so, it was almost on permanent loan to them. The plane he'd flown on his goodwill tours was also studio-owned. Over the hatch were the letters IGMFU. When Ty talked to Rock Hudson about the many hours he'd logged in that plane, he jokingly explained the meaning of the letters: I Got Mine. Fuck You. Those luxuries, however, were no longer automatically available to him.

The house he and Linda bought on Copa del Oro Road typified the impression he wanted to make on the outside world, which was at considerable variance to his privileged, overextended existence. From the road, it looked like a small unpretentious bungalow, incongruously dropped into a prime Bel-Air location. It opened up in the back, however, into an imposing two-story residence, looking down upon a beautiful pool. A terrace sixteen feet wide was built off the master bedroom and study, and it was where the Powers could accommodate as many as one hundred people for a sit-down dinner, as they often did.

It was a lavish life, the Powers and their infant daughter being attended by a butler, a housekeeper, and a governess. Yet it was offbeat to most of the Old Guard.

Then there was the notorious nude statue of Linda, cast in bronze from the plaster model. It created a great sensation when sculptor Peter Lambda exhibited it at a London gallery in 1951. Linda had it shipped to the house in California, where it was set near the pool between some camellia bushes. Some were scandalized, but Mrs. Goetz and her group were amused. "Nobody took it that seriously. There were too many other things to think about, too many things going on."

Much of Hollywood hadn't taken to Linda. Ty was seen as artistic and introspective, while Linda was the publicity-seeking hedonist, the siren luring him to destruction. A lot of friends from Ty's days with Annabella were conservative and didn't approve of Linda's carryings on. She had a flair for publicity, whether positive or not, and carried narcissism to an extreme unusual even for Hollywood. Her extravagance was also much talked about. As one critic put it, "She never met a dress she didn't like."

"For those days, she was very *outré*," Evie Johnson said. "Everyone expected her to behave more circumspectly. They were shocked at the Diego Rivera painting of her. She was wearing a fishnet top and you could see her breasts. It was a lovely painting, but before her time. Ty's old friends didn't approve, but he laughed it off."

During his marriage to Annabella, Ty had become bored with the distinguished continental types his first wife preferred to entertain. Now, he and his second wife were running with a younger, faster group of international jetsam. His first wife had a charming reserve, while Linda was more outgoing, more encompassing, and less discriminating in whom she invited to their home.

This extravagant life called for an equally extravagant income. That's when Ty turned to Bill Goetz.

Louis B. Mayer's son-in-law and his partner, Leo Spitz, merged their young independent International Picture Corporation with the near-moribund Universal Pictures in 1946. Both men served as production heads of the newly named Universal-International Pictures.

The merged studio had no stars, save Abbott and Costello, and Goetz hit upon a plan to acquire more. He and his wife Edie were fellow guests with Lew Wasserman, then an agent, at the home of Harry Cohn, the head of Columbia Pictures.

"I'd like Jimmy Stewart," Goetz told Wasserman.

"Billy," the agent replied, "you and everybody else wants Jimmy Stewart."

"But I want him in a different way," Goetz said.

"How different?"

"I want him for nothing."

Wasserman grinned. *"That's* different."

"If he likes a property that I give him," Goetz said, "it's up to me to make it as best I can. When it's over and the money's in on it, every bit of the profit is fifty-fifty."

"Well," Wasserman mused, "it sounds good to me, Bill. The only thing is he has to see the property."

The screenplay Goetz had in mind was a Western, *Winchester 73*. Two days after the script was delivered, Stewart called on the production head in his office. "Billy," he said, "you've got yourself an actor."

When he heard of the arrangement, Mayer was appalled.

"You're going to ruin the business," he told his son-in-law. "This way we have no control of actors."

"It's the only way I can survive, Dad," Goetz replied. "This is the future of the industry. You're sitting on a mound of gold at Metro. We have to move ahead."

Thus, the Jimmy Stewart treatment was born. It went on for eight pictures with the lanky actor before Goetz left Universal to form William Goetz Productions. Jimmy Stewart made $750,000 in the first film, his take increasing so that he received twice that amount in his eighth, making him as Edie Goetz described him, "a multi-multimillionaire."

Now Ty would be getting the Jimmy Stewart treatment too.

"Here's a script," Goetz told him, "called *Mississippi Gambler*. I've got sets for it. It can be done for a good price."

Ty liked the script. It was a good, swashbuckling role that wouldn't challenge him.

"Who's the leading lady?" he asked.

"There's someone on the lot named Piper Laurie," Goetz replied.

"No," Ty replied, "I'd like Jean Peters."

Goetz, trying not to show his exasperation, patiently said, "Let me explain something to you, Tyrone. Jean Peters is getting the same amount of money at Twentieth, like three hundred a week, that this girl is getting here. If I borrow her to play this, they'll charge me thirty thousand dollars."

Ty didn't feel that amount was untoward in a high-budget production.

"Then," Goetz told him, "you don't understand the Jimmy Stewart treatment. You add that kind of money here and there, and there's no profit at the end."

Ty saw his point. Any such fripperies would affect the amount of money he would take out of the picture. That Piper Laurie turned out to be an extremely gifted actress was incidental to the enterprise.

At home, Linda, who had repeatedly said she had retired from films to become a housewife, was insisting on returning to her acting career. Ty was losing the fight. Linda had read the script and thought she would be ideal for the part that Piper Laurie was about to be given.

"Okay," Ty agreed, "but so there'll be peace at home, would you test Linda for me?"

Goetz agreed to go through the motions. Linda was very disappointed when she didn't get the part. She never realized that she'd never been seriously considered.

Ted Richmond was the line producer assigned to *Mississippi Gambler*. He and Ty got along so well that they later decided to form a joint production company.

The contract players at Universal-International were encouraged to watch the shooting of all pictures made on the lot. Perhaps they could pick up some pointers. As a result, Rock Hudson—well on his way to becoming a star himself—often stood on the sidelines as the saga of a riverboat gambler and his ladies was filmed.

Ty's taste in clothing was casual and conservative. He liked houndstooth sport jackets or tweed ones with leather elbow patches, either type usually worn with gray flannel slacks. He'd liked a cologne Keenan Wynn wore, Aphrodisia, and Evie gave him a bottle. He used that scent from that point on.

Hudson noticed that this was his uniform whenever Ty reported for work. "I found it a little strange that he would dress in a sport coat and tie to go to work at six in the morning, since he'd be changing into a costume as soon as he got there. It was unnecessary really."

Ty wasn't happy that while he was filming *Mississippi Gambler* at Universal-International, Linda was working for Stanley Kramer at Columbia in *The Happy Time*.

Studio head Harry Cohn wanted to team Ty with Rita Hayworth in *Solomon and Sheba,* and thought casting Linda in a studio film might persuade Ty to come to an agreement with the studio. Although he'd make three pictures later at Columbia, the tactic still didn't endear Cohn to Ty Power. The biblical epic fell through and passed on to other hands.

To her credit, Linda delivered an impressive performance. She was working with two actors who were Ty's good friends, Kurt Kasznar and Louis Jourdan.

Ty and Kasznar met through Claude Dauphin. When *The Happy Time* was bought for films, Kasznar was signed to play the role he created on the stage. It was then that he and Ty became close.

"I'd known Ty rather perfunctorily before," he recalled. "I always found him to be very cultivated. He spoke some French . . . he could order immaculately . . . and Italian not so well."

Kasznar recalled that Ty would bring back Tyrolean jackets from Switzerland, and that he wore them with black tie. Jean Negulesco and his wife had a party to open a rumpus room in their Beverly Hills house, its walls covered with works by a painter the director had discovered named Bernard Buffet.

Dauphin announced the guests as they walked in. When Ty, in his Swiss jacket, walked in with Linda, the French actor called out, "Mr. and Mrs. Tyrol Power."

At another party, Ty and Linda were getting better acquainted with Rock Hudson, who had just made a breakthrough as a major star. A butler was passing a tray of hors d'oeuvres, and Linda took a deviled egg. As she brought it toward her mouth, the yolk mixture flew out of her hand and landed in her hair, styled in a poodle cut for *The Happy Time*. Ty, as Hudson recalled, got hysterical. The broad outrageous stroke and the practical joke, and not the subtle witticism one would expect from a man of his refinement, were indicative of Ty's sense of humor. Linda, however, was not amused.

The united front the Powers most often presented to the public was breaking apart. Ty had become involved at the studio with a bit player named Anita Ekberg. Linda confronted him, and demanded he stop seeing the other woman. He wasn't of a mind to, suggesting that he and Linda might start discussing the possibility of divorce. There the discussion ended. The impasse was solved by Bill Goetz, who was unaware that Ty's extramarital affair was causing problems at home. When he discovered its existence, he quickly dropped Anita Ekberg from the picture. Ty still didn't understand. Such frivolities were definitely *not* part of the Jimmy Stewart treatment.

Shooting on *Mississippi Gambler* ended in July. Shortly thereafter, Ty and Linda took a young British couple, Edmund and Tita Purdom, to Mexico on a vacation. Linda and Tita Phillips, who'd danced with the Sadler's Wells Ballet, had attended school together in Israel. Her husband, Purdom, with seven years of experience on the London stage, had come to New York to play with Laurence Olivier and Vivien Leigh in *Caesar and Cleopatra,* and was consequently signed to a featured role in a Twentieth film, *The Titanic.*

Wherever the two couples went, Ty was mobbed. "If anyone asked who I was," Purdom later recalled, "he just waved his hand and said, 'My kid brother,' and they never gave me a second glance."

When they returned from Mexico, the lease on the Purdoms' apartment had expired; they were invited to stay in the Powers' guest house until they found another place. They later moved to a house in Beverly Hills which Bill Gallagher found for them.

The bare-stage reading of *Don Juan in Hell* was considered the greatest triumph of the previous theatrical season. Now, Charles Laughton was adapting and preparing for production Stephen Vincent Benét's narrative poem, *John Brown's Body,* which won a Pulitzer Prize in 1929. It was both an epic and human story, set in the Civil War, of a divided land and divided lovers. Laughton and producer Paul Gregory felt Raymond Massey would be the ideal choice for Abraham Lincoln; that Judith Anderson, who'd played Laughton's consort in the recently completed *Salome,* could supply the female roles in all their infinite variety; that Ty would add visual appeal to the production. The three stars would sometimes narrate events, other times recite poetry, then portray several characters each. They would move back and forth from one microphone to another to suggest movement, while the Walter Schumann chorus sang background music and supplied the sounds of trains, guitars, crowds at a station, and gale-force winds.

Ty was fascinated with the concept, in which the actors and the chorus would be attired in contemporary evening clothes silhouetted against a stark setting, narrating the history of the Civil War.

Publicity releases announcing his association with Laughton stated that Ty had turned down the starring part in *The Robe,* Twentieth's first Cinemascope picture, with its attendant salary of $250,000, to perform in *John Brown's Body.* It was a face-saving distortion, for Ty had actually been passed over—as had Gregory Peck and Laurence Olivier—when Richard Burton was handed the star part of Marcellus. Ty would make three more films at Twentieth. He no longer had any illusions about his influence there. Now that the studio no longer considered him a great star, he could go about his business of developing himself as an actor.

The company started rehearsals at Laughton's house on Curson Avenue in Hollywood. The actor-director's instructions to Ty were particularly apt. "When you come out on the stage," he said, "you will be the fellow who is going to recite some stirring lines and portray some interesting characters. But you will also be the monster, made up of all the characters you have played on the screen. Many people will come to see the monster. You must go out there and dispose of him with a little speech which demonstrates that you can talk and breathe and move. Then you must draw the people along to an interest in the story we're going to tell."

Laughton understood Ty's quiet authority and built on that. He refused to allow him to indulge in theatrics and sentimentality. In training him to deliver his lines with the greatest simplicity, Laughton was helping to create an imposing theatrical presence.

Elsa Lanchester, Laughton's wife, who'd appeared with Ty in two previous films, had never really known him. "Usually, I find good-looking people very boring," she said. "Ty was very kind and helpful and a most gentle man. Yet, I thought he had a womanish streak. There was something very gentle and feminine about his handshake."

She knew Ty no better when her husband was directing him. The English couple had come to an agreement about Laughton's homosexuality. They simply refused to talk about it. They went their own ways professionally as well.

"I kept out of the way of all of Charles's projects," Miss Lanchester said. The living room of their Hollywood house had been walled off and an outside entrance constructed so that Laughton could use it for his drama classes, which met there three times a week.

"Charles didn't gossip about his affairs, and I wasn't faintly interested," she said. "I know Charles adored Tyrone Power as a beauty. He was determined to make this straight actor with a beautiful face into a good actor. Charles believed Ty would become a very fine one. I know they had many long discussions about theater."

Miss Lanchester, although she never knew it for sure, suspected that Ty was bisexual. "Charles protected him on that score completely." She was considerably upset when, after returning from a stage tour, she discovered that Laughton had given Ty a painting by Siqueiros, the Mexican artist, worth several thousand dollars.

"That was very cruel of Charles. He knew I liked that painting better than anything in the house. Looking back, perhaps there was a reason Charles gave it to him. I do know that Ty clung to Charles. He was learning a great deal about acting from him."

The "traveling poem," as someone called it, had its first reading on November 1, 1952, at the Lobero Theatre in Santa Barbara, California. From there it moved to Pasadena and, the Los Angeles Philharmonic Auditorium suddenly unavailable, then to the auditorium of Beverly Hills High School.

Van and Evie Johnson chartered a bus and invited many mutual friends for the performance in Pasadena. Once she saw it, Evie understood why Ty was so excited about the production. It was a marvelous showcase for his voice.

When the production played in Beverly Hills, the same contract player from Universal who'd watched Ty work in *Mississippi Gambler*, sneaked in backstage with a buddy.

"I was a terrific movie fan," Rock Hudson recalled. "I used to see almost every movie. My favorite actor was Spencer Tracy. I'd think of Lana Turner and I couldn't sleep. She was just *it*. I was enamored of almost everybody. There were very few movie stars I didn't like. One was Errol Flynn. It was a silly thing. He reminded me of my stepfather, whom I didn't like at all.

"I liked Tyrone Power tremendously on the screen. He was so incredibly good-looking. His features were sculptured almost. His eyes and eyebrows were his best features. It isn't the spoken word in films. It's what's behind it. Then he had that marvelous speaking voice. I don't think people fully appreciated it. It was so much a part of his charm."

When Ty saw Hudson and his friend backstage, he looked inquiringly at them. "Are you part of this production?" he asked.

"No, Mr. Power," Hudson replied. Sheepishly, he admitted the two had crashed because they wanted to see the show.

Ty invited them to see it from backstage. A couple of chairs were placed for the two young men in the wings.

For Hudson, it was his first time backstage. He quickly became aware of the difference between illusion and reality when, at the end of a long speech, Judith Anderson grandly floated off the stage in her yellow chiffon gown. No sooner was she in the wings than she hawked and spit in a corner.

At the end of the second act, Ty suggested Hudson and his friend sit in the front row, which was almost empty.

Despite Ty's courtesies, Hudson couldn't fathom the play. And yet he would do the same one twenty-five years later.

"I was too young and therefore bored with it," Hudson recalled. "I'd never read it. It was too deep for me. The way it was staged was not very interesting. There was a Greek chorus upstage right, and three podiums in front, behind which the three principals stood and talked, pretending to read it off the script. I only got excited about *John Brown's Body* when I read it later. The writing was beautiful. Benét could describe things in such few words, and that was what hooked me."

The pace was exhausting. In ten weeks, *John Brown's Body* would play in sixty-eight cities. The bus in which the company toured drove through blizzards and rainstorms. Raymond Massey was bedridden by a lingering cold, and Laughton took over his part. In several cities Judith Anderson was sick with pleurisy, but the show went on. Only Laughton and Ty withstood the physical ordeal. Ty had an emotional one to deal with as well. Linda, he was told, had been involved in a scratching, hair-pulling fight with Lita Baron at a party in Hollywood. The other woman objected to Linda's overly attentive behavior with her husband Rory Calhoun.

The tour was interrupted during Christmas week, and Ty headed to Nassau to be a houseguest of friends and to have yet another confrontation with Linda. He wanted a divorce.

Linda countered with an announcement of her own. She was expecting another child. Ty was shocked and confused. After a long discussion, the two decided they should give their marriage another try. As he returned to the tour, which would play several Midwestern dates, he suggested Linda visit her mother in Mexico City.

When *John Brown's Body* played in Cincinnati, Ty ran into Wil Wright, who was visiting in the city. His old friend came away from the meeting with the realization that Ty's age, although he was not yet forty, was beginning to show, and badly. The fast living and hard drinking were beginning to take their toll.

During this period, Ty went for a drive after an evening performance with Laughton and Paul Gregory. They stopped by a lake, and the three men got out. As they paused by the still waters, the very private Ty opened up. He talked about his religious beliefs and his spirituality. Laughton, who was not devout, could barely disguise his contempt for what he considered half-baked theories of the deity and man's place in the universe. Laughton couldn't ignore the contradiction. Ty was talking about his ascetic nature at the same time he was indulging his too worldly appetites. Yet, tortured as Laughton was about his homosexuality, a fact his wife attested to, how much more anguish was pent up in the other man who fervently believed in a disapproving, vengeful God?

That same God, however, couldn't approve of the lack of mutual commitment in Ty's marriage to Linda. At a time when he was gaining more assurance as an actor, he was feeling most insecure about himself as a man. He needed more time alone. Ty wrote to Linda in Mexico City:

My Dearest,
    The news you had for me threw everything into reverse . . . It just seems we are getting farther and farther apart . . . We cannot help hurting each other . . . This is a hated letter to write but I believe it is time to be honest . . . I can't give you what you want most—understanding.

The touring company was based in Chicago, making one-night stands at cities in the area. Linda sent Romina and her nurse back to California while she flew to confront Ty. When she arrived, she discovered another woman had recently arrived in Chicago to also force a decision from Ty. Anita Ekberg. Their affair had never truly ended. Passionate discussions were again held. Ty again agreed to give his marriage another try. The Scandinavian actress returned to California. Linda stayed on.

On January 23, 1953, *John Brown's Body* played at the Orpheum Theatre in Springfield, Illinois. That same night, a local high school was holding graduation exercises.

Weldon Culhane, then eighteen, didn't see how he could attend both events. He went to his principal and asked that the graduation rites be postponed, and was condescendingly told that he was only one person and others wouldn't adjust their schedules to accommodate his.

He went through all the preliminaries for the ceremony—the renting of cap and gown, attending rehearsals—but on that night he was downtown waiting for the touring production to start.

"I grew up waiting and hoping for something to happen in my life," he recalled. "When I knew the play was coming to Springfield, I began collecting all the clippings about it. I saw all of Tyrone Power's movies all over again. I can't say I saw them because they were so fabulous. I went to see him. I wouldn't even hear the sound. I would just look at him and fantasize."

Culhane knew the Orpheum well. He was virtually the manager of a theater on the opposite side of town, because the man in charge of it was an alcoholic and his duties had fallen on the young man.

He made his way backstage to the Orpheum. He went to the dressing room area. The door marked MR. POWER was slightly ajar. Looking in, he saw a makeup table. He was curious to see what was on it.

He was standing in front of it, looking at the eyebrow pencil, the cold cream, a leather notebook, a bound copy of the script, when he saw through the mirror that Ty was standing at the door.

The boy stammered. "I was just looking at your makeup and things." Embarrassed and apologetic, he started for the door.

Ty smiled. "You don't have to leave."

"I don't?"

"No," Ty replied. "Why don't you stay?"

Young Culhane poured out all his pent-up excitement, the missed graduation, his fascination with movies. Ty, by his understanding attitude, made him feel comfortable.

In a short time, Bill Gallagher walked in.

"I have to get dressed now," he told Weldon. "Could you step outside?"

When Ty came out of his dressing room, he asked the boy if he had a ticket for the performance.

"Yes!" he answered. "I have my seat right down there in front."

"Well, have you ever seen a performance from backstage?"

"No."

"Would you like to?"

"Oh, yes!"

Ty asked a stagehand to bring Weldon a stool, and placed it on the edge of the stage.

"I sat there and watched the whole performance," he recalled. "I was totally immersed in this fantasy thing. Tyrone Power, the great movie star, was here. I had shaken his hand. I had talked to him. He had put his hand on my shoulder."

After the performance, members of the audience came backstage. Linda arrived, wearing a long mink coat. "She had the most beautiful face I'd ever seen," Weldon said, "and that beautiful red hair."

Ty disengaged himself from some admirers and walked over to Weldon.

"Did you enjoy the performance?" he asked.

"Yes, Mr. Power," the boy replied.

"We're staying in Decatur," Ty said, "but we're leaving from the Wabash Railroad Station tomorrow morning for Chicago. If you'd like to talk further, I'll be there about ten o'clock."

Weldon watched the other people congregate around the stars. Gradually, the crowd backstage started to disperse. Again Ty came over to him. "Thank you for coming," he said. "Maybe I'll see you tomorrow."

"Oh, yes!" Weldon said. "You will!"

The boy left the theater, walking in the cold and snow to his home. Everyone in the family was asleep. He took out a suitcase, packed some clothes, and walked over to the Springfield bus station. He got on the first available bus to Decatur, then took a taxi to the train station there. He put his grip by a big column and waited the rest of the night until morning.

Several limousines pulled up outside the train station at about the time Ty said he would be there. Girls in the chorus were in the first one, which was followed by a second which bore Judith Anderson and Raymond Massey and his wife. Ty and Linda were in the third, followed by a station wagon with all their luggage.

The group sat down on a long bench. Weldon looked around the column at them. "I didn't know what to do," he said. "In my own fantasy, I guess I'd already been with him. I didn't know if I should face them. I felt that Linda would know. They would all know. I didn't want to embarrass him, yet I wanted to be there. I felt I belonged. I looked around the column one more time. Judith Anderson looked up at that moment and noticed me. She spoke to Ty, who looked over and motioned me to come over."

"This is the young man we met last night," Ty told the others. "I'm surprised to see you here. How nice of you to see us off."

"I wanted to."

Ty rose and started walking away from the group. Weldon followed.

"I thought you'd be here," he told the boy.

"Oh, yes," Weldon said. "I planned on it."

"The train is going to be here in fifteen minutes. We're going to Chicago. Do you want to go?"

"I have my suitcase."

"Good," Ty told him. "I'll get you a ticket. But don't you think that when you leave Chicago, it would be better to go back to Springfield?"

Weldon agreed.

Arrangements were made for the young man to accompany the group on the train. He was sitting in the coach section, when Gallagher invited him to Ty's compartment. Linda was visiting with Judith Anderson at the time. The two talked for a short while. Ty informed Weldon that arrangements had been made for him to stay in the Drake Hotel, where the actor also would be staying.

Over the next few days, Ty would call Weldon, telling him he would be coming down to his room for a beer.

"The first few days nothing happened," Weldon said. "The way I looked at him, he knew I desired him. It was a cat and mouse teasing. I saw very little of Linda. I didn't know if she was there all that time or not, but I was nervous about it."

On the third night that Weldon was cooped up in his hotel room, there was a knock on the door. Ty stood there. He walked over to the bed and lay down.

"I'm tired," he told the boy. He kicked off his shoes. "Why don't you come over by me?"

"That was the first time," Weldon said. "I certainly wasn't well versed on what one was to do. All I knew is that it was exactly what I desired. Ty didn't seduce me. I was perhaps more forward and direct than he was. It was a very mutual agreement about what went on and what we did. I felt warm and close and needed. He cuddled. He liked to cuddle. He filled a tremendous emptiness in my life, and yet he made me feel that I was very important to him."

The day before the troupe left Chicago, Weldon called his mother to tell her where he was. "She was worried about me," he said. "I hadn't even left a note, but I was afraid she wouldn't let me go if I told her. And nothing was going to stop me from going.

I went home. I felt different, more important, bigger. I must have matured five years in that one short week."

As *John Brown's Body* moved East, preparing for the February opening in New York, Weldon got an Illinois state job and started saving his money. Every time he saw a picture of Ty in a magazine, he'd notice the clothes he wore and would copy them. He bought a plaid sport jacket similar to one Ty wore in a publicity picture. He bought V-neck sweaters in all colors and tied the sleeves around his neck, as he had seen Ty do. He had come to know a star intimately, and he wanted to be exactly like him.

After all the trepidation and the self-doubts, the onus of living up to the gifts of a brilliant father, the jangled nerves as he faced the severe Broadway critics, who could take the credit: an actor who had finally realized his potential or a director who molded a performance that was failure-proof? The triumph was the sweetest of his life. No Academy Award could compare—throughout his career he would never even be nominated—with the reception to Ty's performance as *John Brown's Body* opened on February 14 at the New Century Theatre. A standing ovation yet. A few critics would say that the production was too static, but none of them faulted Ty's performance.

Brooks Atkinson of *The New York Times* wrote about Ty, "Let it be said at once that he is worthy of the company he keeps. For he, too, acts with candor, skill and understanding, and he can play a big scene with the authority of an actor who has mastered it selflessly."

"Mr. Power proves to be a performer of outstanding ability," John Mason Brown wrote in *The Saturday Review*. "His range is wide, his skill beyond challenge, and his acting out of the battle of Gettysburg is a virtuoso achievement of the highest kind."

"With his clear, Midwestern voice and manner, Tyrone Power seems the most American, the most unobtrusive, the most effective performer," *Time* concluded. "In contrast, Judith Anderson's manner seems at times a little too elevated, Raymond Massey's a little too elocutionary."

Tyrone Power's triumph was, at last, a promise kept. When interviewers suggested he might be America's answer to Sir

Laurence Olivier, that he possessed the looks and voice and intensity to play similar heroic roles, Ty was overwhelmed. Never had he been so extravagantly praised.

Yet, as he told one reporter, he'd be more interested in "getting a play that would revive what might be called the romantic theater . . . not romantic in the sense of a romance with a woman. But do you remember the great parts John Barrymore played? That kind of theater made a great impression on me."

He was perhaps premature in his presumption. "Ty knew that he was a great movie star," Kurt Kasznar said, "but he also knew the live performance is the most pure acting there is. The greatest tragedy of Ty's life was that he wanted to be a great stage actor. It never worked, except once, in *John Brown's Body.*"

Perhaps the greater achievement had been Laughton's after all. Ty, however, reveled in his triumph. He was also delighted with the news that, although it was not a distinguished picture, *Mississippi Gambler* was Universal's hottest ticket of the year. He already stood to make $750,000 from it, and the picture had yet to be released abroad, where Ty was still hugely popular.

He was on the crest of the wave again. After *John Brown's Body* ended its scheduled tour, Ty and Linda took a two-month vacation in Europe, returning to the United States when she was in her seventh month of pregnancy. His usually somber mood was ebullient. Not even his next commitment at Twentieth could dampen his enthusiasm . . . or so he thought until he read the script of *King of the Khyber Rifles*. There was no way he was going to get mired in that banal dialogue, not after he had soared on Benét's poetry. After much grumbling by studio executives, Ty compromised and his objections were partially satisfied.

Henry King also found the script to be sheer hokum. But if he was going to direct it, he was going to try to make it an entertainment.

When he reported to the Pico Boulevard lot for shooting of interior scenes, Ty found that his old apartment in the stars' building was assigned to Clifton Webb. He never went near it. His old dressing room, still luxuriously appointed, stood empty while he worked on the lot. Here again, he was given one that was far less grand, a smaller lean-to usually assigned to featured players. If this was his punishment for balking at the script, it was a petty one.

The Powers entertained during the filming, and Darryl and Virginia Zanuck were among their guests. Ty might have told Linda about the mistreatment at the studio. Linda wasn't overly cordial to Zanuck, and he and his wife left rather early. Bill and Edie Goetz were still present when Ty started yelling at Linda. "He's my boss! You're supposed to be polite to him!" The Goetzes left soon after. They stopped seeing the Powers for a while.

While on location in Lone Pine, California, Ty gave a revealing interview to John Maynard of *Modern Screen*. About the picture, he said, "I guess it's fine for the studio. I've made enough of them. Dashing fellow under the kepi, and all that. Stand the varmints off and tell the little lady to keep her head down. But the edge wears away and wears away until one fine day you're looking down a one-way street and no room to turn around. That's when you need an out . . .

"Work is the actor's only provision for security. It's his back door, the escape hatch . . . I don't care how well upholstered a vacuum is, it's still a vacuum. Nature hates its guts, as somebody has said before me. And better. You go forward, you go backward, or you die . . .

"I'd be a fool not to know this thing's going to blow up. My association with pictures, I mean. I'm pushing forty. The younger men are pushing up behind me. The kids are rushing up behind *them*. But the trouble with that figure of speech is, they're not boosting me, they're dislodging my handhold, and sooner or later, there's not going to be room for everybody. All right. Last come, first served. That's how I got there, too. But now's the time to get the net ready, the one that has to break the fall. Not later."

From that point on, Ty suggested, he would make his two pictures a year, then remove himself from the movie industry. One of them might be filmed in Rome for his own newly formed production company and would be financed by Italian interests.

Despite his many reservations about *King of the Khyber Rifles*, it turned out to be a pleasant entertainment, fully capitalizing on the potential of Cinemascope. Bosley Crowther of *The New York Times* found it "a lot of picture to look at, and . . . the best one in Cinemascope we've seen." *Time,* on the other hand, observed, "the wider they come, the harder they flop." It had a moderately successful return at the box office.

Twentieth, however, had laid claims to largeness if not to greatness with its innovative process. There seemed to be no room for Ty in the studio's long range plans, which were evolving into a series of excesses. What other studio would, after all, have under contract at the same time such sex symbols as Marilyn Monroe, Jane Russell, and Jayne Mansfield?

Ten days after production of the picture was completed, on September 13, 1953, Linda gave birth to a second daughter, who was named Taryn Stephanie.

"Linda was a very good mother when the babies were little," Evie Johnson recalled, "even after she and Ty went their own way."

Kurt Kasznar agreed. "Linda's girls always had governesses and were overprotected. She brought them up incredibly well, even after the divorce. It was intelligent upbringing, all done without the father. It was Linda's status symbol to bring them up well."

A few weeks after the baby's birth, Anne Baxter replaced Judith Anderson as *John Brown's Body* began another tour. Linda accompanied Ty throughout much of it.

In a telephone interview from Boston, he explained to Hedda Hopper why he had turned to the stage: "I was in a kind of dead-end street and thought it behooved me to get myself another exit somewhere . . . I opened another door, which has allowed me to go on and do some things . . . I had a feeling that some day I was going to have to do something else than develop a strong right arm and a good seat on a horse."

He added that he would only take percentage deals on future pictures.

By the time the tour arrived in San Francisco, Ty and Linda's relationship had forever been altered.

"Some things cannot be measured in terms of blame," she wrote in her autobiography, "only in terms of difference, devastating difference. Had I been prepared for this change, the shock might have been less, for sensitivity had been abandoned wholly for sensuality, as though he had chosen to forget entirely the people we had been, and now wanted to inaugurate a new relationship uncluttered with any vestige of sentiment. I could not fathom his thoughts or what he felt, for he said nothing, but I was left wondering if we could ever know each other again, and after that night; that we were once more man and wife had been made meaningless."

That she should write so cryptically on matters pertaining to Ty, which Hollywood insiders knew about, showed an uncharacteristic reserve on her part.

Ty and Linda hosted Mexican brunches every Sunday. Whenever they planned a more formal gathering, set decorator Walter Scott was called in to dress up the house, bringing in furniture and accessories from the studio.

After one such occasion, a colleague asked Scott, "Did you get invited to the party?"

"No," he replied.

"Well, I hear it turned out to be an orgy," came the reply.

From this sort of idle talk the rumors started building. It was bruited about that sex-related rituals were going on at the house on Copa del Oro Road. British actor Michael Rennie was reported to be deeply involved. Ty's Old Guard friends—Bill and Edie Goetz and the Van Johnsons included—gradually withdrew from his circle. If any of them frankly told him why they didn't see as much of him as they had in the past, he would turn red with embarrassment, then almost choleric.

His private life had been circumspect up to now. Ty's interpretation of what constituted good taste had recently caused him to send a painting, showing him stripped to the waist, to the Twentieth warehouse for storage. Now he seemed to stop caring. His Catholic guilt was overwhelming, suffocating him, demanding retribution. Discretion was forgotten. Sex acts, once private and confidential, turned exhibitionistic. Punishment was near.

Despite his preponderantly gay clientele, Smitty Hanson was also bisexual. He could see that on Ty's side, his was an open marriage, and he wondered if Linda was as sexually active as her husband. Smitty suggested they might make up a sexual threesome

some time. Ty flashed an angry look. "She wouldn't be interested," he curtly replied.

Smitty, while serving at a party, met a blonde European actress who was. "I think he's *fabulous!*" she exclaimed about Ty. The girl refused to believe that Ty had any homosexual leanings. When Smitty set up the evening, he consequently told Ty to play it straight.

After dinner, they returned to a house in the Hollywood Hills, which Smitty was temporarily occupying while the owners were away. Throughout his association with Ty, he would meet with him at a series of such houses belonging to absentee owners, who had entrusted the keys to their homes and their contents to the totally reliable Smitty.

"We got high," he recalled, "and smoked a joint, and we pretended that the liquor made us do something we wouldn't normally do. We didn't really go all out, but got on the fringes a little bit. He didn't really do me. I did him. I was the fall guy as far as she was concerned."

Ty and the girl hit it off so well that they began seeing each other exclusively. When he wanted a girl, nothing would stand in his way. Ray Sebastian recalled a previous entanglement of Ty's. An actress had followed Ty to Europe, leaving another actor in the lurch. The actor angrily confronted Ty. "Look," he said, "I've got about two thousand dollars invested in fur coats and clothes and things for this broad. Now I'm going to lose it."

Ty reached into his pocket and took out a wad of bills. He peeled off some money and handed it to the actor. "Does this take care of it?" he asked. The other man accepted the money and left.

Ty got a bargain in all respects. He was buying cheaply a girl he found more sexually exciting than anyone, male or female . . . though what she would cost him in the long run was considerable. He was preserving the goodwill of an actor he liked and was assured of the other man's discretion.

This wasn't a quality he always found in other people. An article in an exposé magazine had appeared about this time, in which a past mistress was described as having worn Ty out sexually. When Ray Sebastian pointed out the article to him, Ty was incensed. For the first time that Sebastian could remember, Ty described to him in detail a sexual affair of his.

"If that girl had been educated," Ty told his makeup man, "she'd have been a great lay. But she was just an ordinary lay."

Sebastian asked, "Is it true that you couldn't satisfy her?"

"Why should I kill myself," Ty asked, "to satisfy a nymphomaniac?"

The two men discussed what Ty should do about the article. He decided to let the matter blow over, as it soon did. It nevertheless left Ty bitter. He and the girl had parted, seemingly without any mutual resentments. Now it was revealed to the public what the girl had never bothered to directly reveal to Ty. He hadn't known her at all. Otherwise he would have sensed her lack of prudence.

Ty himself, in the company of the girl Smitty had introduced him to, wasn't being discreet either these days. Hollywood is the most gossip-ridden town in the world. Syndicated columnists couldn't help but know that he was involved in orgy scenes. Because they liked him and were generally supportive of the film industry, they chose not to hear and consequently not report the ugly words. Not that other equally famous actors didn't occasionally participate in such group sex. It was that Ty and the girl attended such goings-on with the regularity of a Wednesday-night poker club.

Smitty was among five men and three women at one such gathering. The group was drinking and chatting in the living room of a secluded ranch-style house off of one of Beverly Hills' canyons. At the far end of the living room was a mezzanine loft reached by a ladder, lighted by candles, the deep-pile-carpeted area unfurnished except for a dozen or so floor pillows and a butler's tray holding fixings for drinks.

One of the women had recently arrived from New York, a chain-smoking brunette actress with a well-publicized contempt for the film medium. If Ty was surprised to see this woman, whom he knew casually, he showed no indication of it.

Liquor loosened the few inhibitions the group possessed. Drugs were still not a part of the Hollywood party scene. A deeply tanned young actor made the first move, picking up the girl from New York and carrying her over to the ladder. He climbed only one rung before he and the girl fell to the floor. She laughed, picked herself up, and scooted up to the loft, the actor in mock pursuit.

The others followed. Up in the loft, its beamed ceilings extending from the living room, clothes were hurriedly strewn. The methodical Ty removed and folded his clothes and stacked them neatly in a corner.

The deeply tanned actor, with few preliminaries, was lying on top of the girl, her legs spread as he pounded angrily into her. Ty was looking at the buttocks of the younger man, which were noticeably paler than the rest of his body, as if he'd been sunning for days in bikini trunks. If Ty had the instinct to momentarily caress that erotically thrusting male bottom, he knew better. This was the ultimate taboo.

Smitty looked at Ty's girl. Their eyes met. She finally understood. At this point in his life, Ty had to see and smell the sexual excitement of other males before he too could become aroused. The girl didn't judge. She threw her arms around Ty's upper body. She was happy to have him on any terms.

On a few past occasions, Smitty had brought in another man to join him and Ty. Should he want to see the second hustler again, he always arranged it through Smitty.

"Not that it made any difference to me," Smitty said. "It didn't matter if he wanted to see somebody I fixed him up with on the side. Ty didn't do this. He always called me to arrange the meeting."

Hanson was providing similar sexual service for two other movie stars, one who today is considered one of the immortals of film and the other a popular action hero of the 1940s. All three actors, Ty included, were so circumspect that talk of homosexual activities was almost nonexistent. "Ninety-nine percent of the people wouldn't believe they were gay," Hanson said. "Very few queens thought they were gay. As for Ty, I would venture to say that you could not drum up ten men that he had been with . . . honestly been with. Sure, from time to time, he might even have been with this one and that one. But he was not notorious . . . ever!"

One night, the two were alone. "There were times," Smitty

recalled, "when he didn't look well only because he was putting so many hours in, getting up at the crack of dawn and working. It was just a case of being tired. With Ty, it was also a case of not being able to sleep. He was sitting up in bed, and his eyes were opened wide when I turned over. I woke up the next morning and he was long gone."

As for his appearance, Ty was having more off days than good. If a man is responsible for his face at the age of fifty, his heavy-drinking, fast life and his inner turmoils had caused him to reach that telling milestone ten years ahead of time. When he looked into the mirror, he couldn't have been happy with what he saw. His face was bloated, there were heavy bags under his eyes, and his chin line was so jowly that it was difficult for the movie camera to capture that once classic profile.

What showed now, and what by subtle implications others had gathered, since he would never inflict his misery on others, was that Ty had never been a contented man.

Ty was on a fitness kick. He had to get in shape for a new picture, in which he would age from eighteen to seventy. He was highly excited by the prospect of working with director John Ford.

He was driving Edie Goetz home from a party at Claudette Colbert's and discussing the production. "And get this, Edie," he said, "I'm getting a percent of the gross against the profit." His further explanation of the deal was totally confusing.

Mrs. Goetz, who had been raised in the business, didn't know what he was talking about, but she found his enthusiasm contagious.

"It's wonderful, Ty!" she exclaimed. She was happy for him, but she came away realizing that Ty had never totally understood what Bill Goetz had packaged for him in *Mississippi Gambler,* and what her husband couldn't repeat because he had since left Universal-International.

She didn't offer an opinion. Ty was already committed to the project, and the contracts were signed. All one could do was hope for the best.

Certainly, in Ray Sebastian, he had the most accomplished

craftsman to create most of the seven ages of man Ty would be playing in the picture.

His makeup man, devoted to Ty and his memory, downplayed any talk of Ty's dissipation and its effect on his appearance. "Sometimes he'd get home after those all-night sessions, telling stories, and having a few," Sebastian said. "Not that he came in all boozed up or anything like that. But I could always pull him around to where he was presentable."

It was a particular challenge to make him look convincing as an eighteen-year-old. Sebastian devised a process of squeezing the bags under Ty's eyes together, and smoothing them with a holding solution. Pancake makeup was used to hide the discoloration on his face, and a dry rouge solution was applied to his heavy beard so that he would appear clean-shaven throughout the day. Color was put into his cheekbones to bring them up, and the jowls were shaded down so that they weren't so noticeable.

After he shot some interiors at Columbia, which was producing *The Long Gray Line,* Ty headed East for the bulk of filming at West Point.

Weldon Culhane enrolled at the American Academy of Dramatic Arts in October of 1953. He and Ty had carried on a correspondence since their first meeting. They resumed their relationship when Ty was filming in New York.

The aspiring actor would often be assigned to do readings in class, and Ty would sometimes coach him as they shared a drink. The next day Weldon would follow his tutor's advice.

"How did it go today?" Ty would ask him.

"I was brilliant," Weldon replied.

In recalling those times, he said, "These things that were my problems, they became his. He took them to heart. I look back on them today and realize the tolerance he must have had to put up with that."

At the end of the term, he met with an instructor to get a progress report on his achievements.

"You could make it as an actor," the young man was told, "but the name of Weldon Culhane doesn't cut it."

"My mother likes it," he protested. "Everyone knows me that way."

"How about Granite Culhane?" his instructor asked. In Hollywood, Rock Hudson was making a name for himself. The boy said he'd think it over.

That night, he discussed the situation with his sometime lover.

"Why don't you take my name?" he said. "Don't you like Ty? It's Irish and you're Irish."

Thinking back on it, Ty Culhane—as he is known today—said, "When he suggested it, I thought, why not? I wanted his name. I wanted *him*. It was exactly what I wanted him to say. It helped my fantasy world."

Ty continued work on the picture. Given both his prominence and that of John Ford at Twentieth during the late 1930s, not to mention their common Irish heritage, it's a wonder they'd never worked together before. Now they were together, and at Columbia, a rival studio.

Orson Welles once called the director a poet and a comedian. Ford tended toward conservative politics and a conservative technique, out of which came surprisingly tender and human and comic moments, as if they'd organically sprouted. His view was life-affirming, strong in American traditions like Mother and the Cavalry, combined with a fascination for the outsider who can't respect those traditions. Ford also had a weakness for Irish caricature, a reverence for Abraham Lincoln, a hatred of any injustice done to the Indian, and a passion for the song, "Shall We Gather at the River."

The Long Gray Line was to be Ford's first picture in Cinemascope, and it featured Ty as the spine of the picture, in a taxing part. He was totally unrecognizable as the movie opened, made up as a seventy-year-old man, putting in his bid as a rival to his great-grandfather for Irish comedian honors. With white hair and moustache, a brogue of effortless perfection, and a voice roaming high in the upper registers, the character of Martin Maher, the West Point trainer, was firmly established before the audience came to recognize that he was being played by Tyrone Power, the actor.

Ray Sebastian had performed even more magic in transforming Ty into an old man. He used prosthetic pieces on his jaw and on his cheeks. Sebastian and his associate, Irving Pringle, would each take one side of the face. In this way they could cut down the time of applying the makeup from two-and-a-half hours to less than an hour.

His makeup man, when he looked at Ty one morning, told him he wouldn't need to use the aged makeup that day.

"You already look eighty years old," Sebastian said. Ty had spent the night with the wife of a businessman who'd followed him to West Point.

Sebastian noticed her leave Ty's motel room, located next to his, the next morning, bouncing and buoyant, "as if she'd been drinking a glass of apple cider."

"I think, Mr. Sebastian," Ty said playfully, "that you should mind your own goddamn business."

Sebastian didn't respond, maintaining a knowing look.

"I slept alone, Mr. Sebastian."

"You went to the toilet alone," his makeup man corrected. "You didn't sleep alone."

"Oh, yes, I did."

"Where," his interrogator continued, "on the floor or on the couch?"

"What the hell are you?" Ty asked. "A policeman?"

It wasn't Sebastian who wound up being the accuser, inquisitor, and judge, but the old man.

Ty's work with Henry King and Henry Hathaway—both severe taskmasters—hadn't prepared him for John Ford. The director, considered by many the greatest American filmmaker of the sound era, was given to great displays of rage. At least once during a picture he would reputedly throw his script on the floor and angrily bellow, "Some goddamned actor has been fooling around with this script!"

Ty had gotten along very well with Ford thus far. One day, however, he suggested, "John, look. What would you think if, now that I've reached this age, I smoked a corn-cob pipe?"

Ford fixed Ty with a stony stare. Then he turned around to face the crew. "Everybody sit down," he yelled out. This his workers submissively did. "Now that we have silence," he continued, "I would like to hear some more from this *thinking* actor."

Ty turned a deep red. Ford, a triumphant look on his face,

walked over to his director's chair. He nodded to the others, and they went about their business.

His star, totally humiliated, tried to concentrate on the upcoming scene. He was docile and malleable for the rest of the shooting schedule, and delivered a noteworthy performance.

The last day of shooting, John Ford approached Ty. "I want to thank you for giving me a beautiful show," the director said. "After this performance, you don't have to take anything you don't want to do." He didn't add, as well he could have, "As long as you have a strong director."

Ty was delighted at the compliment and Ray Sebastian was amazed. "I never heard the old man say that to anybody but Ty," he recalled.

"Tyrone Power, whose physical beauty long concealed an honest acting talent, plays the locker-room Mr. Chips in ingratiating style," claimed *The Saturday Review*. ". . . [the movie's] sentimental appreciation of love and duty will wring tears from everyone in the theater but the cashier." Columbia claimed that *Long Gray Line* made $5,635,000 on a production cost of $1,748,000, giving Power his biggest hit in years.

In less than two years, Edmund Purdom had jumped from a featured player to star of Twentieth's most successful picture of 1954. He'd signed a contract with Metro-Goldwyn-Mayer and was brought in to replace Mario Lanza in *The Student Prince,* when the singer proved recalcitrant. Twentieth then borrowed him for *The Egyptian* after Marlon Brando dropped out, rather than play opposite an untried actress like Bella Darvi, Darryl Zanuck's current mistress. The picture would go on to net over $6,000,000 for the studio. Purdom indeed had come a long way since Ty and Linda Power took him and his wife in.

Now, the word was that, as he had replaced two actors in major films, he was standing in as Linda Christian's husband. The affair started during the filming of *The Egyptian,* while Ty was on location with *The Long Gray Line* in New York, and continued as the two were cast together in *Athena* at Metro. Linda had latched onto Purdom's ascending star, being seen publicly with him, reportedly taking a trip to Mexico with him, while Purdom's wife stayed home tending their babies.

That he should be so publicly cuckolded was humiliating to Ty. Whenever he'd strayed, he'd been much more discreet. Linda didn't give a hang for public opinion, and seemed to care even less what her husband thought.

Ty went to Edie Goetz for advice. He was very agitated.

"I just have to get out of this marriage," he told her.

Mrs. Goetz then brought up reports of the sex parties. "Why would you engage in all this?" she asked.

"Who knows what we do when we get involved?" he rationalized. Mrs. Goetz said Ty told her the whole truth of the orgies and his involvement in them, of pictures taken and circulated about town, one of them rumored to have been taken by Howard Hughes on his plane while Ty made love to a blonde actress on the floor.

"Today, of course," Mrs. Goetz said, "all this would be nothing. It wasn't *that* terrible. But it wasn't Tyrone. He was a very discreet man."

She asked him what he planned to do.

"The lawyer says I have to prove about Linda and Purdom," he replied. "I don't like to do a thing like this."

"Tyrone," she said, "You are a gentleman. That's true. But this is a brilliant lawyer. Do what he says."

Mrs. Goetz said that once he had the evidence of Linda's affair with Purdom, he was on his way to getting his freedom.

As with many others before him, Ty buried himself in work as his marriage ended. If only it had been in a more prestigious project.

Henry King had absolutely no respect for the novel by Helga Moray. When the first screenplay of *Untamed* was delivered, he said, "This script is even as bad as the book."

After many script conferences, King and his associates jokingly decided to make an African *Cimarron*. King's original choice was Robert Mitchum, and he'd already shot profile close-ups against the sun of a double who looked amazingly like Mitchum.

When Zanuck saw the rushes, he sent King a cable: "Don't get too close on your double. I haven't signed the contract yet."

The footage, of course, was scrapped when Ty was assigned to the role. In addition to King, he was also reunited with Susan Hayward as his costar, Twentieth Century-Fox, and Cinemascope. It wound up being as depressing a reunion as Henry King had anticipated.

With the completion of his commitment to Twentieth, his last line in the picture was particularly fitting in regard to both the studio and his marriage: "Ready now. Move out!"

Lawyers for both Ty and Linda had been working on a property settlement for a month, but couldn't come to an agreement. They decided to announce their separation anyway, while their attorneys continued trying to divide their assets.

Ty had a meeting with Harry Brand, the publicity director at Twentieth, to tell him that the marriage to Linda was over. The two men worked out the announcement of their separation. Once satisfied with the wording, Ty got into his gray and red Jaguar and drove off.

Later that afternoon, Brand called Linda to read her the wording of the announcement. He was surprised when Ty, whom he assumed had moved to bachelor quarters, answered the phone.

"What are you doing there?" Brand asked.

"We're going out to dinner," Ty replied. With that, Linda got on an extension telephone and the announcement was read to both of them. They blamed the separation on "incompatibility over careers," but said there were no immediate plans for divorce. The joint announcement said Romina, then three, and Taryn, two, would remain in Linda's custody.

Tita Purdon was asked by reporters if she too had separated from her husband. "Absolutely false," she said. "Edmund is still living at home and gossip about a separation is just a storm in a teacup."

When later asked by reporters about a divorce, Ty responded, "I don't have anything to say at this time. We haven't discussed it."

Soon after the separation was announced, Ty went East for his commitment with Katharine Cornell. A publicist stated he had given up three film commitments to be able to star opposite the great actress in *The Dark Is Light Enough.*

Actually, Columbia Pictures granted Ty's Copa Productions a postponement on three pictures: *The Stalk, Lorenzo the Magnificent,* and *The Warrior Saint.* None of the pictures was ever made.

The play was to be a project born of desperation and ending in exasperation. Miss Cornell and her director husband, Guthrie McClintic, felt teaming her with a movie star like Ty would enhance her slipping appeal. She may not have consciously thought so, but there was no doubt that she could wipe an upstart movie actor off the stage. Audiences would come to see the movie star and leave singing the praises of the grande dame of the theater.

While reviews were decidedly mixed, business was extraordinarily good during the ten-city, eleven-week tour which preceded the Broadway opening, and this even included Christmas week in Cleveland. Ty had no family plans to celebrate the holiday.

Miss Cornell, as expected, was getting good reviews during the tour, portraying a kind and noble countess who harbors a cowardly army deserter, played by Ty, who had once been her son-in-law. Ty was enormously frustrated in his role of a graceless, ungrateful scoundrel who felt "good has rejected him" . . . it was uncomfortably close to a thought he hadn't come to grips with in his private life. It was a complex and thankless role, "unredeemed by wit, brilliance, or cleverness," as Brooks Atkinson later described it.

The new verse play by Christopher Fry was pretentious and ponderous. Ty wasn't receiving the help from McClintic that Charles Laughton had given him. Although some reviewers said he possessed one of the best and clearest voices in the theater, the material was beyond him at the same time it was beneath Miss Cornell.

In his unhappiness, he committed a nearly unpardonable act. He exposed the company's dirty linen. In an interview with *Cleveland News* columnist Arthur Spaeth, he said, "We feel the extra something of depth and drive that is missing. I feel sorry for the audience out there . . . When we reach that climax of the drama we feel a need to give them something more and it isn't there to give." He was largely using the editorial we.

The production was playing in Washington when Ty was stricken with infectious hepatitis. He was allowed to finish the run there, a physician in attendance, his performance now more listless and lacking in vitality. Then he was flown to New York for hospitalization.

The scheduled New York opening was pushed back two weeks, until February 23, when Ty, no longer infectious, was still recuperating from the mild case of hepatitis. He'd been drinking heavily, but now he was proscribed from touching alcohol for at least a year. That didn't help his unsteady nerves.

Gathering at the ANTA Theater on opening night were many celebrities, including Eleanor Roosevelt, Marlene Dietrich, Peggy Wood, Raymond Massey, Valentina, Laurence Langner, and a bevy of Vanderbilts, some of them related to Ty's close friend, Watson Webb.

Also on the premises was an unexpected visitor.

Ty Power and Ty Culhane hadn't seen each other for some time. The older man had said he would call or write. Culhane would occasionally get a note, but it was usually brief and noncommittal.

When it was announced that Ty was starring opposite Katharine Cornell at the ANTA Theater, Culhane was elated. The American Academy was next door to the theater. On the top floor, there was a sliding fire door which opened onto the ANTA building.

Ty hadn't called Culhane since his arrival, and the younger man was hurt by the neglect. Yet, he wanted to see Ty, and he devised a plan.

Prior to the performance, Ty Culhane opened the sliding door and walked onto the adjoining catwalk over the stage next door. Looking down, he saw Ty Power come in and walk to his dressing room. He could take in all the conversation below. When it started to fade, as people moved away from him, he crawled further out on the catwalk. By this time, he was covered with dust and dirt and, as he moved, it started falling below. People looked up to see what was causing the dust storm. A light was trained on him.

As he scooted back on the catwalk, he was met by a policeman by the sliding doors. Culhane explained he was a student at the Academy.

"Well, you'll be reported," the cop told him, "and you'll probably be suspended."

"But, I'm a friend of Mr. Power's," Culhane protested. "Just take me to him. He'll tell you."

The cop was skeptical, but he followed Culhane's suggestion. Grabbing him by the arm, he led him to Ty's dressing room and knocked on the door. As soon as he saw Culhane, Ty started laughing.

In answer to the policeman's question, Ty replied, "Yes, I know him."

With that, the cop took his hands off Culhane. "I *told* you I know him," the young man said.

When they were left alone, Ty turned to his young friend. "What *are* you doing?"

"I wanted to see you," he replied.

"Why didn't you just come backstage and ask for me?" Ty asked.

"I don't know. I wanted to watch your performance. After all, you're the one who taught me to watch from backstage. This time I thought I'd watch from above."

Ty was leasing Garson Kanin's house in Turtle Bay at the time, and the affair with Culhane was resumed there. He would occasionally send his chauffeur to pick up the younger man, and they would spend brief times together.

Because the play wasn't as successful as anticipated, Ty was called on to do more promoting than he'd anticipated. He'd tell Culhane he had a lot to do, and that he'd call later.

"I wish I didn't have to do these things," he told Culhane. "I'd rather be with you. You'll understand about these obligations when you start working in the theater."

Culhane waited for long periods between Ty's calls. "I never felt there was anything wrong or dirty or ever to be ashamed of with Ty," he said. "Here was a very important person, someone I thought I was madly in love with. I wonder if it was truly love or fascination."

One day, Culhane turned to Ty in bed. "Will there ever be a day when we'll be together?" he asked.

"Perhaps," Ty replied. "I'd like that."

Nevertheless, when the play closed shortly thereafter—the audiences Cornell and McClintic had anticipated because of Ty's movie star draw didn't materialize—he returned to California and Culhane didn't hear from him again. Ty Power had a more immediate concern. He *had* to get a divorce.

While Ty was busy professionally in the East, Linda was well occupied in Hollywood. After the separation was announced, her affair with Purdom was put on hold, while Robert Schlesinger, the son of Countess Mona Bismarck, the former Mrs. Harrison Williams, paid her court.

Around Christmas of 1954, she accepted jewels worth $132,500 from Schlesinger, including a platinum bracelet set in emeralds and diamonds, worth $35,000; a platinum diamond ring, worth $44,500; and a platinum diamond necklace, worth $53,000.

The only problem with the gift was that Schlesinger's $100,000 check to Van Cleef and Arpels bounced. The jewelers turned to Linda for recovery of the jewels.

She refused, claiming they were a gift. Even after legal papers were served, Linda refused to relinquish the gifts.

In early March of 1955, Linda appeared in court, wearing a nine-carat diamond ring in a gold setting and a heavy diamond-encrusted gold watch bracelet, which she said were both gifts from Ty. She also wore gold earrings, a gold and pearl lapel pin, and a platinum cross set in diamonds.

"Mr. Schlesinger always knew and understood," she testified, "that even though I was separated from my husband, I was married and had no intention of entering into romantic engagements of any kind. He knew that and understood it. I never was alone with him at any time. We were always accompanied by friends or family. These gifts were given expressly as a matter of friendship and only in that spirit were they accepted."

On that day, it was ruled that Linda did not have to return the jewels pending the jeweler's suit to recover them, nor did she have to disclose their whereabouts.

When the divorce suit was called up two months later, considering her previous spectacular appearance in a courtroom, Linda was considerably subdued. Wearing a simple summer dress, she broke down on the stand as she told a Santa Monica Superior Court judge, "My husband was very cool, distant. He wanted to go on trips but without me. He wanted to be alone." Her mother was a corroborating witness.

There were no corespondents named in the action by either party, which was heard on May 4. Ty, who was playing with Cornell in Boston, balked at Linda's demands, but a property settlement was agreed to shortly before the case was called up. He would pay a percentage of his income, not less than $15,000 and not more than $50,000 for the next two years and, after that, not more than $43,000 a year. The alimony would run for eleven years and one month unless Linda remarried. She was given half interest in their Bel-Air home and full ownership of a house in Cuernavaca. In addition she would get 36 percent of Ty's interest in *Mississippi Gambler* and 40 percent of his interest in *The Long Gray Line*.

Linda's attorney, Samuel S. Zagon, said the settlement could amount to well over a million dollars. In actuality it was slightly under that figure, since Ty made $800,000 on the first picture and, because of curious bookkeeping, made nothing on the second.

Linda would get custody of the girls for ten months of the year, with Ty having them for two months.

The divorce judgment entered, Linda left for Spain to make a picture, leaving Romina and Taryn with Ty.

Two weeks previously, Purdom and his wife had agreed to postpone their divorce action for ninety days, in the hope that their marriage could be saved. No reconciliation was now possible, for Purdom was also due in Spain momentarily. Linda declined to comment when reporters confronted her with that fact.

* * *

Ty swore he would never marry again. Never again would he expose himself to the humiliation and the degradation which had characterized his marriage to Linda. He would distract himself with work, taking sex whenever he felt like it and wherever he found it.

He'd been forced to pay $65,000 in legal fees and $16,000 for private investigators in order to get his freedom. With Linda getting such a generous settlement, Ty simply had to return to work. Columbia was discussing several film projects with him and his partner, Ted Richmond, who'd set up their Copa Productions offices in Beverly Hills, at the corner of Dayton Way and Cañon Drive.

More often, however, he was at home with his two baby daughters.

Ty Culhane, in the meantime, had dropped out of the American Academy and moved to California. He took an apartment in Beverly Hills and read with great interest reports of the divorce suit. He would take a taxi to see the house where Ty and Linda had lived, not knowing whether Ty was still in residence there.

Eventually, he gathered up his nerve and called the number Ty had once given him. A houseman took his message. He received a call two days later, Ty inviting him to the house on Copa del Oro Road. Linda was no longer living there.

Within a few years, Ty Culhane would become known as one of southern California's most accomplished interior designers. He already had very decided tastes, and they didn't coincide with the one-time residents of the house. "I thought it was furnished terribly. It didn't look like what I thought a movie star's house should look like. Neither Ty nor Linda had good taste.

"Whenever he saw me, there was a great apology for not keeping in touch. I didn't think of him as a great actor. I looked on him as my lover. Rather than his ever pursuing me, I certainly was the one who pursued him. I made up my mind from the first night I met him that he'd be mine. I wanted to see him all the time. I wanted to move in.

"If I read in a paper that Ty was going to be at a party or staying at a hotel, I would make a point of being there or leaving a note. One or two days later he would call."

Ty laughingly told him, "I've never met anyone in my life who's as persistent as you are."

"If I want something," Culhane replied, "I go after it."

The younger man, however, was now at the point where he realized their affair had no future, even though he never had that feeling when he and Ty were together. He had come to realize that Ty could never feel an exclusive emotional commitment to another man. Neither could he promise an exclusive sexual commitment to a woman. Tyrone Power had never felt that he had the best of both possible worlds in his bisexuality. His whole existence was in contradiction to that belief.

The meeting between the two was to be their last intimate one. Ty said he was going East to make a film. Culhane wasn't bitter about the parting. Ty would reach out and caress people, making them believe he cared. It wasn't necessarily a sexual gesture, as it had often been with Culhane, but its spontaneity had long endeared Ty to all who knew him. That was what Culhane would always remember.

"I don't know anybody who knew Ty who didn't love him," Rock Hudson said. "I don't just mean like him . . . *love* him. With all that magnetism, there was no self-centeredness and no conceit. I'm sure he knew the effect he had on others. I know a lot of actors with magnetism who don't necessarily have warmth. Ty had *great* warmth. You felt the friendliness of him just by being around him. With Ty, you knew he was a nice man and that you could trust him. You knew, for example, if you told him a confidence that you wouldn't have to preface it by saying you didn't want it repeated. He instinctively knew that."

His role in *The Eddy Duchin Story* was a return to unabashed tear-jerking, with noticeably less subtlety and depth this time out, under the direction of George Sidney, who'd been borrowed from Metro by Columbia. It emphasized the most doom-laden aspects of the pianist's life, as in quick succession he lost jobs promised him, his wife to illness, and finally his own life to a debilitating disease.

"The real tragedy of Duchin's life," Ty told *The New York Times* when he was filming on location, "was his dying at such a young age, only forty-two. I knew Eddy quite well. Working right here across from the [New York Memorial] hospital reminds me of how I used to visit him over there when he was a patient, toward the end."

Ty's next birthday would also be his forty-second. Considering his own premature death, the statement now seems portentous.

Duchin was known for his "dizzy fingers" specialty of crossing hands and playing the melody in bass. Carmen Cavallero was hired to play the music. Ty spent eleven weeks, coached by pianist Nat Brandwynne, learning how to "play" on a dummy keyboard. It was arduous work, allowing director Sidney to shoot full figure shots of Ty at the piano, expertly fingering the instrument. He learned twenty specialty numbers for the picture. If only others had brought equal preparation to their work.

Always the complete professional, his patience wore noticeably thin with those whom he considered less so. He would not comment on his differences with Kim Novak, his costar, other than to say, "Confusion between temperament and bad manners is unfortunate." When the company returned to California, he sequestered himself from the crew, which was not typical of him, staying behind the closed doors of his dressing room, playing the mood music on his record player full blast.

One of the few times when he ventured out of his dressing room was when he hosted Taryn's second birthday party on the set. Romina, four, joined in the celebration. Linda returned from Europe one day too late to attend the party. She was in the company of Edmund Purdom.

The two lovers returned to California to find themselves virtual social outcasts. With their sophisticated continental auras, they were expected to handle themselves with greater finesse. Their continued association was considered distasteful by much of Hollywood. People wanted to think the worst of them. It was generally said that Ty had been instrumental in getting Purdom the starring role in *The Egyptian* at Twentieth. This wasn't true. As Edie Goetz said, "He didn't have that much influence, frankly." And certainly not in that period, when his commitment to the studio was winding down. Linda had a genuine acting talent, and Purdom was even more gifted. They defied public opinion and forfeited any chance to advance their careers.

As for Ty's, it was moving along splendidly. *The Saturday Re-*

view would say about his current film that "for a movie based upon known facts, it has an unaccountable air of unreality, a lugubriousness, a prettying-up that eventually becomes morbid and offensive." But not to the public. It earned $5,300,000 for Columbia and put Ty in a great bargaining position with his Copa Productions films, which Columbia would distribute.

It seemed a natural transition that in his return to the stage Ty would be playing a pianist-composer, this time in *A Quiet Place,* opposite Leora Dana, Kurt Kasznar's wife.

The models for the play were Leonard Bernstein and his actress wife Felicia Montealegre. Bernstein agreed to coach Ty in piano playing. Another pianist backstage would actually play during the performance. Through his past experience in *The Eddy Duchin Story* and Bernstein's coaching, Ty became proficient enough to play the piano himself. The backstage pianist wasn't needed, but Ty insisted he stay on, for he didn't want to do him out of a job.

Kasznar, at the same time his wife and Ty were involved in the out-of-town tryout at the Shubert Theatre in New Haven, was himself being directed by Tyrone Guthrie at the Phoenix Theatre, getting a scale salary of eighty-five dollars a week, in *Six Characters in Search of an Author.*

Because of their same first names, Ty was convinced that he and Guthrie were related. Kasznar introduced them over the phone, and the two men agreed to meet during a weekend performance of the Guthrie play, at a time when Ty's own production was dark.

When he and Leora Dana arrived at the Phoenix, Kasznar told them, "I'm so uncomfortable. I feel like I'm inside a washing machine."

"Don't worry," Ty assured him. "When Ty Guthrie wants you to be noticed, you will be."

When the two Tyrones met after the performance, they compared family backgrounds, and decided they were distant cousins. Ty was thrilled to be finally meeting the distinguished Guthrie, whom he considered the greatest theatrical director alive.

Yet, if he'd had him for *A Quiet Place,* even Guthrie couldn't have saved it.

"Ty and Leora were cooped up for fifteen weeks in this play

that couldn't be fixed," Kasznar said. "It was dismal for everyone."

The play closed out of town at the National Theatre in Washington, just prior to Christmas. Its dejected stars returned to New York, their mood anything but merry.

Kasznar decided to throw them a party, inviting as guests the cast of his company.

"I bought eight hundred red roses," Kasznar recalled. "At eleven o'clock on Christmas Eve you can get these things for nothing. I also got some white candles. I put the roses and the candles on the tree. I must admit it was the most beautiful Christmas tree I'd ever seen."

It was a gesture stage actors could well appreciate, Kasznar giving his wife the roses that would have been her due at the curtain call of each performance.

Decades of such traditions are what distinguish the theater from motion pictures, which were and are in a constant state of flux. The only constant in Ty's film career had been the dreary repetition of similar roles. Now, as he prepared to star in the first picture for his production company, which Columbia would distribute, he was caught up in a new wave of motion picture making. Like other major stars—Kirk Douglas, Burt Lancaster, Robert Mitchum—he was becoming his own boss. He was involved in all the preproduction activities. What the stars were discovering was that not only would they make more money, they would also keep a larger percentage of it. It was such an effective tactic that even studio executives started turning to independent production.

In February of 1956, Darryl F. Zanuck stepped down as production head of Twentieth to form his own unit. Except for his brief stint in the military during World War II, he had run the studio since 1935. His action was based sheerly on financial considerations. As one of the highest paid executives in the country, he was in the 90 percent tax bracket. As an independent producer, he would be in the 25 percent, long-term, capital-gains bracket, just as Ty now was. Twentieth would distribute any pictures Zanuck produced. Buddy Adler was named to succeed him.

Ty's next project, *Abandon Ship*, was a daring venture into deep waters, a role rarely assigned to him. To make it possible, it was necessary to film it in England. It was a savage tale of a second in command of a sinking luxury liner who, with the captain dead, faced the harrowing responsibility of deciding which of twenty-seven survivors were to be allowed on a lifeboat capable of handling only fourteen people. It was a grim, unsmiling, Darwinian business of eliminating the weak and injured and keeping the strong who had a chance of surviving an upcoming storm.

His haggard looks stood him in good stead in this unconventional portrayal. Ty was proud of his performance, though it won him few new fans.

It did win him, however, a new lover, Mai Zetterling, the Swedish actress, who'd appeared in the picture with him. Ty found her as sensual as Linda and as strong as Annabella. She was an uncommonly brilliant woman who would make her own mark as a film director some years hence. Ty for the first time since his divorce was deeply involved with another woman.

Echoes of his past rebounded while he'd been filming in England. He saw much of Annabella during this time, sparking talks of a rekindled romance. He would always retain a great fondness for his first wife, but they could never revive the love they'd had for each other. While Linda had been able to obtain her final divorce decree on May 4, 1956, she didn't pick it up until August 8. She was elsewhere preoccupied.

Robert Schlesinger, the man who'd given her the jewels and used a rubber check to pay for them, was indicted in a $330,000 oil-stock swindle. The check he had given Van Cleef and Arpels would have been good if the businessmen accusing him of bilking them hadn't stopped payment on a check for $150,000. Schlesinger, however, was not to be found, and a police alert was sounded in fifteen states.

Then, Linda was subpoenaed to give a deposition about a trip she took to Mexico with Purdom in 1954, while each was still married to others, in Tita Purdom's divorce action against her husband.

In the meantime, Schlesinger was found in Canada and extradited to the United States. He pleaded guilty to two to eight counts of grand larceny in the oil-stock deal and was sentenced to the maximum term of five to ten years in prison. The jewels by this time had been returned, Linda getting a settlement of $25,000 from Van Cleef and Arpels.

Early in August, Linda announced plans to marry Purdom after his divorce was final. One day later she said she had no plans to marry Purdom. Three days later, she picked up her final divorce decree from Ty.

Ty was now involved in narrating a film for John Ford, called *The Rising of the Moon,* a three-part feature shot in Ireland and using members of the Abbey Theater Company. Ty served as host and narrator of the three episodes, affecting a flawless brogue and following it with his professional narration. It was a short-lived, totally joyous experience for him.

He stayed on in Britain to star in a George Bernard Shaw play.

Kurt Kasznar felt that Ty should have been ideally cast for the rakish part of Dick Dudgeon in *The Devil's Disciple,* which he portrayed at the Manchester Opera House and the Winter Garden Theatre in November of 1956.

He called Kasznar and his wife Leora several times during his engagement.

"I'm miserable," he complained. "It's pouring rain and I can't play the part. I *cannot* play a swashbuckler. I'm a klutz. I'm bumping into everything. I sure wish you were here."

The telephone call lasted for forty-five minutes. When it was completed, the Kasznars poured themselves a drink.

"What are you doing next week?" he asked his wife.

"Nothing."

"Then let's call British Airways."

They sent Ty a wire: GOOD LUCK. NOTHING CAN GO WRONG. WE REALLY ARE WITH YOU.

The Kasznars left New York on a Monday, figuring they would arrive in England just in time to get to Manchester for the Wednesday evening performance. Because of bad weather, the plane landed in Prestwick, Scotland, instead, at three in the afternoon. Ty's agents had been alerted, and a limousine was ready to drive them to Manchester. They got to their hotel forty minutes before the curtain, changed into evening finery, and were whisked to the Opera House.

They were seated in the fifth row. Ty's first appearance was greeted by a heavy round of applause. The audience had come to see a movie star whom they adored. However, he gave, as Kasznar recalled, a totally forgettable performance.

When Ty's dresser admitted them to the dressing room after the performance, Ty was so taken aback that Kasznar claimed his heavy makeup seemed to fall off his face.

His friends, who'd shown how truly devoted they were to Ty, spent the next three days with him, commiserating with him over the inevitably bad reviews. He was holding back in his performance, Ty now believed. "I have to let go," he insisted. "I *have* to."

He couldn't, however. It was the story of his life.

* * *

Romantically, his affair with Mai Zetterling might have approached talk of marriage if it hadn't been for the complete turnabout in their relationship. She was the dominant one, and he was the one treated as the pretty plaything, and not a particularly bright one at that. He went with the Kasznars to Brighton, where she was doing an Anouilh play. Ty took notes during her performance. When he went backstage with Kurt and Leora, he started offering suggestions. "I can't hear what you're saying," he told Mai. "What are you saying?" Then, he started referring to his notes. Mai couldn't possibly accept his criticisms. What did he, a mere movie actor, know? It was the beginning of the end.

Linda had taken up with a Spanish Marquis, Alfonso de Portago. He was separated from his American wife, Carol McDaniel. Elsa Maxwell wrote snidely about Linda, "She does have great talent for attracting men and an apparently irresistible desire to do so."

Linda was in the stands in May of 1957 to cheer on the sports-lover Marquis de Portago as his Ferrari took off in Italy's Mille Miglia road race. Forty miles from the finish line his car went out of control and smashed into the crowd. He and twelve spectators were killed.

"A few days ago," she told the press, "I was praying in a church in Rome and suddenly had a terrible premonition that God would take 'Fonso from me. But I never imagined it would be in such a terrible way as this . . . I loved him because he was a true nobleman in soul."

The widow of the Marquis made the flight with the body for the funeral in Madrid. Linda, too, emerged in black from her hotel room and took an Italian passenger plane to Madrid, driving to the cemetery for the burial ceremony, succeeding in upstaging the widow and his family.

Another line circulated about her after this spectacle: "Linda Christian, star of stage, screen, and funerals." Whoever was handling her press relations should have been fired.

After his divorce, Ty never said a negative word about his ex-wife. He always wired her good wishes on her birthday and on holidays. Mai Zetterling had accompanied him to Mexico City for the shooting of *The Sun Also Rises,* yet it was only proper that he wire Linda his condolences over the death of her lover.

On the basis of that thoughtful act, Linda told *The Los Angeles Examiner* that she and Ty might remarry. "When we were divorced it was Mr. Power who wanted his freedom. I have no idea whether we can have a reconciliation because he seems to be stuck on his freedom."

Ty, in denying such a possibility, tried to soften the rebuff. "The divorce is final," he told the Associated Press. "The rumors of a possible remarriage doubtless arose over the fact Miss Christian is en route to Mexico City to be with our two daughters, who are staying with her mother while we are filming here."

With her departure, the affair with Mai Zetterling was interrupted. Katy Jurado seemed to have dsplaced her in Ty's affections. Reports of a romance with Juliette Greco, one of the other stars of the picture, were totally erroneous, for the French chanteuse had displaced Bella Darvi in Darryl Zanuck's affections.

Shooting of *The Sun Also Rises* had to be an anticlimax. Darryl Zanuck, in his second picture for DRZ Productions, wanted Ty for the role because, as his biographer Mel Gussow put it, "Power . . . was the truest, the handsomest, the best of the lot. He was a good choice for the part, except for his age—forty-three."

One of the few satisfactions for Ty was that he was making $275,000, equal to a year's salary when he was at his prime as a

Twentieth star, which he was getting for working a few months. Whether Ty was the actor to play Jake Barnes, the disillusioned, sexually incapacitated World War I hero, is obscured by the fact that almost every other choice in the movie was so obviously wrong, particularly its director.

Henry King was an ornate, detailed director of the full and filigreed Victorian School, working with material written by a writer, Ernest Hemingway, whose lean and spare style was a rebellion against the whole Victorian tradition.

There was nothing lean and spare about the picture's budget, at $5,000,000 the most expensive location picture ever financed by Twentieth. Cinemascope was the wrong process for a story made up of carefully selected details. The canvas was too large. After all the rewrites, the script still didn't capture those elusive shards of meaning in the apparently trivial exchanges of Hemingway's dialogue. Power and his associates—Errol Flynn, Ava Gardner, and Eddie Albert—were the wrong age for members of the Lost Generation. When these middle-aged people claimed to be veterans of World War I, it's logical to assume the story was taking place during World War II.

The Sun Also Rises was a prestige production that didn't work despite its lofty intentions. Ty was effective in holding the screen with nothing more than condemning eyes. Some critics found him sensitive. Others said he was spiritless.

Regardless, Ty was well aware that Errol Flynn's boozy portrayal was the more showy one. "Errol Flynn is likely to walk off with an Academy Award for his work in this picture," he told Hollywood columnist Dorothy Manners.

From Mexico, shooting of the picture moved on to Europe. Both Ava Gardner and Errol Flynn had to stay out of the United States for eighteen months to get a tax break. The company, instead of going back to California to shoot interiors, moved over to France.

When Henry King arrived, he discovered that Zanuck had been directing Ty and Juliette Greco in a street scene. The director didn't take issue with Zanuck's meddling.

"What if the Director's Guild hears about this?" the film's business manager asked him. "What are they going to say if they find out Zanuck directed part of the picture?"

"There's no direction anyway," King said. "They'll never notice."

What one of Ty's friends did notice was the way his looks had deteriorated. Jacque Mapes saw him in Rome, shortly before the company moved to Spain to wind up filming. He was shocked by Ty's appearance. "He looked unwell. I don't know if alcohol might have been a problem, but I'd heard reports of his heavy drinking. It wasn't just his age. He was probably already ill. He didn't have that dashing look. He'd always had a look of vitality and a sparkle in his eyes. Now he was tired and looked older than he actually was."

CHAPTER

11

Hollywood, June 10 (AP).—Tyrone Power, who has been away from Hollywood for two years, returned today to costar in a movie with Marlene Dietrich.

Power's arrival from Europe by plane touched off more rumors that he and actress Linda Christian might become reconciled, but he denied the possibility.

A FEW MONTHS PREVIOUSLY, WHILE HE WAS ON LOCATION IN Mexico with *The Sun Also Rises,* Ty had been visited by independent producer Arthur Hornblow, Jr., and sounded out about playing one of the leads in the film version of *Witness for the Prosecution.*

Agatha Christie's play was playing concurrently on Broadway with two other productions with courtroom settings: *The Caine Mutiny Court Martial* and *Inherit the Wind.* It had been bought for $430,000 by Hornblow and his associates and would be released by United Artists. Billy Wilder would be the director.

Two of Wilder's past hits, *Sunset Boulevard* and *The Lost Weekend,* had revived the careers of its male stars, William Holden and Ray Milland. The former finally emerged as a major star and the latter won an Academy Award for Best Actor in his role as an alcoholic. The directors of Ty's last few films had been either talented and tired or hopelessly mediocre. Wilder represented a change of luck which was long overdue.

As the director recalled, it was Hornblow's idea to cast Ty in the picture. "It was a good suggestion," Wilder said. "Ty liked the part, he filled it, and he played it."

The two men had known each other casually for some time. The continental Wilder, though he found him to be greatly underrated as an actor, was more impressed with Ty as a gallant. "He was one of those rare occurrences in Hollywood," Wilder said. "He was an absolutely total gentleman. The one thing I admired more about him than anything else was his manners. There was a style about him, and I admired it greatly.

"He had facets to him that couldn't be put on film. Virtue is not photogenic. And Ty had many virtues. There was nothing petty about him. There was a genuine shyness about him. He liked to blend into the wallpaper. He wanted to be an actor, not a star. He was excellent and professional and prepared and intelligent . . . totally impeccable in his professional life. Ty wanted his father to be proud of him. He was, after all, a crown prince. It was preordained that he would be an actor.

"He would never say anything bitter or cutting or derogatory about anybody. He was absolute perfection . . . placid . . . collected.

"With very rare exceptions do I get close to actors. I try to keep it like a lawyer-client relationship. Ty became a close friend. The picture we did together was one of the few joys of my professional life."

The main players and the director were so chummy that each would take turns catering lunch for the others while they filmed at the Goldwyn Studios in Hollywood. Charles Laughton and Elsa Lanchester might supply roast beef and salad one day. On another, Marlene Dietrich would cook an entire meal. "She was a great cook," Wilder recalled, "and took more pride in being a hausfrau than an actress." Ty's Mexican cook would cater another day. Billy Wilder's wife Audrey would send over a *salade Niçoise* on yet another. Their work over, they would meet every evening in Wilder's office to drink bullshots. They were so caught up in their work they all hated to go home.

Ty was embarrassed by Dietrich's attentions to him. It was part of her craft to fall in love with her leading men. If he said 'he liked a particular wine, she'd send him a case of it the next day. She also gave him an extravagantly expensive gold cigarette case.

When reminded of Dietrich's infatuation, Wilder said, "Everybody had a crush on Ty. Laughton had a crush on him. I did, too. As heterosexual as you might be, it was impossible to be totally impervious to that kind of charm."

Ty was top billed in the picture, but he willingly became part of the ensemble. He offered suggestions on his characterization, some accepted by Wilder, but he didn't assert himself any further.

"Ty's evaluation of the picture and his role was absolutely in focus," Wilder said. "There was nothing surface about it at all. Also, he didn't have that now prevalent insistence on being the whole picture. Nobody like Ty would weigh and count the lines he had and compare them to the long theatrical speeches of the barrister played by Laughton. We only talked of the end effect. Would it come off? We were putting together a cocktail in a Waring blender. Ty and the others were the ingredients."

Ray Sebastian was again doing Ty's makeup and acting as occasional cook at the daily lunches. It was a snap assignment for him, since Ty was acting in modern dress and was required to merely look like himself . . . and he was looking much better than he had in years. Dietrich's makeup was considerably more complicated. Through the use of face straps, her skin was lifted to emphasize those immortal cheekbones. They had the opposite effect, however, making her look older because they confined the movement of her head. Midway through the picture, the straps were loosened up, as was Dietrich herself.

All the actors were as good as, if not better, than they'd ever been. Ty too rose to the demands, bowing to the histrionics of Laughton and Dietrich, while remaining the emotional core of the picture, playing the innocent commoner caught in a schemer's web he couldn't control. As a man who may have been wrongly accused of murdering a wealthy widow, he was defended by Laughton as the barrister and confounded by the hostile testimony of his actress wife, played by Dietrich. It might have been a claustrophobic film, the great bulk of the highly verbose action taking place in a seventy-five-thousand-dollar Old Bailey court-room set created at Goldwyn. With its twists and counter-twists, however, *Witness for the Prosecution* was one of those rare motion pictures generally conceded to be better than the stage play on which it was based. Wilder was understandably proud when Agatha Christie said it was the first good screen adaptation of anything she'd ever written.

Wilder talked to Ty about two or three projects they might do in the future. "He was on the verge of hitting it actually big," Wilder said. "Ty knew the craft inside out. He was maturing into something. I only wish he were alive now and we were doing something together. I saw him playing slightly older leading men, past fifty or fifty-five. I'm absolutely sure he would never have done the Cary Grant thing . . . to say, 'I've had it,' and retire. He would have functioned to the very end."

It is more often the case that once the film ends, despite the promises to keep in touch, coworkers drop out of each other's lives. This the three men decidedly didn't want to do. They had worked so happily and so well together that they vowed to continue the relationship. When the picture was completed in October of 1957—United Artists rushed it into release so that it would qualify for that year's Academy Awards—Wilder, Laughton, and Ty took a holiday to Europe.

They flew to Paris that fall, rented a car, and Ty acted as chauffeur as they drove to take the baths at the Austrian spa of Badgastein. From there they drove to Vienna, then flew to Berlin, doing a little publicity for the picture along the way. The three, however, largely mapped out culinary highlights to enjoy on the trip.

"We talked about a mixed bag of subjects," Wilder said, "about what we were going to eat, what kind of wine to have with it, Shakespeare, music, art . . . We laughed all the way. It was The Three Stooges in Europe.

"We were climbing up and down mountains. That's pretty heavy hiking, and not just going on a stroll through the Wiener Wald. Ty had no problems. That's why I found it hard to believe later that his heart was bad."

Despite their great conviviality, Wilder had no way of knowing

whether Ty was a happy man. "He was a man full of tact," the director said. "He would not spill out what was eating him. Surely
something was. *Everybody* is eaten up by something. He was private and discreet. He never talked about himself. He was unobtrusive and easy. I found him pretty placid."

Some of his friends felt Ty wasn't an exceptionally bright man.
Wilder disagreed. "I considered him intelligent and perceptive. He
just didn't do the phony thing. He didn't try to appear smarter
than he really was. He never just talked. He said *things.*"

About his poor choice of properties, Wilder said many intelligent and learned actors are notoriously bad judges of what is best
for them. "The fact Ty exposed himself on the stage was a big
plus for him," Wilder said. "No one was going to say, 'Cut! Let's
do that again.'"

As fond as the two men were of each other, Wilder came away
realizing—as others had in the past—that Ty's inner core was
somewhat elusive to grasp.

"I know very little about his amours," Wilder said. "I'm sure
that with his looks and charm there must have been a string of
glamorous females wanting to get their hands on him."

In the brief period that they were friends, Wilder never sensed
any homosexual leanings in Ty. Neither did Ty's makeup man,
Ray Sebastian, who worked closely with him for twenty-three
years.

"I'm fully aware that if someone doesn't make a pass at me,
that doesn't prove he's a heterosexual," Wilder said. "He may
happen to be a homosexual with excellent taste. I'm not protect-
ing Ty now. If this was Ty's problem, I find it totally understandable. And I'm full of compassion . . . certainly for a man
like Ty, whom I genuinely loved.

"There's no extraordinarily good-looking man who doesn't feel
the pressure from other men. They are tempting to homosexuals,
and traps are set. When you think of the handsome actors in their
younger years . . .

"Did Ty jump into marriage so as to obliterate his real colors?"
Wilder asked. "Who knows?"

Perhaps only Ty knew. He had come to believe bisexuality, and
not homosexuality, as Oscar Wilde maintained, was the love that

dare not speak its name. There was little he could say in defense of such fragmented passion.

Ty and the director stopped off in New York, while Laughton flew on to California. Audrey Wilder was there to meet her husband. So was a young girl named Debbie Minardos, whom Ty had met while making his last picture.

When the four had dinner, Wilder found it ironic that Debbie talked about her passionate crush on Elvis Presley, while Ty, the movie star in her life, was sitting beside her.

Early winter of 1957 was one of unusual contentment for Ty. *Witness for the Prosecution* looked like a certain hit, his resources as an actor being duly appreciated, and he was preparing for a stage tour opposite Faye Emerson and Arthur Treacher in George Bernard Shaw's *Back to Methuselah*. In the offing were several pictures for his production company as well as the semi-commitment to Billy Wilder. Staying on in New York after the Wilders returned to California, he took a small apartment on East Seventy-second Street, where he and Debbie entertained at small parties. Hanging in the foyer were posters from his father's stage plays.

Deborah Montgomery Minardos, at twenty-six, was divorced from Nico Minardos, a young Hollywood actor, and the mother of a ten-year-old daughter. She was Mississippi-born, neither as sophisticated nor as cultivated as Ty's ex-wives. Her coloring was as dark as his. Friends said they looked so much alike they could have passed for brother and sister. His feelings for her, however, were anything but fraternal.

Of all the women in his life, as much as he came to like her, Kurt Kasznar thought she was the most unnatural choice for Ty. "I never asked him why," he said. "Debbie must have done something that pleased him."

Ty would noticeably cringe at her gaucheries which, when analyzed, weren't that offensive. She was outspoken, and her opinions, though often valid, sounded ignorant when spoken in her cracker accent. Had Annabella or Linda spoken the same words they would have sounded sophisticated. He would never be so cruel as to ridicule her in front of others, but his friends were well aware that he was vaguely embarrassed nonetheless.

Rock Hudson had just separated from his wife, and at the invitation of Kasznar and Leora Dana, decided to spend Christmas in New York as their guest. During the round of holiday parties, he got to know Ty better.

When he returned to California, Hudson considered Ty more than an acquaintance and less than a close friend. "He was a man of few words, yet he always knew what to say at the right time. He loved to laugh. I was impressed that he never made references to his ex-wives in any way, good or bad." Ty's only failing, as Hudson saw it, was his impossible desire to please everybody. He never gave vent to any anger or frustration. It seemed unhealthy to hold so much in.

Prior to embarking on the eleven-week, 8,200-mile tour in January of 1958, Ty was interviewed in New York by William Glover of the Associated Press. In describing his four roles in the George Bernard Shaw epic drama, Ty said he was touring as a rebellion against "soft living."

"Mass means of entertainment have made it all too easy for the actor," he said. "Some players have become seduced by the ease of living that movies permit today. But the toughest thing in the world is to have all that ease and have to do something you hate."

Performing on stage was something Ty definitely didn't hate, despite the realization that many were coming to see him because he was a movie star and not because they regarded him as an accomplished man of the theater. "I don't think it is important, the motive why they may come," he said. "Your responsibility is to leave them with something. If a half dozen in an audience are impelled to think further because of the play they've seen, it is well worth the effort. If you advance the frontier of thinking a fraction of an inch, that is enough."

Arnold Moss cut down Shaw's ninety thousand words and nine hours of playing time to thirty thousand words which took two hours to perform. Unfortunately, despite its truncated form, *Back to Methuselah,* which had failed in its original 1922 Theatre Guild production and hadn't been revived up to now, still played like a philosophical tract. Shaw's thoughts on the future of mankind opened with Adam and Eve in the Garden of Eden and ended in 31,920 A.D. They seemed to take almost as long to unfold for squirming audiences. The hinterlands turned out to see Ty and his colleagues, accepting their interpretations as Culture, overlooking how ponderous and unplayable Shaw's work still was. Reviews were decidedly mixed out of town, although the production made back its investment before it opened in New York on March 27.

By this time, nominations for Academy Awards had been announced, and *Witness for the Prosecution* figured prominently in the proceedings. It received four major nominations, for Best Picture, Best Director, Best Actor (Laughton), and Best Supporting Actress (Elsa Lanchester). The Academy overlooked Ty's performance completely, opting instead for Laughton's showier characterization, which was a compendium of wheezes and shaking of wattles . . . a totally juicy part. It wasn't Ty's nature to resent the accolades being received by his friend, but he must have felt some resentment that his peers still hadn't gone beyond his good looks to discern the talent beneath.

What Broadway critics discerned was that Ty, with the exception of *John Brown's Body,* had never been an effective player in the theater, despite his great promise. He was in a better position to choose his stage properties than he'd been in films, and yet his choices were invariably wrong ones. Ty, in trying to prove his worth, had opted for the roles which vividly contrasted with his film-star image, and he hadn't been able to pull them off. Critics found potential in his stage work, but several pointed out that he had yet to learn how to sustain a role. *Back to Methuselah* folded within a few weeks.

"He was heartbroken over these failures," Kurt Kasznar said. "If he'd been a successful stage actor, Ty would have been a happy man."

At this time, when his professional future was still up in the air, Ty and Debbie had settled into a solid personal relationship. His sister Anne came down from her home in New England to meet Ty's new lady. The two women saw each other again on a weekend at Marblehead, then once in California, but Anne never knew Debbie well.

Ty and Debbie ran into Ty Culhane one day in New York.

"Hello," Ty called out. "Good to see you." He and Debbie continued walking.

"That was kind of it," Culhane said. "I obviously took it more seriously than he did. Yet, he never made me feel he was amused by our affair, or that he was laughing at me. He was a very kind and gentle man. He treated me with great respect. Because he did that, I never felt uncomfortable or out of place with him.

"Thinking back on it, I don't think Ty had a strong sex drive. Certainly, because I was younger, I had a stronger one. He could have anyone he wanted, yet I was never aware he was involved with other people. When we were together, I was the only one. Yet, he never told me the words I wanted to hear. As a result, I never said them either."

That sort of commitment was about to be made with Debbie. They would get married immediately.

The wedding was held in Debbie's hometown, in the chapel of the Tunica, Mississippi, Presbyterian Church. Debbie wore a black dress and carried a Bible with an orchid in her right hand. Ty was in a dark business suit. Afterward, they flew to California and checked into a bungalow at the Bel-Air Hotel.

Van and Evie Johnson honored the newlyweds at a party, and many of Ty's friends got a chance to meet Debbie for the first time. Because she was Ty's wife, they wanted to like her.

A month later, the Powers announced they were expecting a baby in February of 1959, and that they were hoping for a boy. In the meantime, while they awaited the baby's birth and the start of Ty's new film assignment, they would be spending most of their time aboard *The Black Swan*.

One day, Debbie called Rock Hudson, who was then living in Malibu, and invited him to join her and Ty on a sailing jaunt to Catalina Island. "He wanted to be the skipper," Hudson said. "I knew nothing about sailing. I'd never been on a sailboat before. Therefore Ty was the skipper."

That summer, they became truly close. "I don't know why," Hudson said, "other than he was a very warm man and I just felt the friendliness of him by being around him. I wish I'd known him longer."

As a result of that first weekend with the Powers, Hudson too became a sailor. He was soon introduced to Claire Trevor and Milton Bren, two of Ty's closest friends, who, in turn became his intimates. "They had a sailboat identical to Ty's, which I bought," Hudson said. "I'd been telling Ty and Debbie of a terrible movie I'd made with Piper Laurie. She was called Khairuzan, which means good fortune in Arabic. Debbie suggested I should use that name for my own ketch."

The boat was christened in an unusual way. The Powers invited Hudson to join them early one evening, so that they could run a film after dinner. The picture, of course, was the abysmal one Hudson had been trying to forget, in which Khairuzan was the leading female character.

Kurt Kasznar joined Hudson one day and observed as the actor washed down his boat. "What kind of movie star are you?" Kasznar asked. "Ty doesn't wash his own boat. He gets someone to do it."

Throughout the summer, Ty and Debbie were amid a loving group of friends. As the time neared for them to depart for Spain, Ty was honored at a combination bon voyage and belated birthday party at a restaurant in Newport Beach. During dinner, a woman came up to the table and asked Ty for his autograph. Politely, he replied, "Madam, today is *my* day. No, I will not." Rock Hudson was astounded. It was the only time that he'd seen Ty be anything other than gracious and accommodating.

As September rolled around, Ty was promoted to major in the marine reserve. Like all other aspects of his life, he hadn't told friends of his pride in being a marine. "Ty wasn't the type to brag about his exploits or flash his medals," Billy Wilder said. Yet, it was a source of obvious pride to him, for his continued attachment to the marines was a verification of his manhood.

In the middle of the month, Ty and Debbie were off to Spain for the new picture. It didn't hold great promise, other than the financial one his healthy percentage of the picture assured him, but there were so many others to look forward to. As an actor, he was just beginning to hit his stride.

Had a lifetime of unearthly repression contributed to the tragic implosion or was it his ignoring of the family's health history, as well as his own, that doomed Tyrone Power to his too early death? Bill and Edie Goetz, on location in Nevada, were unable to get to California for the funeral, but Mrs. Goetz consulted with Houston heart specialist Michael DeBakey about what might have been done to save Ty.

"It was such a terrible waste," she stated. "Dr. DeBakey said rheumatic fever often causes valvular damage to the heart years after the illness, with no symptoms in the meantime. Open-heart surgery could have been performed to repair the valves and Ty would have been completely cured."

He should have known of the possible damage to his heart, and monitored it constantly, yet Ty chose to overlook the symptoms. His Irish sense of impending doom made him a fatalist, passively accepting what, with a fight, he could have conquered.

Thus the stage was set for the indignity, the final circus in his life cycle, which was his funeral.

Jean-Pierre Aumont, in his autobiography, *Sun and Shadow,* wrote about a conflict between a cosmetician at the morgue and Tyrone's personal makeup man, as to who would prepare Ty's body for viewing. He wrote, "These two artists were debating who would add the last touch of pink in the cheeks of the unfortunate cadaver. 'I'm the one who always makes up Mr. Power,' said one. 'I know what he likes.'

"The other would answer, 'Corpses present different problems than live people. I've never had the least complaint about my work.'"

Ray Sebastian totally refuted Aumont's account. "Debbie asked me to make Ty up," he said, "to look as he had as a young man. I didn't know if I would be able to do it.

"There was a sergeant on duty at the mortuary. He had already embalmed Ty when I arrived. He had never made up a cadaver. He usually embalmed it, put it in a box, and shipped it to the United States. He asked if he could watch how I did it. I shaved off Ty's beard, then put the makeup on him. I carried on a conversation with Ty the whole time I was there. That was the only way I could get through it. When I was finished, I offered to leave some makeup for the sergeant to use. He said that was one responsibility he didn't want to take on.

"Before Ty died, you'd see priests everywhere you turned, but we hadn't been able to find one to give him the last rites. Before I left, I said my own prayer for him."

There was no available casket, so Sebastian suggested Ty's body be placed on a wooden plank, which would be supported by sawhorses, over which blankets would be draped. This was the way the body lay in state until the memorial service at the United States Torrejon Air Base the day after Ty's death.

The body was then placed in a makeshift casket, which was covered in gray canvas, and was accompanied back to the United States by Ty's widow and Bill Gallagher.

Linda flew from Paris, stopping over in New York where she was met by television entertainer George De Witt, before she went on to California for the funeral. Romina and Taryn, in the meantime, were flown in from Mexico City.

As spokesmen for United Artists were stating that no decision had been made about the future of *Solomon and Sheba,* the producers were frantically looking for a replacement for Ty. Gary Cooper, Robert Taylor, William Holden, and Charlton Heston were reportedly approached. All were unavailable.

Finally, Yul Brynner was persuaded to take the part, if only as a memorial to Ty. "No one who was asked to do such a thing would be able to say no," he stated. The money was an added inducement. Brynner's terms were double those of Ty's, and his work would have to be completed by February 15, 1959, because he had a commitment to start another picture on that date. He would be getting $700,000 as Ty's replacement, in addition to 15 percent of the gross over $9,000,000.

The private funeral services were scheduled for noon on November 21, 1958, at the Chapel of the Psalms. Debbie at first agreed to seat one thousand uninvited guests outside the chapel, with the ceremony to be carried to them over a loudspeaker. Then she changed her mind.

Because she believed that Linda had made a spectacle out of the Marquis de Portago's funeral, Debbie asked her to stay away from the services. "Ty belongs to me now," his widow stated. "Whatever anybody else does is of no concern to me any more."

Linda's reaction was caustic. "I am happy for her if she can find peace in that belief." She and her two daughters celebrated mass at the Blessed Sacrament Catholic Church eight blocks away.

The invited mourners started arriving to pay their final respects. Among them were Henry King, Henry Fonda, James Stewart, Gregory Peck, Billy Wilder, Danny Kaye, Clifton Webb, Brian Aherne, Herbert Marshall, Robert Wagner, and Natalie Wood. Loretta Young, on a lunch break from filming her television show, arrived wearing Oriental makeup. Yul Brynner had already started growing a beard for the role in which he would be replacing Ty. When he arrived, the gathering crowd burst into applause. He glowered at them, and they quieted down.

Inside, an organ filled the chapel with music associated with Ty's career: "Always" from *Alexander's Ragtime Band;* "Mam'selle" from *The Razor's Edge;* "The Battle Hymn of the Republic" from *John Brown's Body;* and Eddy Duchin's piano theme.

The Philippine mahogany casket was kept open during the military funeral. Debbie, in a straight-back chair, her back to the other mourners, held Ty's hand throughout the half-hour ceremony.

Cesar Romero read "The Promises of America" by Thomas Wolfe, which Ty was to have read to airmen in Spain on Thanksgiving Day. After the reading, Romero said a few words:

"Ty was a strong, vital man who never spared himself. Everything he did, he had to do well and to the best of his ability, whether it was in his personal life, in his professional career, or in his service to his country.

"He constantly gave of himself, until one day he gave a little too much. He was a beautiful man. He was beautiful outside and beautiful inside. We shall all miss him.

"Rest well, my friend."

After the services, six marines carried the flag-draped casket to the burial spot beside a small lake in Hollywood Memorial Park Cemetery.

Only then was the full force of the vulgar carnival impressed on the minds of the mourners. It was a grisly recreation of the crowd scene from Nathanael West's *The Day of the Locust*. As their favorite stars appeared, the crowd started cheering. At its outer edges, families were seated on the lawn eating box lunches, oblivious to the crying of several children among them. A little girl was getting a hula hoop lesson from her father. A small boy, trying to get closer to the activities, fell into the pond, screaming and sputtering as he scrambled out. The crowd was effectively pushed back as the body was interred.

The ceremony over, the invited mourners gradually dispersed, to be followed by the crowd. All in all, it hadn't been totally out of control. Only one woman had fainted.

Hours later, Linda and her two daughters visited the grave, leaving a five-foot cross of white gardenias.

When they were married, Ty and Linda had entertained dozens of Hollywood's most famous names. She learned how short or unforgiving the memories of those she once considered friends actually were. During the few weeks that she stayed on in southern California after Ty's funeral, she heard only from Henry Hathaway, Joe Pasternak, and Delmer Daves and their wives.

It was a disquieting, disturbing time for all who had known and loved Ty, and it was no better reflected than the description by *Time* magazine of Ty's military funeral: "Major Power deserved the attention; he had served his country well during World War II. As an actor, he had been better than many of Hollywood's handsome heroes. As a private citizen, he had certainly been no worse."

Epilogue

THE LATE FALL RAINS HAD COME ON UNEXPECTEDLY, AS USUAL, beating softly rhythmic tattoos on the hardened southern California soil. After a week, they were gone. The sun filtered through the rain clouds, which were beginning to lift, as a group began to gather at the once grand, now unkempt, Hollywood Memorial Park on November 15, 1978, to commemorate the twentieth anniversary of Tyrone Power's death. Ray Sebastian had coordinated the event every year since then.

Half an hour before the service was to begin, a woman of endless self-fascination began expounding on the singular greatness of Valentino, also buried in the same cemetery; of her closeness to the Power family; but most importantly, of her choice of dress. "I always wear black and white," she remarked to no one and everyone. Today there was a difference, she explained, for the black and white was in a new configuration for her—polka dots—and the dress, with its tight bodice, reached the ground. On her head was a black-brimmed hat with white streamers, under which dangled gold hoop earrings.

Floral arrangements were beginning to arrive for the twelve-thirty ceremony and, as each was placed by the grave marker, which is in the shape of a white marble bench, the woman rearranged it to her own liking, then sat down. From the other side of the small gathering, another woman rose from her metal folding chair to re-arrange the rearrangements more to *her* liking, after which she too sat down. This was the cue for Our Lady of the Polka Dots to rise, to return the sprays and bouquets to the places where she'd originally set them. Neither paid attention to the other as each alternately waged her silent battle of the roses, carnations, and daisies.

Others were straggling toward the outdoor setting—the group would total fifty in all—and never was there a more stereotypical microcosm of the crowds that had followed Tyrone Power in life: the bespectacled student of film, long and lanky and intense; the girl with the black-rooted platinum hair, bearing a disturbing resemblance to the murdered girl friend of a British rock star; the suited anonymous factotums from the movie industry, past and present; the plain, dowdy women who had worked with their hands, while standing on their feet, all their lives.

Near the lectern stood a stocky, gray-haired man, Italian in looks and gestures. Talking to him was a fastidiously dressed Latin in a brown checked suit of over-contrivance, with dark brown epaulets and collar. Nearby was a funereally dressed man of indeterminate age, the pallor of his face and the blackness of his obviously dyed hair suggesting he should be lying in a casket instead of standing beside one.

Soon a very pregnant Taryn Power arrived, a back-to-the-earth vision, her apparel suggesting the mothball-scented chest from which it was apparently recycled. Over it she wore a fake fur coat, true to her ecological beliefs, which she would soon be taking off as the sun broke through the clouds.

The service began. A minister who was to deliver the eulogy had been detained elsewhere and Norvel, the funereal-looking psychic-astrologer, stepped in to offer oracular tones and improbable verbiage as those gathered lowered their heads.

A captain from the United States Marine Corps, preceded by an honor guard, then placed a wreath of red carnations at the grave marker. He talked briefly and stolidly of Tyrone Power's meritorious service as a marine pilot in the Second World War.

Next, Norvel delivered his overblown rhetoric, phrases jumping out at the listener in unctuous insistence: "Tyrone Power's sign was ruled by Venus . . . he was a glittering star in the diadem of civilization's light . . . another soul under Venus was Rudolph Valentino . . . the Venus person not only captures the hearts, minds, and souls of the multitudes, but perpetuates them . . Ty was terribly interested in the mystical . . . his belief was celestial in its intensity."

The man in the fussy brown suit then rose to speak about Tyrone Power's special standing among Hispanics. "We always felt he was one of us." He went on to talk of the many Power pictures in which he had been given small parts, through the star's intercession, and of their first meeting.

The occasional actor had taken a job as a clothing salesman at a Beverly Hills men's store in the mid-1950s, since acting jobs weren't coming readily to him. Tyrone Power walked in one day and noticed him. He pointed in the general direction of the modish Bermuda shorts the younger man was wearing and said, "You've got what I want."

The twenty-minute service ended shortly thereafter on that questionable note, and people congregated around Taryn, who graciously shook hands and even, at the insistence of one fan, signed autographs.

Three people—Tyrone Power's daughter Taryn, his sister, his son—are bound together by a distinguished and colorful family history. Yet, at this writing, they have never met. In vainly attempting to compartmentalize his professional, family, and secret lives, Tyrone Power tore himself apart instead. He doomed himself at the same time that he was unwittingly creating family schisms that, twenty years after his death, have yet to be bridged.

Immediately after Ty's death, however, steps were taken to salvage *Solomon and Sheba*. Because the picture had to be totally refilmed, Fireman's Fund, the insurer, settled with United Artists for a total of $1,229,172, the largest insurance company loss in the film industry up to that time. The finished picture was recently singled out as one of *The Fifty Worst Films of All Time* in the book of that same title, with a special award given to the man who was billed as "Orgy-Sequence Advisor."

Patia Power never learned of her son's death. She was moved to her daughter's home in New Hampshire. "Mother had been the victim of many minor strokes," Anne Hardenbergh said. "She could not communicate. The speech centers were damaged. She was bedfast and could only take a few steps into a wheelchair." She died in September of 1959, ten months after her son's death.

Anne Power Hardenbergh, after divorcing her second husband, moved to Florida, where she has carved out a new life and career as an artist.

Ty's first wife, Annabella, today commutes between her homes in Paris and the Basque region of southern France. She made a highly visible return to California in 1964 when she accepted an Academy Award for Best Actress on Patricia Neal's behalf.

She was Watson Webb's houseguest during this visit. From that point on, she totally retired to private life. Her son-in-law, Oskar Werner, told an interviewer in 1966 that she had become involved in prison-reform work.

After several well-publicized romances with others, Linda Christian, in 1962, married Edmund Purdom. He was the man believed to have broken up her marriage to Ty; neither the industry nor the public forgave him. His once-promising career virtually evaporated. So did his marriage to Linda, for they were divorced within a year. Since that time, Linda has remained an international nomad.

Romina, only seven when her father died, was pushed into an acting career by her mother while still in her teens. She rebelled to marry an Italian pop singer, and lives today with her husband and two children outside of Rome.

Taryn was five when Tyrone Power died. She had a brief acting career too, starring in several pictures, but she also opted for family life, having recently given birth to a daughter. She and her man live in West Hollywood.

Debbie Power married Arthur Loew, Jr., a year after Ty's death. Her new husband adopted Tyrone Power IV, who was born on January 22, 1959, two months after his natural father's death. The young man was nurtured and protected by his adoptive father, who, after he divorced the boy's mother, went into court, insisting that Tyrone Power Loew retain that name.

Tyrone Power's only son continued to have Loew's love and

encouragement through his growing-up years, even after Debbie Power Loew married Loew's cousin, David Lawrence, with whom she now lives in Mexico City.

Tyrone Power IV—the name Ty's son reclaimed—had no plans to become an actor, thinking he might become a concert pianist instead. As he approached his college years, however, he decided to claim his birthright.

Today, he is a junior at Pomona College, majoring in drama.

Rock Hudson took a group to see his godson perform in a campus production of *Macbeth,* in which the twenty-year-old played Malcolm. The accomplished Tyrone Power voice was there. As would be more apparent after the performance, his father's brows and eyes—ringed by the same double lashes that enraptured women of all ages—are also very much the son's. Yet his movements during the performance were lumbering and untrained, lacking the grace of the preeminent swashbuckler of an earlier generation.

Nevertheless, one of the group said on the way back to Los Angeles, "Think of the doors that kid's name is going to open."

"Yes," Hudson agreed. "That legacy is a doorway. But he has a lot to live up to, and he'd better be more than ready."

Bibliography

Adamson, Joe. *Twentieth Century-Fox Goes to War*. Unpublished, 1976.

Arnold, William. *Shadowland*. New York: McGraw-Hill Book Co., 1978.

Aumont, Jean-Pierre. *Sun and Shadow*. New York: W. W. Norton & Co., 1977.

Barrymore, Diana. *Too Much, Too Soon*. New York: Henry Holt and Company, 1957.

Barrymore, John. *Confessions of an Actor*. Indianapolis: Bobbs-Merrill, 1926.

Belafonte, Dennis, with Alvin H. Merrill. *The Films of Tyrone Power*. Secaucus, N.J.: The Citadel Press, 1979.

Binns, Archie, in collaboration with Olive Kooken. *Mrs. Fiske and the American Theatre*. New York: Crown Publishers, Inc., 1955.

Blum, Daniel. *A Pictorial History of the American Theatre 1860–1970*. New York: Crown Publishers, Inc., 1969.

Bowers, Ronald. *The Selznick Players*. South Brunswick and New York: A. S. Barnes and Co., 1976.

Brockett, Oscar G. and Robert R. Findlay. *Century of Innovation*. Englewood Cliffs, N.J.: Prentice-Hall, 1973.

Carpozi, George, Jr. *That's Hollywood: The Matinee Idols*. New York: Manor Books, 1978.

Christian, Linda. *Linda*. New York: Crown Publishers, Inc., 1962.

Coudert, Jo. *The Alcoholic in Your Life*. New York: Stein and Day, 1972.

Crawford, Mary Caroline. *The Romance of the American Theatre*. Boston: Little, Brown, and Co., 1925.

Curti, Carlo. *Skouras*. Los Angeles: Holloway House Publishing Co., 1967.

Davis, Fitzroy. *Quicksilver*. New York: Harcourt, Brace and Co., 1942.

Directors Guild of America. *An Oral History with Henry King*. Unpublished, 1976–1978.

Dunne, John Gregory. *The Studio*. New York: Farrar, Straus & Giroux, 1968.

Eells, George. *Ginger, Loretta and Irene Who?* New York: G. P. Putnam's Sons, 1976.

Flynn, Errol. *My Wicked, Wicked Ways*. New York: G. P. Putnam's Sons, 1959.

Fontaine, Joan. *No Bed of Roses*. New York: William Morrow & Co., 1978.

Fowler, Gene. *Good Night, Sweet Prince*. New York: The Viking Press, 1944.

Frank, Gerold. *Judy*. New York: Harper & Row, 1975.

Graham, Sheilah. *The Garden of Allah*. New York: Crown Publishers, Inc., 1970.

Graham, Sheilah. *How to Marry Super Rich: Or Love, Money and the Morning After*. New York: Grosset & Dunlap, 1974.

Gussow, Mel. *Don't Say Yes Until I Finish Talking*. Garden City, N.Y.: Doubleday & Co., 1971.

Harris, Radie. *Radie's World*. New York: G. P. Putnam's Sons, 1975.

Higham, Charles. *Charles Laughton*. Garden City, N.Y: Doubleday & Co., Inc., 1976.

Kobler, John. *Damned in Paradise*. New York: Atheneum, 1977.

Langner, Lawrence. *The Magic Curtain*. New York: E. P. Dutton & Co., Inc., 1951.

Marx, Samuel, and Jan Clayton. *Rodgers & Hart. Bewitched, Bothered, and Bewildered.* New York: G. P. Putnam's Sons, 1976.

Merman, Ethel, with George Eells. *Merman.* New York: Simon & Schuster, 1978.

Morella, Joe, and Edward L. Epstein. *Lana.* New York: The Citadel Press, 1971.

Mosel, Tad, with Gertrude Macy. *Leading Lady: The World and Theatre of Katharine Cornell.* Boston: Atlantic-Little Brown, 1978.

Moses, Montrose F. *Famous Actor-Families in America.* New York: Thomas Y. Crowell & Company, 1906.

Niven, David. *The Moon Is a Balloon.* New York: G. P. Putnam's Sons, 1972.

Palmer, Lilli. *Change Lobsters and Dance.* New York: Macmillan Publishing Co., Inc., 1975.

Parish, James Robert. *RKO Gals.* New Rochelle, N.Y.: Arlington House, 1974.

Parish, James Robert, and Stanke, Don E. *The Swashbucklers.* New Rochelle, N.Y.: Arlington House, 1976.

Ringgold, Gene: *The Films of Rita Hayworth.* Secaucus, N.J.: The Citadel Press, 1974.

Sheppard, Dick. *Elizabeth.* Garden City, N.Y., Doubleday & Co., 1974.

Solomon, Aubrey. *A Corporate and Financial History of the Twentieth Century-Fox Studio.* Unpublished. Research Associateship, Center for Advanced Film Studies, Louis B. Mayer Film History Program, Beverly Hills, California, 1975.

Springer, John. *The Fondas.* New York: Citadel Press, 1970.

Steinberg, Cobbett. *Reel Facts.* New York: Vintage Books, 1978.

Stempel, Tom. *An Oral History with Henry King.* Unpublished. Beverly Hills: American Film Institute, 1972.

Winter, William. *Tyrone Power.* New York: Moffat, Yard and Co., 1913.